MANHATTAN SEERESS

MANHATTAN SEERESS

Lorraine Saint Pierre

Luhrenloup

Luhrenloup

This book is true to my recollections. Some names have been changed for reasons of privacy. Otherwise the book is faithful to my experience.

First Luhrenloup Edition 2019
www.luhrenloup.com

ISBN: 978-0-578-43663-0

Cover design by Bien Swinton

Walking the tightwire is living;
everything else is waiting.

Karl Wallenda, patriarch
of The Flying Wallendas.

TABLE OF CONTENTS

FIRST THIRD

0. The Fool 1
1. The Magician 13
2. The High Priestess 49
3. The Empress 64
4. The Emperor 86
5. The Hierophant 112
6. The Lovers 133

SECOND THIRD

7. The Chariot 167
8. Strength 180
9. The Hermit 192
10. Wheel of Fortune 205
11. Justice 220
12. The Hanged Man 239
13. Death 256

LAST THIRD

14. Temperance 277
15. The Devil 294
16. The Tower 314
17. The Star 338
18. The Moon 351
19. The Sun 367
20. Judgment 377
21. The World 395

Preface

A seeress is one who sees, one who knows. It's not something one talks about. In the talking one reduces this "awareness" to the questioners' ability to grasp something foreign to them; it becomes trivialized. For the past few centuries, humankind has turned its back on non-rational ways of perceiving. There are many names attached to this area of human experience, shamanic, psychic, mystical, intuitive, spiritual, religious, superstitious. This other way of perceiving is at odds with the rational world and is rightly seen as a threat.

Science rules our present era. Any opposition to the rational is quickly dismissed, condescended, ridiculed, attacked. Yet it is here, a part of every human being's experiences. We have no true words for these unexplainable happenings. A seeress is someone who uses that way of perceiving the world as her guiding force. She is aware of many separate worlds she navigates in, aware of forces in the universe with rules that must be obeyed in order to survive, protect oneself, live a rich, meaningful life.

I am not alone with this gift. There are others. When we meet there is that flash of recognition, yes, he or she or he is one of us. The word psychic is one that I detest, but is the only way I can make myself understood by most. My gift is easily lost; the everyday life overwhelms; the everyday life has its comforts, its known fears, one is soothed, caressed, fed, loved, one is ill, broke, fired, attacked, despised, one will die.

Seeing is about pulling that mask off, and truly being there at that moment, it's that part of self that you understand as ancient, has always been, will always be, the one who knows you, the totality of you.

From the start, I've looked for a seat at the table; I wanted to partake of the feast and add my voice to the conversation. So I came to New York with an open heart hoping to find my way. On the surface, my journey was the typical NYC story of a grad student living in poverty on the Lower East Side, looking to find time to write.

I had tested the seriousness of my intent to speak my mind and enter the conversation by going on a vision quest before coming to the city. It starts with a camping trip through my home state of Maine. After a week alone, without the comforts of home, my programmed life begins to deteriorate; I become more connected to the earth, sunrise, sunset, time to get up, time to turn in. On an old logging road, I sense a presence, is it the sorcerer? It occurs to me that my mind is filled with thoughts from morning till night, because life is too fearful otherwise, without boundaries, chaotic. My plan is to find an appropriate place to go on the vision quest. I spend 4 days and nights alone in the woods fasting.

And what is New York to such a person moving to the city? It is affirmation, the truth swept out from under the rug. NY is ugly, vulgar, filthy, it's a tart in a too short skirt looking for a good time, it is the streets and avenues I've read about, the violence, the architecture, the art, the beautiful people, the best of the best and the lowliest of the low; it is terrifying and desirable. I have arrived at the banquet table! Its inhabitants don't doubt for a moment what is commonly known as psychic phenomenon. How else can one survive and even thrive here?

Midway through my MFA in creative writing at Sarah Lawrence College, and out of money, I look through the help wanted ads in the Village Voice, and I come upon this:

> Psychics Wanted, set your own hours, work as little or as much as you want in the privacy of your home giving readings over the telephone. Psychic Reader's Network, 1-800-***-****.

Thus begins my career as a Manhattan seeress. It was not something I sought out. Like the trickster Coyote, I stumble in inadvertently. It was only going to be a summer job. The psychic networks provide me with incalculable training as I spend evenings counseling client, after client, for hours on end. From the beginning, I love the work, and at some point the parts meld, and I am no longer a writer, and separately a spiritual person. My ear is tapping into the heart of America, its passions, fears, obsessions, its poetry and mystery, its stories.

What is the rationale for this book?

It is about power and spirituality. I am not a guru with a product to sell, or directions on how to attain nirvana. I will not take you to the Himalayas or Machu Picchu to connect with the ancients, that is a journey taken alone, but I will point out some signposts along the way. How one becomes a seeress is what I chose to explore in this memoir. I have specifically selected stories to illustrate, from the sublime to the practical, a spiritual journey introduced in each chapter by an atout, the Tarot's major archetypes. From the Fool, the first of the atouts, to its last and twenty second atout, The World, our human journey with its risk and folly unfolds. The development of a seeress becomes a hodgepodge of stories about power and the lessons one collects, or formulates, about rules, attention, listening to the untold story, tapping into other worlds, other ways of being; it's about commitment. There is also an artist here alive to her new world seeking inspiration among artists on the Lower East side, learning the ways and foods of her Chinese neighbors, falling in love.

Lorraine Saint Pierre

THE FOOL

-0-

Arms outstretched, a white rose in one hand and a knapsack in the other, the Fool gazes heavenward not realizing he is about to step off the cliff and fall deep into the chasm. The horizon beckons and a small sack of knowledge is all he carries. He is pure ideal and potential, the white rose, a symbol of his spiritual quest.

He begins his journey with a carefree attitude. Undoubtedly, this is not his first; his lofty vision gained after a long withdrawal. He is free now and the bundle of his past is light. He's forsaken the solitude that so long nourished him and seeks only to share the beauty he's found.

A dog snaps at his elbow to remind him of the sensual pleasures that await. The Fool pays no heed, he prefers to stumble along, open to adventure, not realizing it is almost over. It began when he withdrew from life degraded and broken, wanting only a corner to hide, never thinking he would find his way back. How he managed this return to innocence is the real adventure.

Before him the sweet path of life unfolds. It is time for new thoughts and understanding. Later, he will be depleted once more. Faithless, he will drag the heavy burden of his past and fall deep in the abyss. Not this time, no harm will come to a Fool whose only device is a rose.

Upright: A new beginning, innocence.

Reversed: Journey delayed, cautiousness.

Put your money down, girl, I want to see some green stuff, is the slut's mantra. I've always liked bad girls with their saucy ways and their penchant for shocking behavior. Maybe, just maybe, they're on to something that eludes most. New York City is the only place I know of where you fall in love with her because you are able to survive her adversities, and what's more, to thrive and succeed in spite of them. It's the slut's test.

Eight o'clock Sunday morning, the police arrive at my apartment in Greenwich Village, "How long have you been living here?"

My roommate Elizabeth, after having accepted my half of the deposit money and rent for our new apartment, has called the police.

The answer to the officer's trick question is . . . *More than 30 days.* Less than that you are classified a guest and are at the mercy of your host. She has surreptitiously negotiated the lease in her name only.

"That's right lady, get your stuff out," says the officer.

The Fool

Standing in my nightgown, arms flailing, I make a lot of noise about being a paid tenant to convince the two men who think there are more dignified ways for them to spend their time than being involved in domestic situations. Murders, bank robberies, that's what they're looking for.

One of them is uncomfortable with my appearance "Go put something on," he says.

"I want to speak to your captain!"

I've arrived in the city with an invitation from Sarah Lawrence College to take part in their MFA program in creative writing. I haven't thought too clearly how I'm going to support myself, but I'll find a way. What's important is that I'm here in New York, a city I have always wanted to live in. My writing, the whole of it, is in this room in files and diskettes, my sound system, all of my music, my books, my Seth Thomas chiming mantel clock, kitchenware, pots and pans, lamps, my desks, the most basic things and the most cherished.

"Look Captain, obviously I'm not just a guest in this woman's home or I would not have brought all of these things here. If she has no compunction about putting me out on the street after I've paid my share of the deposit and rent, why should she care about returning my property?"

He agrees and gives me till evening to clear out my possessions. Out on the street, I find my shoes and boots scattered on 7th Ave. Someone's broken into my car, messed up the locks on both doors so I can never lock them again, stolen a portable radio, some of my clothes, the shoes and boots which the thief obviously was not impressed with. The car is on its downward trajectory and won't hold out much longer. I have arrived in NYC on a wing and a prayer.

Waiting for my roommate at Grand Central Station on my first day, I listen to Eduardo Martinez Guayanes play guitar and sing in the large hall. The music is so beautiful that all of Grand Central seems to sigh in its ambiance. He sets a serene, yearning tempo that pierces my heart. I cannot understand the Spanish words, but I buy one of his tapes nevertheless. Friends tell me it's about the land, and our love of it, its beauty, its secrets. A small town girl from the state of Maine, I watch amazed, as respectable, silvered gentlemen in three piece suits run madly to their trains.

Why have I come? All I know is that I need to be here.

In the center of the maze we call New York City, my two-week apartment is in Greenwich Village, on Barrow Street. Yesterday, I took a bike ride in the neighborhood and as I stopped to tie up my bicycle, an older man came over and chatted. He's new to the city himself, about to sign a lease on an apartment tomorrow. We talk for a while and he asks me to dinner. The night is cool, and after our meal we walk through the Village exploring our new city. He buys me a dozen roses and we agree to meet for brunch this morning at his hotel. When I arrive with my sad story, he immediately finds a storage space to put my things and makes arrangements to secure it. Afterward, we have champagne and strawberries for brunch. He has come to New York with a play he wants staged, a short bull of a man, a teaser and a flirt. His wife died a year ago. Coming to the city is a big move for him too. I will never see him again, I don't even remember his name, but our meeting is fortuitous.

I leave the hotel intent on returning to Barrow Street to start packing. On the way, I meet up with Emmanuelle, a sculptor I met at The Farm, an artist's colony for women in Poughkeepsie. She's visiting galleries canvassing the competition. I sketch out my situation as we walk to the apartment.

"I'll help you get your stuff to the storage unit," she says.

A very hot day, sweat is pouring from us as we move boxes down five flights of stairs; I am working strictly on adrenaline. We get the car filled up, then over to the storage unit to unload. Trip after trip, there is no plan beyond this task. Once we get the last box out of the apartment, I hear the bolt click into place as the door lock shuts me out forever.

I have a storage unit, my aging red sportscar, Felinas, a bank account with $300 in it, and I am homeless. One is truly alive at such a moment, and tuned in to psychic energy to an astonishing degree, signs, omens, their significance and indications. A great part of being a seeress is being able to read the moment. There are many explanations for this phenomenon; I lean toward Carl Jung's theory of synchronicity.

Since recorded history and before, the practice of divination has involved the dispersal and reading of diverse material, sticks, bones, tea leaves, coins, runes, tarot cards. What occurs at such a moment is a co-incidence, a meaningful coincidence. The coins, runes, sticks, or what-have-you, will reflect the circumstances of the person or situation one is exploring at that very moment. Synchronicity bears witness to the myriad of meaningful coincidences that are a part of life. A synchronous event occurs when two incidents happen at the same time and are connected in some manner.

Meeting the man who comes to my rescue on the day before I lose my apartment and then coming upon Emmanuelle on the street who not only helps me pack, but lets me stay with her a few days till I can make other arrangements, are two very good examples of synchronicity. Psychologists refer to a gestalt, an assemblage of events, phenomena, occurring simultaneously that are interrelated. Gestalt is the study of their relationship to one another. The laying down of cards as one sits with a client to give a reading will always reflect the client's situation and give a correct interpretation of it. To be sure, the reader's expertise or lack thereof, her depth of thought and understanding, her character and wisdom will also play a part, enriching or further confusing the situation.

The artist and writer, Kate Millett, a friend and mentor, hears of my troubles and invites me to stay at The Farm in Poughkeepsie. This women's art colony is a working community. Artists are invited to stay for a summer, paying board and room and also work The Farm 4 to 5 hours a day to provide for its continuance, shearing its crop of Christmas trees, keeping the grass and weeds around them mowed, repairing and expanding the existing structures. There's a photography studio, a really decent woodworking shop, a recording studio, a silkscreen room, a pond where women swim. A lot of young artists come to The Farm, mostly they are women at turning points who, when their season is over, will not go back to their former lives. I came to the Farm when I was still living in Maine.

After my experience, I packed my bags and headed for NYC.

Kate had given me the yellow room of the main building during my summer. It's in the original farmhouse, very old, big fireplaces in the front parlor and an upstairs bedroom (which is named the "Simone de Beauvoir" room because she stayed there one summer.) I had driven from Maine with my cat Hermine in a van, camping along the way. When I got there Kate greeted me at the door; she looked like a hippie with long white hair, loose clothing, shit-kicker boots and a leathery outdoors appearance. We were 12 that summer, and I must say, living with women who are on the edge of making major decisions in their lives requires fortitude. Democracy was never so severely tested and found wanting. Nevertheless, we were trying to do something noble, to create a bit of beauty. I was beginning revision of my second novel 53. There were great dinners out on the decks with kerosene lanterns casting their glow late into the night as we ate, drank lots of wine and had endless discussions about art, politics, the immediate crises of the day. I have returned to The Farm many times since my first stay and have become friends with Kate.

"I've been away all summer," she says. "Mother was trapped in a nursing home after she got sick. Getting her out of that terrible place and dealing with lawyers and the court system, I spent the season traveling back and forth to Minnesota."

Artists were not invited because of the Minnesota troubles hence no work was accomplished. The Farm is in bad shape. None of the Christmas trees have been sheared. And her mother has just died.

"I've rented the main house, the cottage and the Lavender House for the fall and winter to some students from the Culinary Institute, and an Indian couple who teach at Vassar are renting the main house. We'll have the gallery and connecting barn where you can store your things."

On the night that I arrive, feeling shaken and vulnerable from my New York experience, I approach the Lavender House, the only building on the premises with lights on, to find a party in progress. Just a friendly get-together between the tenants and

Kate, except that these are culinary students and a feast has been laid out. The Indian couple has also contributed food from their culture. Kate welcomes me and introduces me to the gathering in the warmest of tones as someone special she is honored to know. I take my place at table with the group feeling close to tears, in awe of the magic that protects me.

The very next day Kate and I set to work shearing, getting the trees ready for Christmas. With its many fields and varieties of evergreens, it takes 10 to 15 colonists, working 5 hours a day, 5 days a week, the whole of the summer to get the job done. In no way are the two of us going to be able do it alone, but we don't talk about the impossibility of our task.

I became acquainted with Kate after I read her book "The Loony Bin Trip." I was living on campus at the University of Maine in Orono as an artist-in-residence at the time and wrote her a note about the book. To my surprise she responded, and after we exchanged several letters, she invited me to The Farm. The book impressed me; she assumed risks coming out as a person with a "mental affliction" at a time when this was not done.

I have worked as a psychiatric social worker/mental health clinician and was part of the Emergency Team in a community mental health center and later in the emergency room setting of a hospital. My job was to counsel people in crisis, evaluating patients with psychiatric or social problems in emergency situations, recommending treatment, be it a program of counseling, commitment to state hospital or private facilities; I'm adept at dealing with distraught, unstable adults, children, their families, friends and police.

The world Kate wrote of was familiar to me, a world as yet mapped and charted. We know that certain medications have the effect of pacifying those afflicted for short periods, but patients are reluctant to take them. I was fresh out of college with a degree in psychology when I started working in the profession. What an eye opener! In some way it may have been the best job for me after graduating with a head full of idealistic notions ready to make my mark in the world.

THE MAGICIAN

-I-

A virile man wearing a red flowing cape and a golden ribbon round his forehead stands majestically holding a wand up to the heavens. His other hand points its attuned energy to the ground. The Magician's stance is bold, yet graceful. On the table before him are the tarot symbols for earth, fire, air and water. It is with these basic tools that he makes his magic.

The Magician approaches his task with no prospect of success. Having submitted to the trial, he gropes in darkness yearning only to achieve grace. Above his head is the golden lemniscate of dominion and immortality. Therein lies the clue. Only when he is able to release his grip on life's rewards and submit to a power greater than his, are his actions imbued with light.

He awakes in the morning to a warm sun; a community reaches out to greet him. Able to remain detached, he sees the unfolding design and perceives his desires within reach. Prepared to stand fast for his integrity, he has mastered the art of stillness. The superb showman's actions are dramatic and bold, belying the difficulty of his task.

Upright The power and tools to achieve one's desires.

Reversed: Acting from a sense of need and distrust;
motivated by insecurity.

> Not until the selfish, game-involved nature of man is completely mastered is he safe in using [psychic powers.]
>
> "The Psychedelic Experience"
> Timothy Leary

I was working with professionals, naive enough to expect the scintillating intellectual debates of college to continue. What I found was a group of 9 to 5 working stiffs who, having heard every conceivable story, with few remedies to provide, preferred to discuss the goings-on of their favorite TV programs.

And staff meetings? -- Barracudas with the scent of blood.

But the patients fascinated me. Since childhood, I have had the ability to discern things about others, have been able to communicate with a deeper, secret part of them. I explained this to myself, and still do, as another dimension of human reality, an ongoing form of communication that few are able to tap into of their own volition. A great trauma, psychedelic drugs, or long periods of isolation may force it upon one. People experiencing psychotic episodes often exhibit marked psychic abilities. I approached my work as an innocent. Patients recognized an affinity to me; I was one of them. What mattered that a person carried the label of schizophrenia, neurosis, bi-polar disorder? They were human beings worthy of respect. Being crazy did not mean they were stupid. Many psychotic patients, like myself, were able to navigate two worlds. I brought one patient to a hospital, looking to have him admitted to their psych unit and sat with him in the admitting station. As the two office workers warily filled in the information I was able to provide, the patient rambled on to the walls and the world at large, gesticulating wildly. The women typing away at forms looked up periodically, first at the madman, then at me. After the admitting process was over and we walked out of the office, he smiled and winked, "Gave those two a scare, hunh!"

Was he a rational man pulling a fast one on us? No, he was traveling both worlds and each was equally valid to him. Who am I to say that his "psychotic" world does not exist, that it is caused by child abuse or chemical imbalance? It's like explaining dreams as products of indigestion.

We have a quick breakfast at 8 then up to the autumn fields. A riot of fall colors, and in the far distance are the Catskills, I am surrounded by beauty in all directions. Hawks circle overhead looking through the fields for prey; one sees an occasional deer that Kate protects with signs, PRIVATE PROPERTY, NO HUNTING ALLOWED. The air is cool, crisp, a far cry from shearing trees in summer, sweat running down your back, yet covered in protective clothing head to toe to ward off the poison ivy of summer whose serpentine runners are propped like silver garlands on tree branches. After several weeks, no matter what precautions, potions, or salve used, one is covered with the rash.

Tree, after tree, shears in hand, trimming branches to establish a well proportioned cone shape, thousands of them, checking the leader, making sure there is only one by cutting the surrounding branches. No one wants a tree without a leading branch at top to hang a star, or an angel. These peaceful mornings in the bosom of nature are the best part of my day. We work in silence for which I am glad. Kate mourning the loss of her mother and I, the loss of the home and life I have left behind in Maine; we are orphans who find solace in the land, the skies, the workaday world of the farm. I have lost my identity and am living in limbo, not yet in the city and the new life, not quite out of Maine psychologically.

I commute to Sarah Lawrence College in Bronxville twice a week on roads packed with cars heading for the city. Huge multi-lane highways with kamikaze drivers weaving in and out of lanes with reckless abandon. I admire their sang-froid and am training myself, like them, to just shove my way into another lane and not look backward or hesitate mid-maneuver. Turning on the radio, I discover some weird guy named Howard Stern spewing forth craziness and filthy talk. He keeps me company as I learn to assert myself on the interstate.

Then there are my descents into the city to get a P.O. box where I can forward my mail to; try as I might this never works out. Maine holds my mail without a forwarding address for a month and when the 30 days are up they chuck it out. Good-bye to Maine. Driving into the city is nerve wracking. I don't have the confidence I had when I first arrived. The buildings, the noise, the difficulty in accomplishing small bureaucratic tasks overwhelm me. On a street corner feeding quarters into a phone trying to find a live person in the tangle of press 1, press 2's and press 3's, driving and driving to find a spot for the car, the never ending crush of human beings; *how am I ever going to manage this?*

I was at one time married with a child, a suburban homemaker. Once it was over, on a camping trip through Maine, an incident guided me to the path I find myself on today:

On the seat next to me are a couple of books I've picked up at the library, Celine's "JOURNEY TO THE END OF NIGHT," then some interviews, published by the New York Quarterly, of poets about their craft. It's the extent of my planning for the camping trip. I'm heading north up Route Four to Livermore Falls and then on.

It's been three days since I've moved out of the house, its memories of married life, raising a daughter and the divorce, and I'm still in mild shock. The veil had lifted exposing a painful reality, and I didn't like what I saw. Friends and acquaintances seemed inaccessible, still in the old way of being. Everything they said belonged to a past I no longer inhabited.

Throughout spring, when I knew I had a sure buyer and steps were being taken, I began to look at maps and drive to different areas of Maine trying to find a likely region to move to. I've been across America but I don't know my own state well. The wilderness up north, the Great Allagash and Baxter State Park are a fantasyland I've always heard of.

I found a log cabin in the western mountains; a small, secluded house presently occupied till the end of the month; I've decided to camp out till then. I'm not sure what attracted me to the cabin except I sensed good vibrations. Finding it was a stroke of luck.

I stop at Lake Wasookeag and park my red sports car, Felinas, at the rest area near some picnic tables. Alone, I strip down, put on my swimsuit and bathe in the lake. Afterward, I make a supper of a baguette with radishes, scallions and some cheese. A family comes to the picnic area and chooses a table far from mine. Good. The solitude feels right, even necessary. I've decided to spend the next two weeks exploring Maine.

There must have been a million crickets at my campsite off the highway outside of Monson, but peaceful and secluded. When fixing breakfast, I realize I'm poorly equipped to camp out, a last minute decision. I have no sharp knife or utensils and have to use part of a nylon stocking as coffee filter.

Then it's on to Greenville, the last outpost of civilization, to stock up on equipment. Every other building is a great wilderness outfitter. Two banks refuse to cash my check, but the A & P does so readily. It takes a while to get all the things I need and I leave Greenville at one thirty in the afternoon without coffee filters.

The great northern wilderness and Lilly Bay are up ahead. I spend the night at a gorgeous spot across from the water, but I have difficulty falling asleep when it gets dark and there is nothing else to do by 8 PM. I spend hours tossing and turning. On this night something comes to my tent. I can hear its rhythmic panting.

By morning, I've gotten into camping mode, losing my city ways grudgingly. Breakfast consists of scrambled eggs, burnt toast and coffee -- delicious! Afterward, I head for Kokadjo traveling a private logging road, dirt, wet down to control dust. Felinas gets caked with a half inch of mud clear up to the windows. The road comes to an end at a forest gatehouse where a woman takes down my plate number and asks where I am going, and how long I plan to stay. She wants to know where I'm from. We chat for a while and I tell her my plans. I had wanted to head northwest and on to the Gardner-Debouillé public land area, but the old woman tells me most of the trails on my map are privately owned logging roads and I won't be able to gain access to them. I will have to take the northeast route where I can visit Baxter State Park for the day. The old woman writes it down in her log book. That's good; I'm not going to die in the wilderness unknown to the world.

Baxter State Park is a long ride through rough country, but beautiful. Katahdin dominates the southern part; every turn in the road brings me face to face with that mountain and there are several camping areas. When I head up the narrow dirt trail it becomes wilder, unspoiled. That's when it happens. I'm going along, about fifteen miles an hour when I see a bear scamper across the road in front of me, a black bear.

Jesus! I wish there was someone with me to share this experience.

Surprisingly, I'm not frightened. Rather, I would like to be a bear too, to go tumbling and running in the woods with it. My Hollywood image was of creatures that stand on hind legs and roar menacingly, not this shaggy black ball scampering on all fours. It's surely an omen. When I first started writing I had terrifying dreams about a bear who came crashing through my safe middle class life wreaking havoc, its powerful claws tearing into walls, destroying all in its path.

No sooner have I parted with it then I come round the bend and see a doe and her young one in the middle of the road. The fawn takes off, but mother stays to examine me. It's as if I've stepped into another world. On leaving the park, I speak to the ranger who estimates the bear's age at two or three years, a young buck.

"It's rare to spot these bears," he says.

Come evening, I camp about three miles down an old logging road, a short way from Patten, off Route Eleven. I have an eerie feeling being there; psychic forces are at work. I take a walk on an overgrown, abandoned road, find some raspberries, eat several handfuls, then run for a half-mile.

After I've set up camp and had supper, I sit on a rock thinking about the underworld and how hard I work to keep it down, to ignore it. But still it's with me and pierces my reality when I least expect it. I think about psychic energy; I can feel its presence in the rocks. It occurs to me that my mind is obsessed with "relationship," that my life revolves around my relationships, and perhaps this is so because the world is too fearful otherwise. It holds unlimited possibilities -- chaos.

It's been a long driving day. I crawl into my tent and fall asleep in short time, but am awakened in the middle of the night, freezing. I try to rearrange my sleeping bag, put on my chamois shirt and wool socks and then the damn tent falls on me, full of dew. My sleeping bag and even my clothes get wet. I get up and go to sleep in the car.

A scary dream awakens me:

People pursue me with faces wrapped in gauze and I'm asked for identification, my driver's license with a picture, but I can't find a picture of myself without others in it.

In the morning, I discover the car has a flat tire and the battery is dead. I think to walk to the highway, but for some reason I'm a bit apprehensive. Once there, I decide if I have no luck after flagging down five cars I'll go back and maybe there will be enough juice in the battery to get it going. Number four car stops. A man with soft, curly grey hair greets me.

We look at each other for a moment; he's OK. "My car's parked a couple of miles down this road," I explain. "I've got a flat tire and my battery is dead."

He nods. "I'll go take a look," reaching over to pop open the door on the passenger side of his automobile, motioning for me to get in.

Once the tire is changed and the car's running, he hesitates . . . as if not wanting to part with me. I try to explain my trip to him, but my explanation lacks clarity. It doesn't matter, because

I can see he has understood the nature of the adventure I've embarked upon and he wants to share a small part of it. This service he's rendered will suffice him before he reenters the every-day world of his life in Patten.

It's back to Route Eleven, pouring rain. I head past Eagle Lake toward Fort Kent and Madawaska, to the very tip of the Maine border, then down through French country, Presque Isle, Frenchville, Van Buren. The terrain is very different here, miles and miles of flat land, potato fields and sugar beets. I listen to French songs from the Québec station just over the border. The farmhouses are great two and three story structures. I love the large open porches and half buried potato barns.

When my daughter came back from college, there was a strange look on her face when she arrived at the house. "You gotta get out of here, Ma," she said in an ominous tone.

And so I've left my dead house.

I'm not well. It started in the morning. I feel dizzy, weak, stomach is sick. I decide to spend the night at a rest area and information station in Houlton. I don't want to be far from help if I need it.

I awake the next morning not feeling any better. The camper parked next to me moves back and forth. At first I think it's my dizziness, but no, it's the wind. What a job trying to make coffee with the propane stove! It takes forever getting the water up to boil.

I spend the day in the parked car reading some poetry essays, Levertov and Rukeyser. And some of Céline's book, a stream-of-consciousness story from a guy living on the edge. The Levertov article was written in the sixties. She takes a righteous stand, belittling the rich kids and their experience at the Ivy League school where she taught.

I was more impressed with Rukeyser. Still, I find very little of substance concerning craft in both interviews. Before I knew very much about poetry I used to read Whitman, Dickinson, Poe, Bly. There was no plan to it, even later when I read every poet I heard of. Had someone asked, *Did you learn anything from it?* I would have said no. Perhaps there is a subconscious plan. I find that a poem writes itself if it is true. But how to arrive at truth? For me, it is learning to be quiet, learning to listen.

During my year of waiting for the house to sell, I realized that from the beginning what most interested me were the words. It was my reason for entering college. I had wanted to learn the words to speak my soul, and more than that to free me from the constraints of the identity imposed on me. I had wanted to master those specific words that are used to imprison and shackle the defenseless, and I've done that. Yet, I realize this isn't enough. I want to be able to touch people with my words.

I fix myself a big breakfast the next morning with a pot of coffee, some stir fried carrots, onions and potatoes, and a couple of toasted egg sandwiches with cheese, a sure cure for what ails me. I swear, on my deathbed I will be eating five course meals. Afterward, I take out some fruit for my midday snack straightening things out in the car, and go to wash up in the rest room.

Driving down Route One, I think of spending four days in the woods fasting, as the Indians do. A vision comes to them from the experience and it shows them the path they must follow in life. Usually an animal or bird is part of the vision and is adopted as that Indian's totem; it's incorporated in their name.

I want to do this. I've thought about it this winter, lying in bed at night thinking about starting a new life, wanting guidance for a new direction. This fast may not be easy to accomplish. I've got to find a place where I'm not going to meet up with people. And then there's the queasiness, I feel somewhat better today, but still in the bathroom, the room started swimming when I exerted myself.

To my left, off the highway, is a winding dirt road that I decide to explore. Rough going, some fresh tire tracks and many old apple trees along the way. I drive for a mile through woods and when I come to a clearing, I park the car and continue on foot. The area is fresh mown grass, flowers, and vegetable gardens.

Oops! I can see an old man working among the pole beans. *I'm on someone's property.* But another inlet leading to the gardens opens and I go back. Mr. Shey introduces himself, tells me he is a retired railroad man. He wears one of those striped engineer hats and looks like Santa except he hasn't got the beard.

"This is a beautiful area, Mr. Shey. The vegetable and the flower gardens are gorgeous.

You must have worked a long time to accomplish this."

"I have time. This is my private corner," he tells me with a wink. And it is that. No one traveling Route One would suspect there's an Eden behind the woods.

We chat for a while and we are silent too. I'm a bit uncomfortable, but I trust him. We lean on the hood of his truck and I notice he is inching close to me. I don't know what to think of it, but I don't have an urge to move away.

"How would you feel about my camping in
the woods back there?"

"I wouldn't mind at all."

"I'd like to stay for four days."

"That's fine. Come," he motions, "I'll get you some vegetables for your evening meal."

He gets me corn and tomatoes, some cucumbers and beans. Then he takes me for a walk beyond the clearing to the woods in the back.

"You can get water from that stream," he points down beneath a stone bridge where cool, dark water runs through a winding path of rocks. "There are three miles of woods beyond this, and then a couple of lakes -- all of it uninhabited, and miles and miles of woods beyond that."

He leaves then, his house being way back on Route One. I immediately set out for the woods. There are many trails and I walk quite a while looking for just the right spot to set up my tent. I take my clothes off along the way. Back at the clearing, I lie naked for a couple of hours, sunning myself and reading another essay. Erica Jong speaks about getting published and what it meant to her, that talent isn't enough, you need perseverance too, how she knew good writers in college who never followed through and weren't writing anymore.

Later I have my last meal, clean out the ice chest and get rid of the perishable food. I pack the things I will need for my four days in the woods and set out.

* * *

It starts raining during the night and by morning it is pouring. The tent leaks badly. Everything is soaked, my sleeping bag and all my clothes. Then all of a sudden a loud roaring noise;

sounds like a motorcycle. It's Mr. Shey coming up the road in an all-terrain vehicle.

So much for four days of fasting, solitude and peace.

"I got worried that you got lost in the woods."

Reasonable assumption, there is some responsibility about my camping in his woods, and he doesn't know me.

After he leaves, I put up a clothes' line and hang out the sleeping bag, my extra pairs of socks and my hat. But it's no good because it continues to rain on and off all day. I'm miserable, no place to stand or sit, rain, rain everywhere. I'm cold and there is nothing to be done about it; everything is wet. So I sit inside the tent on the plastic air mattress with rain coming down on me and all I can think of is home, but there is no home left, and of food, food, food, vegetables, eggs, thick sauces, fresh fruit with cream, cakes and pies.

I give up at five PM, bring in my wet sleeping bag and turn in. I'm beginning to get sick and have a bad headache.

Ω

Cloudy, overcast second day. I hang the sleeping bag on the line with little hope of it drying, then cut some pine boughs and fix myself a place to sit down. Later I take a walk, but it's hard going. I'm weak and tiring easily. What's more, my sneakers are getting soaked, so I sit around most of the day. The food cravings seem to be gone, but the headache continues.

I notice when I close my eyes that the imagery is vivid. I see wild, crazy pictures, wilder than dreams. I try to figure if they make up a story. They don't seem to. Do they reflect momentary feelings? I don't know, they're so outrageous it's hard to decipher them.

Mr. Shey drives up in the afternoon. "It's gonna be a cold night, about 30 degrees," he tells me.

Oh gosh, that's discouraging! Well, I'm going to have to do something about it.

He tells me his daughter is coming up from Connecticut this evening, which he's looking forward to. After he leaves I get to work preparing for the cold night by cutting some pine boughs to put underneath my air mattress, figuring it will put me that much higher off the ground and maybe I can put some on top of me.

Five o'clock and I'm exhausted. I check the sleeping bag, a few wet spots otherwise it's fairly dry. But the real luxury is that my woolen socks are dry. There is a towel and a pair of shorts in my pack. I wrap one around each foot then lie down.

It takes several hours till I fall asleep. All of a sudden, I'm awakened by the sound of the all-terrain vehicle.

Jesus! What is it now?

"Hello! Hello!" comes the impatient voice outside. While I'm in the process of opening the zippered screen, then the zippered flap, the voice, irritated, says, "Hey! Hello!"

I get things unzipped and see a young man with red hair sitting on the vehicle. "You must be Mr. Shey's son," I greet him.

"No, I'm the grandson."

He asks what I'm doing "way the hell up here."

"I don't know."

"You don't know!"

At this point, I close the flap to my tent. He can't start his all-terrain vehicle and mumbles something about it. His penis has wilted.

Good! I hope he gets stranded in the woods overnight.

And now I'm ill, violently ill. My stomach is going crazy. I keep wanting to throw up; surely it can't be food. I spend a long miserable night.

ΩΩ

Fairly warm third day, but windy: After awakening, I force myself to go outside. The sound of that wind is oppressive. Weakness is causing me to totter. I walk to my spot in the sun and am warmed. The tiniest field mouse, no more than a biteful, comes to check me out. Then many birds park themselves in surrounding trees, sparrows mostly. They're starting to trust my presence.

I hang out my sleeping bag to finish drying and see Mr. Shey driving up the path for a visit.

"I'm really impressed with what you're doing," he says. Marvel and affection are written all over his face.

I nod, "I feel the same way about you. You're a kind, gentle man with a trusting heart. I enjoy these visits."

"I do too."

It isn't that we talk so much, but rather we seem attuned to each other. I feel at peace when I'm with him.

Before leaving he gives me the weather report, "It's gonna be a cold night, but warm day tomorrow," then he starts his machine and heads out.

My energy runs out at three PM. I try to stick it out till four but at three thirty I decide to turn in. I put on my two pairs of socks and sneakers. Tonight, everything is dry. The minute I lie down the vision begins. I see a man dressed in a phosphorescent robe. On his chest is a scroll with calligraphic writing on it. It's a map. From each side of the man's throat grows a young tree, both reach up to form the antlers of a deer.

This man is a sorcerer who gives off a cool, glowing light in the dark. His identity, worn on his chest, is the *words*, beautifully written. It serves as a map to guide others. Indians have visions of animals; I have one of a sorcerer. I understand the vision is guiding me to the world I know but dare not acknowledge or speak of. It's the underworld, the world of chaos, without boundaries, that I glimpsed on the logging road.

The vision continues and I see jaws, the open jaws and teeth of what appears to be a fish or alligator, a Batman with his mask, several Batmen snapping their long fangs. Then it is eyes, a face with an eyeball wet and slimy. A hand reaches in to pull it out; it turns into a little fish. And next a face that looks like a mask, the right eye is missing.

This part of the vision is the other side of the coin, the life without identity, wearing a mask, rapaciously hungry, without sight or wisdom.

Ω Ω Ω

I awaken at 9 AM on the fourth day. A coyote came close to my tent during the night and sang me a lullaby. It isn't my puny energy it crooned to but that great feminine astral power in the sky. Tomorrow morning I'll be making my way down to the clearing and the gardens. I'm concerned about my ability to make that trip with full pack, the tent and my sleeping bag.

The day is warm, full sun. I sit quietly for a while and write in my journal. Afterward I take my clothes off and sunbathe but I can only stay for a while, I'm exhausted. At noontime I crawl into my tent. My mood is peaceful; the forest has an order that induces this. I find that I don't think very much, it's more intuitive. In the city my mind spins and spins until at times I wish I could remove my head to get a rest.

This morning when pissing on the ground I noticed a rock with a small natural puckering hole in it that looks like an inverted belly button. Turns out it's an old Indian scraping tool used to abrade hides and such; fits perfectly in the hand. Whoever made it shaped it in such a way that it looks like a fish with the belly button pucker as its eye. When I leave here I'll be driving through Indian territory, the Micmacs'. I had wanted to buy myself something; the scraping tool is much better, made when Indians roamed America, Children of the Earth that nourished them and this simple tool a part of it.

I think about that first day in the gardens with Mr. Shey. I could see that although my work is there, I don't want to go back to the city for a long while. It saps my energy just to maintain balance in all that craziness.

My daily visitor comes at three thirty. I crawl out of my tent and stand for a while but find I can't sustain it and go to sit by his side on the red machine he disdains so. "It's my son's," he always points out.

We have a long visit and talk about simple things, about nature and animals, the habits of certain birds. It's ending and both feel sad. I confide in him about my fast and vision quest.

"I suspected you were doing that. I could see there were no cooking utensils here. I wanted to bring you a sandwich several times."

I smile at this offer.

"I'm truly amazed you've done this and stuck it out."

I don't know why I'm not afraid in the woods only that it's a fact. I tell him about the coyote that came to my tent in the night.

"I hear them in the evening from my house. They travel in packs. That's how they hunt."

He doesn't warn me or try to coax me out of the woods because he knows I'm free and treats me with respect.

"Will I see you tomorrow?" I ask, pointing out that I'll leave around noontime.

"I won't be able to come in the morning. My daughter's visiting and we'll be going to church. But why don't you stop at the house when you leave?"

I can tell it's important to him; he wants his wife to meet me, but I don't want to do that. What with the grandson's visit I figure I'm being thought of as a curiosity at his house.

At night the visions are of women. I see a sorceress in a long white gown. The woman wears a crown that springs off her head and is structured into a triangle, richly decorated with lights around it. Then come a series of pictures of one woman. It's a friend back home, a woman who's lost her power in the world. She appears soft, feminine, happy, not this woman's way for many years now. She is hardened and emulates men's ways in the city.

In the first scene, she wears a wedding gown but hides her face. When she does show it, there are small tree fungi all over, and also on her gown. She wears another wedding gown in the next scene.

It has a bluish tinge and the crown of her veil is encrusted with large bluish pearls. She is walking at the edge of a cornfield.

The last scene depicts the bride sitting at her vanity, radiant. She arranges her face and hair. There follows a series of pictures of women, all beautiful; one is a painting of a woman holding a yellow flower, a living, moving painting with red, red lips. The flower is presented; it is live.

The sorceress with triangular headpiece brings unity and light, warm light to me. She shows me the way to become whole through the example of my friend who is transformed and given a new identity by becoming part of the woods, the cultivated soil, through solitude and refinement of the soul.

And I understand, the beauty of woman ultimately is the flower she presents to us, not the way she appears.

Ω Ω Ω Ω

This is the morning! I crawl out of my tent; make my way to the blackberries across the path that I've been eyeing for the past four days. Their tartness grabs at my throat and I retch. I drink some water and sit in the sun for a bit and rest.

Then I start packing for my trip down, making everything as compact as possible. The plastic water jug is emptied and I latch it to my pack. Bedroll is tied so I can carry it like a suitcase. Only the tent is cumbersome. Although it folds up compactly and slips in a pouch, the pouch has no handle.

I gather the pine boughs I had cut and use them to repair part of the path that is gutted and collects water. Slowly and rhythmically I make my way down, never stopping once all the way. I can see the clearing ahead. I start to cry -- because I am glad? -- No, confounding human nature, I am sad to leave the woods.

Felinas waits faithfully. My breakfast consists of herb tea with honey and I have an orange to eat. Throughout food preparation, I scurry back and forth through the gardens and fill my cooler with vegetables as Mr. Shey has advised.

The sun overwhelms me and I sit in the car to rest. I pull out a crisp, clean sheet of paper and write a poem to Mr. Shey. I include a note and pick some goldenrod and black-eyed Susans that I stick in the scarecrow's hat.

Back on the road, tooting wildly as I pass Mr. Shey's house, I drive by the Indian reservation and am overwhelmed with sadness. They have now become the Children of Government. They live in identical brick houses all in a row, all facing the highway.

I turn the radio on, want to get acclimated by degrees, but find I cannot listen to hard news. A plane crash has occurred in California killing fifty people; and over in South Africa thirty Blacks have been murdered for refusing to leave homes after being given eviction notices. This information is given in a rhythmic, singsongy way. No feelings, hard.

Click! I shut the thing off.

Around five o'clock I decide to stop at a store and get some supplies, then find a place to bed down for the night. Oh god, what a shock I encounter when I step into the store! I've lost my way of being in the world. Stimuli bombard me from all sides. Words! Letters! Signs! Exhortations! I feel like an African bush woman suddenly transplanted to the Grand Central Terminal. Against the back wall is an icebox with butter, I get two sticks and make my way to the counter. I want to protect myself from all the stimuli. Furtively, I look at the counter girl as she slowly counts out my nickels and dimes and then I run out.

Once outdoors I make a quick assessment of my physical appearance: wild hair that I stick beneath a straw hat to no avail. My body looks emaciated. A normally slender woman, this weight loss makes me look anorexic. I can finally say without equivocation that I have a flat abdomen. And my inner thighs so long a source of concern at the gym, the skin just hangs from them now. What's more, I haven't bathed in five days.

I stop at another store, make my way to the icebox; *there's that Wine Cooler I like.* As I reach in to get it a young man comes over and says, "No Ma'am, you can't take that."

"What have I done?" I jump back.

Seems they don't sell wine on Sunday in this town. I'm completely unnerved and mutter something about getting ice.

"Yes," he says. "You can get ice."

I quickly make my way out of there too. Eventually stopping at two other stores, each time gaining more composure. My walk becomes slower, sexier. People's looks are less strange when they see me. I keep driving and driving, but can't seem to find a place to bed down for the night.

Finally around 7 PM in desperation I make my way to a boat access and launching area in Searsport. A big lot, tarred with marked lines for parking cars, big overhead lights, potted flowers and a picnic area with corrugated metal tables, grills and a tiny lawn. But the view is stupendous, ocean all around, about twenty five boats moored in the water, some with sailing rig, a long, large wharf where people are coming back from boat trips.

There's much activity in the lot, cars pulling in and out. Some just come for the view, others are going home with their catch. Two women and a young boy in a beat up car pull up next to mine. Mama and her girlfriend, sitting to my right with the window open, are discussing LOVE. The kid's got an enormous ice cream cone in one hand and a large drink in the other. I watch him playing for a while. He finishes his ice cream then throws stones at the sea gulls. I have to control an urge to push him over the rock edge he skirts and send him hurtling into the ocean.

At bedtime, I park under the big light next to the camper trailer making sure all doors are locked.

Morning sun streams down on me; people are bustling through the parking lot. I sit up, again the outstanding view. I notice people are less frantic than the ones I saw in the stores yesterday. About fifteen of them are fishing off the docksides.

I make my way to the corrugated metal tables and start coffee. An old woman comes to greet me and offers chitchat. I acknowledge her and reply briefly, trying to protect myself, to control incoming messages. Something happened to me in the woods -- I don't want to lose it, don't want to go back to being crazy in the world again.

I sit with my coffee and begin to write. The old woman and her husband take the table next to mine. They are having lobster. He unfolds a lawn chair facing the sea and cracks open a book, a pampered man, handsome, lean, with full white beard. His wife faces corrugated metal and begins her attack on the lobsters. She works steadily and quietly save for an occasional query about her husband's well being. She speaks with an accent too faint for me to distinguish. The morning passes like so. The man removes his tee shirt, nice, well-proportioned chest. He sees me watching and struts a bit. I'm amazed at the amount of meat the old woman has managed to extract from the lobsters. Everything's been pulverized. I notice she didn't save the tomalley -- an out-of-stater.

It's time to head home. I chart my route and head inland. The closer I get the more anxious I become, not wanting this time to end and bracing myself for the ride into town. I would like to go immediately to my cabin, but doubt that it is ready yet.

I decide to go to the Silver Gym, take a shower and afterward get supper, hoping staff is not present so I won't have to chitchat. Again the violent shock as I enter, hard black iron strewn in long rows on the floor, heavy black iron machines everywhere, and the whole of it set off by mirrors all around reflecting it twice and three times over.

I pass a body builder and his girlfriend on my way to the locker rooms. Both give me the once-over and disdain me. Three weeks ago I was a peacock strutting this floor. I still remember the combination to my locker and the door opens to reveal an electric blue body suit with stripes, smoke colored tights and salmon pink leg warmers hanging there.

I pack everything up except the toiletries I will need for my bath. The shower lasts thirty-five blissful minutes and afterward I blow dry my hair, put on a dress and heels examining myself in the mirror. I look good; my face is strong.

Chinese dinner at the Jade Fountain: I see hardship in the faces of people around me and I remember the glib comment made by a visiting celebrity. "A depressed mill town," is how he phrased it. Two fortune cookies inform me that my outstanding trait is versatility and the way of the heart is the most profound way to speak.

I head for the cabin, stopping along the way to pick up a bottle of champagne. What an incredible sight it is when I get there! A big bouquet of wild flowers with oak leaves sits on the picnic table, several smaller ones in the house. The place has been spruced up and polished.

I sit quietly outdoors for about fifteen minutes taking in the white tipped, blue mountains, the lake, the tall pines. I light the outdoor fireplace that's been prepared with newspaper and kindling. Then I become frenzied like the lobster woman and bring in the things I had stored in the pump house, hang all the bedding, area rugs and pillows to air out, put the food supplies on shelves, in cabinets. I decide to leave my office furniture and equipment for another day. I am too weak to move the filing cabinet and desk.

I proceed to the car, uncork the champagne bottle and pop it against the front door. Then I completely unload the car by firelight, bringing in the vegetables from Mr. Shey's gardens. I wash them up and cook the beet greens so as not to lose them. At four o'clock in the morning, with everything straightened out, I hop in bed. In the still and quiet I am aware I have entered the chaotic darkness of my life, my new home. I begin to cry, deep heart wrenching sobs, and I do not stop for a long time.

THE HIGH PRIESTESS

-II-

Woman has been the object of adulation since the beginning of time. Before Jesus and Mohammed, before the Great Gautama, people gathered round the sacred fire to invoke her power. Now women speak of the intricacies of relationship, of children and the comforts of home, but of the One who has taught them to weave and to cast spells, they wisely say nothing.

Like mother before them, they are slow to declare their debt and acknowledge Her influence. It's not mother but the Seeress who comes to teach in the night. Having forsaken the warm bosom, they are ready to make use of her powers. She sits regally in front of two pillars across which hangs a veil separating us from the Unknown.

The High Priestess is dressed in long blue robes, her feet firmly planted on a large crescent moon. Its orb, pale yellow, is repeated in miniature form on her crown. Her beauty is striking and hypnotic. Deep blue eyes cast a penetrating gaze as she points to the scroll on her lap. "Come," she beckons. "Come and see. You cannot continue your life without this knowledge."

Upright: Connecting with one's psychic power.
Laying confusion aside. Intuitive wisdom carries one further.

Reversed: Rejecting one's psychic power.

After a morning of working in the fields I retreat to my private world in the 'Chicken Coop', an artist's studio that was once home to a cackling brood. It is here that I have placed my files, the books I cannot live without, the novel I am working on, my poetry and essays. Here, I imagine, a new identity is forming as I work at school essays and my novel, "53". The coop, attached to the Lavender House, has a pitched roof slanting down towards the outside wall and is covered with large windows, a room drenched in afternoon sun. Hermine lounges on the long design table below the windows. She has been to the Farm many times and considers it a vacation home.

My cat would be greatly offended to be thought anyone's pet. A country neighbor back in Maine, herself a transplanted New Yorker gave her to us. The egg woman as we called her, did a little farming, raised some chickens, selling their eggs. The woman's name was Hermine, so I named the little kitty after her. I did not consider her my cat; she was free to attach herself to anyone in the house, or to remain unattached if she so chose. In the course of teaching her that she was not living in the wild and did not have to fight me for every scrap of food she saw, I sustained some nasty scratches the first few weeks she came to live with us. Then early one Friday evening, I was alone in the house, sitting in the living room with a glass of wine after my day's work; she came to the room and stopped by the entry looking at me, a beautiful cat, intelligent, lively. It occurred to me that I loved her. What an absurd thought, a little furry creature, independent, even bitchy; she had only been with us a couple of weeks! How could I possibly have feelings for her? We continued to look at each other for a long moment, and then she walked over and jumped on my lap -- something she had not as yet done.

I was hers, she knew it and claimed me. And so it was from that moment on. Witches speak of a familiar, an animal said to serve and protect one. In many cultures, the cat has been regarded as a supernatural, a bringer of good fortune or as an omen of evil, especially a black cat. Hermine is not black, she is a brown striped tabby and I do consider her my familiar. Too many events have occurred indicating that our relationship was more than one should assume from a cat. She has taught me to be aware of a person's energy as opposed to their words, actions or appearance. What energy does a person bring into a room when entering it? Does the energy increase or dissipate with time?

I could not understand at first the animosity she felt towards individuals I perceived as innocuous, but slowly I began to decipher a pattern in this group, a certain falseness, and an imbalance that made for adversity. She taught me to be more observant of my senses, and she surely saved me once that I know of, and maybe more than that. She let me know there was someone outside about to break into the house one night. As I walked to the entryway trying to figure out what was so upsetting her, a man opened the door intent on robbing me. I was blocking his way and he ran off. Had he walked in unchecked, only to discover me unexpectedly, I would have had a bad time of it.

After my vision quest, I settle in my cabin by the mountains and start work on my first novel, "COMICS." I also seek to learn something of others who have taken similar spiritual journeys. I study with the anthropologist and shaman, Michael Harner and I attend a conference in Boston and later at Cape Cod where I meet Margot Adler, the National Public Radio correspondent and granddaughter to the Viennese psychiatrist and Freudian disciple, Alfred Adler. Margot is a longtime witch who has written a definitive book on the history of witchcraft, Druids and paganism, entitled "Drawing Down the Moon." I also study with Starhawk, another witch and psychologist from California. As a nature based spirituality, witchcraft celebrates the eight witches' sabbats, the turning of the wheel as it is called, which occurs at times of seasonal change, one celebrates the solstices, the equinoxes, the cycle of planting seeds, harvest, the approaching darkness and cold. I find celebrating the sabbats a meaningful experience, a time to ponder the harvest I have reaped in the fall, in spring, a renewed sexual energy, and acknowledging loss on Hallow's Eve. I am a child of the earth.

Our technologically based society separates us from planetary revolutions, but it does not shield us from them. They do affect us; better to acknowledge and understand the change earth and its inhabitants are moving towards or away from.

I am not an astrologer, but can see merit in accepting the fact that we are part of a universe that encompasses even the lowly human being on planet earth. Surely, we cannot remain untouched by this planetary system. Witches speak of magic. It has been said that they *make* magic, but magic is not something one makes. It is all around us, one has to learn to tap into it. I do not waste energy on clients who doubt, want to be convinced, demand proof. It has to start with faith, faith that magic happens and that one is capable of harnessing it. Magic will not bring you to a destination you're unwilling to put effort in attaining, nor will it present you with inappropriate choices. One of the tenets of magic is based in knowing what is appropriate for oneself and one's milieu.

I attend a workshop with the witch, Zsuzsanna Budapest in upper New York. The woman who owns the property where this conference takes place is also a witch, a green witch, one who's power lies in knowledge of herbs and plants for healing, nourishment and awareness. Her apprentices work all summer and participate in many of the ongoing workshops and conferences. They are the cooks who feed us excellent meals using weeds, flowers, and goat cheese.

The Green Witch raises goats, hence the cheese, longhaired white beauties, and has found a way to create a unicorn. Not a matter of reproductive genetic engineering, rather a physical operation to create the unicorn on a goat's forehead. The property is off in the wilderness set way above a fetid, slimy green pond, and on the ground underfoot are scattered pieces of dark slate. Apparently had been a slate mine in the past. The sun never comes out once during my stay. Thankfully, I have the van with bedding and all its facilities. Others camp outdoors in the rain. There are places in the house for people to sleep, but no one wants to put up with the Green Witch.

The dampness, the fetid green pond, the goats baah-ing, baah-ing, and I on the deck of the Green Witch's meeting house every morning early, playing a cassette of Ottmar Liebert's haunting guitar pieces and doing my exercises, is what comes most vividly to mind of the time. Zsuzsanna has initiated the witch Starhawk, whose book "The Spiral Dance" is considered a classic among pagans and witches. Those of us with psychic power sense it immediately when meeting another gifted person. A beneficial exchange of energy travels between us. The short time that I was with Starhawk was a wonderful experience for both of us.

Starhawk's mentor, Zsuzanna is the daughter of a woman who had been a practicing witch in Budapest. She herself is responsible for reviving the craft in the United States. A tough bird, currently involved with a woman, and in her past had been a professor's wife, part of the academy. I take her seriously and write down everything she says. She speaks about power, how to get it, how to use it, how to protect oneself. And she speaks about the ancient one, the one beyond mind and intellect, before language, way back in the first brain, she who lives for pleasure, and drama, and ritual; a sensual woman who takes pleasure as her right.

When it comes time to leave I'm approached by a jolly looking, silver haired, rotund woman wearing an apron, "Are you going to Maine?" she says. "Could I ride with you?"

How can I say no? I'm her only way home. But the thought of spending 6 hours with a crinkly, jolly-cheeked little grandmother is not appealing. She hasn't packed her belongings yet so I walk over to help her. Her bed is a fishnet hammock tied to a couple of trees in the woods.

Must've been difficult when it rained.

We get her belongings loaded in the van and off we go. Out of the woods and into the heavy traffic of a nearby city, I slowly inch up, stop light by stop light, to the intersection that will lead to the turnpike. The light changes to red just as I'm about to turn. Now, as anyone who has had a Ford Econoline van knows, the gears get stuck at times and you have to go out, pop the hood, jiggle them back in their slot, while someone inside presses on the clutch.

At that very intersection with three thousand cars behind us in which sit drivers, eyes riveted on the traffic light, I can't get in gear when the light turns green. I explain the situation to Freyja as best I can to the accompaniment of three thousand blaring car horns. Once I step out of the van with my wrench, my neighbors get the message and drive by screaming profanities and spitting. But the old woman's cool, doesn't let it faze her. She even gives them the bird.

We get to talking once we hit the highway. She tells me she's a witch, but has never been initiated, a sex witch.

"I beg your pardon?"

The plump Mrs. Santa Claus has devoted years and years to the study of sex, contributed articles about it to erotic magazines, has created pornographic cassette tapes and experimented extensively in the field. She sees herself as a sacred slut. She's also an excellent artist in all media with a series of water colored cunts in their many moods. I have notepaper with a reproduction of one of her ecstatic cunts in its lower right hand corner. She's also a potter and a naturalist. There's a photographic art show created by an artist that features her corpulent fleshy body, naked, in the act of creating pottery that's been exhibited in a number of galleries.

When we get to Maine she asks me to drop her off at a friend's house, her own place being over an hour out of my way. We unload her stuff which looks like the gear for a Lewis and Clark expedition, parfleche sacs, carpet bags, the rolled up hammock -- sturdy, quality material.

Knock, knock, knock, nobody comes to the door. We wait and wait. Nothing.

"I can't leave you out here with all your stuff," I say. "I'll give you a ride home."

What I see when we arrive at her aerie by the Atlantic Ocean is a true witch's house. Disney could not have done it better. She lives way, way up in the trees, three long flights of stone stairs as we ascend into the foliage, cutting our view from the road below. At the second level is a sauna built below the deck of her cottage. The property once belonged to her and her husband, a summer home for the family. Freyja chucked family life, hubby and the kids on the day she received her master's degree from art school. Walked out on all of it, moved into the summer cottage, and with a bank loan, she built a large pottery studio, the deck and the sauna. There is no running water and no phone. She heats with wood that she hauls up to her tree aerie with a motor driven Rube Goldberg contraption that lifts it up and deposits it on her deck.

When we finally arrive at her door there's a witch's broom of twigs nearby, gorgeous flowering plants all over the deck, tools, split wood, an altar with candles and purple linen. Inside her house is a veritable junkman's dream. Stuff is piled everywhere. You cannot afford to be squeamish in the filthy place. I will spare you the details of what the kitchen looks like.

After several trips back down to the van to get the rest of her things in, we settle down to a pot of herbal tea and we make a pledge to follow the rituals, the ways of knowledge, and the eight sabbats of the craft that will lead to initiation in a year's time.

Our sabbats become wonderful celebrations with theater, fantasy, the very best food, wine, and flowers. Nature surrounds us, the trees, the ocean, the birds; it's a magical time in which we spend most of it living out on the deck.

Of all the rituals we perform, one comes especially to mind. It's a lesson on the powers of sexuality that she passes on at the sabbat of Yule (the winter solstice, December 20-23.) I'm artist in residence at University of Maine in Orono at this time and travel over to spend weekends with her. Once I arrive and we have deposited the goodies I've brought for our celebration, she suggests we visit her neighbor and friend who lives down below, close to the sea.

Chuck's a good ol' boy, recently abandoned by some decent woman. He and a bunch of his buddies now share the little house the couple occupied. Beer flows freely, reefer smoke in every room, flashes of male aggression, a typical boys' clubhouse.

"I got some good whiskey for Christmas Freyja, why don't you and I, and the redhead," he points to me, "have a glass of cheer."

We have a drink and the guys do too. Yak, yak, yak, first thing I know Freyja and I are in the kitchen washing men's hair under the tap. They're standing in line waiting their turn. Everybody's stoned, getting really groovy, into the scrubbing, the white towels, patting their hair dry. The sex witch winks at me.

I am in a small house with about six or seven good ol' boys, rough necks, outdoor workers, fishermen, carpenters, who only travel in one direction if sexually aroused. Not comfortable, a situation I would not put myself into willingly. I make sure I keep an open path to the outside door. Sure enough, signs of aggression, guys shoving each other; someone says this is all a tease. Out of the blue, Freyja starts recounting an article she's read about the intelligence and communicating abilities of whales.

What is she talking about?

The men laugh at her and her new age ideas. She goes right along with them. I don't know about whales, but animals when cornered show their underbelly, their vulnerability, so as not to be attacked. As in the case of animals, the current of energy changes in the room so that shortly we are having the most intimate talk about Christmas, where we stand in our particular lives at this present holiday, and what it means to us, some sad stories, told with grit and the pride of machismo men, a truly memorable evening.

As the old witches' saying goes, Where there's fear, there's power.

THE EMPRESS

-III-

A woman sits in a garden by a waterfall; a deep red heart at center of her chest separates a small, lovely bosom. She is heavy with child. All of her resources are committed to nurturing this small beginning. She will cherish and give succor to it long after others have lost interest.

The Empress, at one moment soulful and receptive, can be a willful menace if she sees her progeny threatened. This is not reflected in her warm, youthful face, which promises a life of bucolic pleasure. There isn't the least hint of ravage in the blooming pink lotus, along with several strands of wheat she holds in her left hand, or in the sensual way her long blond hair caresses bare shoulders. Like the many-seeded pomegranate at her feet, there is only endless possibility for beginnings in this wonderful garden. And the child's time is short before the full force of life must be acknowledged.

The Empress has one foot resting on a crescent moon. She sits with her legs spread widely, the cloth of her robe clings to strong, heavy thighs. One's gaze is drawn between those thick legs, where it all begins, deep into darkness, in an underworld of desire.

Upright: Commitment to growth; fecundity, nurturance, protection; the garden of earthly contentment.

Reversed: Psychological problems, lack of commitment, disloyalty.

With teachers and fellow apprentices at Sarah Lawrence, we dissect our own writing and that of the story collections we read to see what works and why. Later in the chicken coop studio, I work in bed facing the desk I set up but do not use. Notebooks, scraps of paper, pens, file cards, and a pile of books surround me. Hermine at my feet likes being close to the creative energy of my writing. Later, Kate and I critique the stories I am reading for classes over dinner, Henry James, Jorge Luis Borges, Flannery O'Connor, among a host of others, share our meal. With New York City on the back burner for the time being, I luxuriate in literature, that and being out in nature shearing Christmas trees.

We are making progress in the fields and it looks like we may be able to get all the trees sheared for the harvest. Kate is invited to discuss her writing at a conference in Germany and during her absence, in my time alone out in the fields, and at the evening dinner table, I contemplate my return to the city. I would like to leave when the farm work is completed.

Someone drops a newspaper on my windshield on one of my trips into the city, a weekly crammed full of events, announcements, classifieds and, a 'for rent' section with listings from people looking for roommates.

I could afford to do that.

I check the weekly's address and head over to Houston Street looking for New York Press. At the receptionist's desk, I compose an ad seeking a roommate situation for Hermine and I, listing The Farm telephone number where I can be reached.

The receptionist looks it over, changes a few words, "It'll come out next Tuesday," she says as she walks off with my scrap of paper.

Every joke and wisecrack I've heard about rents in New York, most especially Manhattan, turn out to be true. They are merely scratching the surface. In 1890 William Dean Howells wrote a book now considered a classic, "A Hazard of New Fortunes" in which the main character, March and his wife, arrive in New York thinking they should be able to find accommodations in a day or two. It It took Howells almost 3 chapters to elucidate the difficulty of their search. I am just as naive as the Marches a hundred years later when the situation is a hundred times more wretched.

After showing me the room I would occupy, one roommate tells me that I will not be allowed in the rest of the apartment, but that I'm free to use the bathroom. To cover the prohibitive rent prices, tenants are forced to take desperate measures; some living in studios looked to share their one room apartment with me. Manhattan is where everyone wants to live and I am no different. I could just as easily have stayed home as to live in Brooklyn, the Bronx or Queens. Below are lines addressed to my immigrant father who was always served the meat platter first at our table:

UN MORCEAU DE VIANDE

Je me rappelle de toi, Papa
Assis à la table avec Simone
Qui t'offrait toujours premièrement
L'assiette de viande, pas à moi et my petits frères.
Tu m'avais dit "Je suis l'homme dans cette famille:
C'est à moi la viande."

Guardes tes Christ de grillades de lard
Salées, tes rôtis de porc, tes tourtières,

Papa; garde tes privilèges du Canada. Je m'en vais
En Amérique, pi je m'en fishe!
Tu n'as pu le droit du Seigneur sur moi.
Ce qui se passe dans me culottes

C'est mes affaires. Tu comprends tu?
Tu pensais me vende en mariage à un Seigneur
Pour que je lui passe l'assiette
À mon tour, les janbons, la dinde de Noël
Les saumons du passage St. Laurent. Non!
C'est à moi la viande, Papa. Tu comprends tu ça?

Le riz gommeux, les petits radis rouges, la sauce blanche,
c'est les pâtées de ceux qui vivent en prison.
Pas moi! J'vais m'sauver; j'vais prendre
le train qui va jusqu'au coeur des États-Unis;
j'vais manger à mon goût; j'vais danser et chanter;
j'vais parler les mots que tu m'as defendu.

Can such a girl aiming straight for the heart of the United States settle for the boroughs? I want the Big Apple. After visiting many apartments and prospective roommates, I settle for an arrangement on the Upper East Side with an editor who has a house upstate and only stays in the city two days a week, a nice apartment in a good neighborhood that I will have to myself most of the time. Kate and I celebrate my good fortune with a steak dinner and a bottle of red wine. I leave with a promise to return on harvest weekends to help out when buyers come to tag their trees and later retrieve them.

Back in the city, there is much to learn, the subway system, the busses. Everything is fast, fast, fast, people running everywhere, eating on the street as they walk to their next destination. A game of 'chicken' is played between pedestrians and cars at every stoplight to see who owns the street. The crowding and pushing, the shoving, the bumping and the interminable 'excuse me's', I have excused myself more times in my first month in the city than I ever did before in my life. And the people are amazing. You see the most beautiful women in the world on the street, and the most wretched human beings, every skin shade, every nationality, every language is represented; they wear turbans, burnooses, hijabs, abayas, kimonos, sarongs, silk pajamas, berets, kaffiyeh, hoodies, and yarmulkes, so many accents, my favorite being the native New Yawka's. I find myself after encounters with such individuals walking off down the street repeating the words just heard, trying to grasp the accent, fuggedaboudit. It's OK, most people talk to themselves on the street too.

The adventure of my life exhausts me; I come home early evening and crash in bed.

Neighborhoods retain much of the 19th century flavor lost to the rest of America through its small businesses, markets, its bodegas, and its city of walkers. All of these enterprises sitting on the most expensive real estate, in an island that is difficult for delivery trucks to navigate into and out of, makes for expensive goods.

Having received training from Hermine, I am keen on energy and quickly notice that there is a certain carefulness, a privacy to people on the street that I don't sense elsewhere. It's not that people are afraid, or overly protective, I would use the word alert, like an animal is alert. I fall in love with New Yorkers from the start for their pragmatism, their reasonableness, their sense of fair play and their ironic humor. In a city with so many voices, so many needs, one gets to the heart of the matter quickly, (out-of-towners might say rudely,) resolves the matter and moves on.

I have decided to take my former Greenwich Village roommate to Small Claims Court to see about getting my money back. I should tell you that the idea of New York as opposed to the fact of it overwhelms me at times. I walk the streets, look at skyscrapers around me and think, *Yes, I'm in New York; yes, I'm in Chinatown; Yes, Times Square, Macy's, Delancey Street, Bloomingdale's, Sardi's.* Every square inch has been filmed, analyzed, dramatized, compartmentalized.

Will court be like the TV shows?

I fill out the papers, collect the necessary proof and head down to Centre Street for my appearance on the appointed date. Huge dramatic buildings with sculptured friezes, Greek columns and majestic stairs leading within to all manner of courts, civil, criminal, superior, federal dot the area. I find the right building; no this is not like court TV. The hallway is packed with grim people clutching whatever evidence they've brought to win the day. Actually it is night, everyone looks tired and miserable, except for the lawyers who are preening among their peers. The doors open and we file in to a courtroom the size of an auditorium. There will be no friendly chat with the judge here. When my case is called I'm informed that my former roommate has telephoned ahead and canceled, a much-abused tactic in Small Claims Court, the thought being to wear down your opponent with postponements. I am not a quitter. At the second court hearing, she appears with her father in tow. Roommate is wearing a scruffy pea coat and a pair of jeans, apparently hoping to impress the judge with her penurious circumstances. I, on the other hand, am dressed in a black suit, nylons and high heels, having learned through experience that the court system favors middle-class, responsible-looking adults.

Dad, a lawyer presently taking graduate courses in divinity at Harvard, moves for another postponement. The judge is ready to go along with this in spite of my objections until he notices the address on my petition, which is Kate's address at the Farm.

"You've come all the way down from Poughkeepsie for this hearing?" he says.

Why I had put the Farm's address escapes me presently, but I say, "Yes, Your Honor," and am granted my hearing.

I choose to see an arbitrator rather than take a chance of being heard by the judge and risk another postponement. My opponent agrees; the benefit for their side is that there is no possibility of appeal if I fumble my presentation and lose the case.

The arbitrator sends us out in the hall to see if we can come to some agreement. Dad and I talk back and forth; he looks down to the files in my hand as I gesture with them unknowingly to make a point.

"OK," he says when I propose to extend the payments over the next four months.

We go back to the arbitrator and present our agreement.

"Include your address in the document," I say to Elizabeth's father.

He demurs.

"Put your address down," says the arbitrator. He watches as Dad fills in the information, "No post office box, a real address," he points out.

A divinity student, hunh? I can see where roommate learned her tricks.

I don't have any money. There's a mix-up at the school financial aid office, and although I make a lot of noise, it gets me nowhere. Kate's lover, herself a student, advises me that she is able to get food stamps and a small stipend from the city. A pretty grim prospect, still I have to do something and I call the number she gives me. When I get to the building, it is like a scene from bedlam. Filthy, cavernous halls populated by confused, brain-addled individuals, homeless supplicants unable to comprehend what the system expects of them, the forms, the protocols, and the hopelessly poor who understand only too well that they are being made to humiliate themselves for society's regalement. There is no one to answer questions or give directions; I stand on line for hours just to find out where to go to apply for food stamps.

One woman loses it and screams at a worker who 'disses' her, "Without my black ass you wouldn't have a job!"

The cavernous hall explodes in applause. I join in whole-heartedly.

When my turn comes, I am sent upstairs where a roomful of people sit on metal folding chairs waiting their turn to be called by a battalion of welfare workers on the other side of the partition. I put my name on the sign-up sheet and go to take my seat with the others where I face another predicament. I find myself heading toward the only other white person in the group.

What does this mean? Am I a bigot?

Maine has so few black people that I never laid eyes on one until I went to college, and even in that circumstance they were only a handful that kept to themself and were seen as exotic. My ideas about blacks and the black experience are a cliché picked up from the media that permeated my susceptible mind like water to a garden trench. I saw myself as a liberal-minded person who wanted to do the right thing. Yet I'm not even comfortable enough to go sit with them. One has no idea how we become racist, how we learn to harbor secret ideas about others, how we are informed of our place in society relative to them, our standing in the scheme of things.

The food stamps and stipend, the first check from roommate and my financial aid package for the past semester all arrive on the same day. I go out and buy myself a computer and a printer. What a thrill! I owned many things when I was married, a house, several sets of china, a variety of stemware, kitchen gadgets, linen of all sorts, a roomful of books, the furnishings of a six room house, a beautiful Duchess Atlantic wood burning cook stove as well as a Franklin fireplace, my grandmother's pedal sewing machine, wood boxes, a pick-ax, seven or eight good shovels, a couple of hoes, rakes, a lawn mower, outdoor furniture. I gave some of it away and put the rest in storage. With each move I lost or gave away more and more, letting go of my previous life by bits and pieces.

The first thing I bought myself after the vision quest, living in the cabin, was a sound system, speakers, a receiver, cassette deck and turn table. With a new life must come music. That system which I have added to, and now the new computer has given me more pride of ownership than all that I possessed in the past. I gave much thought to these purchases, knowing they would give me good service and pleasure. The life without identity, wearing a mask, rapaciously hungry, the snapping jaws in my vision quest are behind me now.

My village in the mountains, bisected at its center with a + sign formed by the only roads leading in and out, has a population of two to four hundred individuals, their houses clustered around the + mark. Driving down to the valley in icy winter is a steering wheel clutching adventure. Who but the old with severed ties to the workaday world, and one writer living on the proceeds of the sale of her house, could afford to live in such an isolated community? I know not a soul. For the first time in my life I am utterly alone. What the vision quest has taught me is not to run away from discomfort or unhappiness, but rather to embrace it, take it to heart, let it work its way through to a rightful outcome.

I live a monastic life, out running every morning, long walks in the woods often sighting groupings of moose, deer, fox, a bear, a bobcat. Our paltry human presence in the village does not intimidate the animals and it's not unusual to see one sauntering across someone's yard. I spend afternoons in my writing room working on my first novel, COMICS, writing poetry, and essays, Hermine keeping company in her tanning salon under the desk lamp. After work, I get myself a glass of red wine and share cheese and olives at my desk with her.

The hardest part of the day is crossing over to the living area afterward. Never having been a fan of the box, I have no TV nor do I have a radio for quite a while. Society will have to do without my interest in it. I sit in the easy chair until dinner, afterward it's back to the easy chair till I'm so bored there's nothing left to do but go to bed. I lie awake in the dark room and think of the life I have left behind.

I had imagined that I was in charge of my life, an ambitious, competitive woman who made things happen. It's America's philosophy, *Pull yourself up by the bootstraps, you can make a change and become whatever you want; the possibilities are endless.* The possibilities are not endless, there is only one right path, the trick is in discovering what that path is. Having found my way, my attitude seems not so much passive as accepting. I'm doing what I'm supposed to be doing, therefore I have confidence that what happens to me is correct and proper. I needn't struggle against life; I will be taken care of, and if not, then that is how it's supposed to turn out.

I experience a sense of peace I have never had previously.

My workshop with the shaman Michael Harner, an anthropologist and professor who has done fieldwork in the Upper Amazon, the Canadian Artic and Lapland, is held in Boston. On the first night of my arrival, he speaks of the journeys a shaman takes to the upper world or the underworld, seeking solutions, cures, and answers to bring back to the supplicants of his tribe. As the evening wears on I become guarded and a bit paranoid. *How have I gotten into this?* I had thought to find a spiritual/psychic teacher, a guide. Going out searching for one, I felt was not the way to go about it. Rather, I decided that if I needed a guide or teacher, Spirit would bring the appropriate one to me or point one out.

On one of my journeys down the mountain to pick up supplies, I stop at the Colby College library to check out some books. In the crook of the easy chair I sit in is a copy of Michael's book, "The Way of the Shaman." After reading it, I decide it's the sign I have asked for.

A part of me rebels against exploring and exposing the spiritual core of my being, and I find it hard to write about the shamanic experience. This fear is Spirit's way of making me realize that something important is unfolding and I must commit myself to it wholeheartedly. My entry into the city is an example of that phenomenon. Spirit made me understand, through the initial shock of finding myself homeless and my struggle to come back, that moving to New York is an undertaking that will involve a complete turnover in my life and needs full commitment on my part. It's a rite of passage.

The next morning Michael sends me out in the yard to find a rock the size of a grapefruit, a special rock that holds some appeal to me. He then has me read the story held in the rock. I proceed focusing on the indentations and protuberances, the streaking and their meaning in a colleague's life. In teaching me to use a rock as a tool of divination, he shows me that the power of divination is within myself not in the tools I use, as for instance the Tarot cards I employ. Many of the things he speaks of are familiar; one's connection to special power animals is no surprise. Animals have been guiding me through dreams since I was a teenager. Michael teaches me how to become aware of these guides, how to court them and how to understand their method of communication.

What I learn that has been of great help in my practice is the ability to journey. What is journeying, and where does one go when traveling to the upper world or the underworld? These are realms that one may glimpse at times of great terror, suffering, or near-death experiences, when one loses the connection to everyday reality. It is a way of knowing that surpasses the ego's great drive to control the phenomena one experiences, but more than that, it's beyond the world we have created and maintain with our thoughts. One may call such a journey an out-of-reality experience. Knowledge and communication is imbibed instantaneously. Notice the word imbibe; no one speaks words to me in this realm. I somehow take in information that will have to be digested. Both worlds have particularities in that they are populated, and have landscapes.

When journeying for a client, or myself I am directed to the spiritual basis of my query and a way to resolve the obstruction. A guide may choose to show me a number of scenes to help clarify a situation or I may meet hindrances, dark spirits who do not wish my supplicant or me well.

The universe is a mystery I will never resolve as my only source of knowledge is gained through the narrow prism of my senses. Science has forced us to deny and even ridicule the spirit world so long a part of our ancestors' system of knowledge. They were not the ignorant, superstitious lot they have been painted as, or our species would never have survived. Our modern world, that more and more separates us from the living earth, dulls our intuitive capacities. Few of us could survive if forced to forage or hunt for our own food. And why should we, you say, with supermarkets full of provisions? Science has given us some baubles, but taken our freedom and independence in the bargain.

The writer Milan Kundera has said that, "It's been some time now since the river, the nightingale, the paths through the fields have disappeared from man's mind. No one needs them now. When nature disappears from the planet tomorrow, who will notice?"

If tomorrow morning we should wake to find our televisions, computers and cell phones no longer function, there would be some annoyance. After a week, psychological and physical problems would emerge, and in a month's time we would have a crisis on our hands. We have lost the ability to be still, to be quiet. Our senses have become dulled from the sensory overload of modern life. We have lost the tools our ancestors possessed.

My next venture is to a witches' conference in Cape Cod. It's held at a campground by the ocean. Although there are cabins one can stay in, I prefer camping out in my van, and so does Hermine. The witches use its main gathering building, a large sunny open space with lots of windows and double doors open to the elements, to create altars. They drape them in fine linen, place flowers, candles, statues, some needlework, crystals, precious stones and all manner of artwork on them. These exquisite altars are strategically placed in the four directions.

Some things I've heard: Witches have mysterious, dark powers, and are repulsive. They perform secret rituals, cast spells, and are part of an occult underworld. One consults such people in the late hours for dubious reasons. They have been said to eat babies, perform orgiastic rituals and are thought to be in league with the Prince of Darkness.

One of the women whose table I join for lunch explains how a witch gets her power from the earth, the cosmos that surrounds her, the planet she lives on, from the rising of the sea, the changing of seasons, the animals, the trees, the plants, the herbs to heal and to bring on ecstatic states.

That woman is Starhawk, who I would call the Jesus figure in the trinity of significant women in the craft for her environmental work, her peace and justice activism in the lay community. The other, whose book I mentioned earlier, Margot Adler ("Drawing Down the Moon,") I would define as the Holy Ghost for her wisdom and great knowledge. God, the father and creator, or in this case, the mother, is surely Zsuzsanna Budapest, the person most responsible for bringing the craft to America.

Raised as a Catholic convent girl, I have experienced the power of ritual and its ability to bring about profound change. During the conference we perform many rituals that are new to me, yet in some ways similar to the ones I had experienced as a child. Witches work with the element of magic. How does one come to grip with phenomenon that is unexplainable? Is there a father up in heaven watching over us, or a mother as a great many witches believe? Is there a GOD, a Great Eagle?

From the beginning, in the beautiful Catholic Churches I attended as a small child, I did not believe. I could sense that churches themselves (i.e. the physical structures,) had power, and perhaps what the people did in them is what gave the buildings their aura. All religions hold a piece of the puzzle in some convoluted manner. People who believe in God and perform rituals can bring about magic just as well as a pagan. Repeating the many prayers of the rosary leads one to a trance-like state, or rocking back and forth while chanting monotonously ushers in a condition of hypnotic lethargy. One seeks to escape the confines of "reality," to achieve a connection with spirituality, the spirit world.

It is essential in the making of magic to separate oneself from everyday cares, needs, desires, of conventionality and propriety, indeed to look on with disinterest at the very thing one hopes to achieve. In such a state, one is more open to the power dynamics of one's situation, a warrior poised to act in a heartbeat. It is power itself that will determine the outcome if one behaves impeccably, and it will be called magic.

THE EMPEROR

-IV-

Warned that he is heartless, that he bases his decisions on external evidence only, one approaches with care. A silver breastplate outlines the ripples of his muscular chest. Even the scepter in his right hand is a symbol of male potency. Perched on his throne wearing knee-high brown boots, he has one leg jauntily crossed over the other.

The Emperor leans forward, as if momentarily he will bound up and execute the plans he's mulling over. His red chair displays an eagle forming its left side, talons clutching the black balls at the end of its legs. The eagle's head is repeated on the crown above the man's face. It's the same fierce look with piercing eyes. He is handsome with prematurely white hair and beard framing a face that reflects a tinge of compassion in the full lower lip.

One follows the hand as it curls round the armrest with ram's head and back curling horns. A stubborn animal, like the Emperor whose firm resolve establishes his purpose. He has pledged himself to become love's protector. The sword in his left hand is planted solidly in soil; his clothes reflect the rich ochres and burnt sienna of the earth and the sheer cliffs circling his empery. Trust this man, he stands his ground.

Upright: Responsible, strong, protective.

Reversed: Immature, unstable, avoids responsibility.

The Emperor

For those unused to the cities,
being in New York is like freebasing
the known universe.
William Monahan

The editor's fifth floor apartment consists of an entryway, a good-sized living/dining room, a small kitchen pantry, a master bedroom, with an adjoining small room that he uses for office, and my small bedroom. There is no direct sun in the apartment, but a large window in the main room with the trunk and branches of a dead tree framed plumb in its center. Most would consider it good fortune to have found such a place. And I do too, but living in someone else's home is an alienating experience. It is not my sofa, or my dishes, or my taste in decor. I am sitting in someone's apartment that is not my friend, my lover, or part of my family. What's more, he and his wife are not here enough to give the apartment a sense of habitation.

Thankfully, I am pretty busy with schoolwork and learning my way around the city. During school breaks, I spend long hours writing to friends back home, and on weekends I take off for the Farm. Harvest season starts on Thanksgiving weekend and we are out in the fields with customers as they choose and mark the trees they will come to cut down later. It has become a tradition to go tramping through the fields with kids in tow choosing just the right tree. Hot cider and cookies await the kids, and a shot of rum in the cider mug for grown-ups after they've tagged their tree.

There are three ways of entering the city by car, the Henry Hudson Parkway on the west side, the Harlem River Drive, and the Major Deegan Expressway coming in from the Bronx. The contrast between Farm and city is never more apparent than coming back at weekend's completion. The closer I get to the city the filthier it becomes no matter which road I have taken, trash, broken bottles, abandoned cars on the side of the road, buildings splattered with graffiti, some with broken windows, missing doors, the institutional projects, vacant, overgrown lots, the squalor of poverty. I gird myself for the experience by acknowledging that this is also part of New York's character and contributes to its edge.

Sometimes I travel by train that is quite nice going out. I take Metro North at Grand Central which journeys underground till it gets to Harlem and then I am up in the air and light looking down at the streets below, boys in high tops shooting baskets, a view through someone's kitchen. Soon the scenery opens and buildings disappear, sky all around, the river's edge, bridges; America beckons. I kick back in my seat and loll in the profusion of nature's colors. Coming back on the train I go through the reverse process arriving at Grand Central at night; everybody's rushing to get to their train, the colorful ski parkas, mittens, snow boots and ski caps are replaced by three piece suits, trench coats, meticulously coifed and made up women dressed mostly in black with sleek boots reaching up to the knees, the sophisticated look of experience, even among the poor. Past the onslaught of noise and bodies, the rush and tension, I make my way down to its lower depths to catch the Number 6. Millions of people travel these stairs and stand on the platform everyday waiting for their train. Underground, standing with a lot of tired, frazzled human beings, I look down at the tracks below and see a couple of rats scurrying amidst filth and detritus. At these times I think that living in New York is similar to the rats' experiences in the underground tunnels of the city.

Will I make it here; will I find my way to the light?

Although I am physically in the city, I stand outside of it, going to museums, galleries, attending concerts as a visiting stranger who does not know a single soul, and always, the sentence comes to mind, *I'm in New York City.* Not that I want to meet anyone at this time, I am comfortable in my protective cocoon. There is too much to take in and no time or energy to give to others.

My second novel is based on my experiences as a child growing up in a Catholic convent. Mother died of TB when I was a baby and later when I was 6 years old my father came down with it and had to be hospitalized. Our home was broken up; my brothers went to live with a relative and I was placed in a convent. On my first day, standing in the sewing room after Sister Mason secured my belongings, she pointed toward a set of double doors down the corridor, "Go on," she said.

I walked over, opened the playroom doors, and was deluged by a towering wave of sound, a large hall packed full of girls running, laughing, playing, screaming. It was like opening the doors to hell. I made my way to the less populated side of the room where the books were kept. I didn't know at the time that only the big girls were allowed in that section of the hall, but no one bothered me on that first day. In the afternoon, I was given an identification number to distinguish me in this community, 53, which is what I have named the novel.

The experience of being in New York is similar to opening the doors to the convent playroom that first time. It looks like a good time, but it is all too loud and overwhelming on first exposure. And like the convent, New York is a world onto itself. I don't remember very much of my first year in the convent, and I probably won't remember much of this year either. I walk around in a daze much of the time, imbued in the lives of characters in my novel. They have taken up residence in my head carrying on their lives, regardless of what I am doing.

Felinas, the car, has become a major problem. The gas tank has a hole in it and the mechanic tells me it is not worth the price of the car to have it repaired or to install a new one.

"The hole is at the top of the tank," he says. "If you don't fill it up completely when you go to the gas station, you should be OK."

I am now driving a potential bomb, and an uninsured one to boot. The doors don't close well since it was broken into and I have to enter it from the passenger side. Felinas was a treat from my other life, a fire-engine red Toyota Celica GT sports car that I adorned with a license plate that said, LUHREN. It has a sound system to die for, with an electric sunroof and cruise control for the long haul.

Having a car in the city is as practical as having a snowmobile. One has to run out every other day and move it for the street sweepers. People have developed a procedure for dealing with this. One has to case out the streets to know which ones get swept at what hours and what days; it's like playing musical chairs. On the morning that I have to move my car, I drive over to the other street, which has just been swept, but is not technically free to park in yet. I have an hour's wait in the car with coffee and newspaper till it is legal to leave it. At the appointed time, the car doors from one end of the street to the other open to release their drivers.

I have accumulated $500 in parking tickets while trying to figure out the routine. Returning from school at night when 99% of the parking spots are filled does not help matters. I am spending a small fortune on gas driving around looking for a parking space.

Having a car in Maine is akin to having shoes on your feet; you're not getting very far without it. I bought my first one when I was 17 and got my license a month later. It was a hipster's car and had the advantage of beating out every boy who dared challenge me at the red light. One's car is the most personal of possessions. In the privacy of its enclosed body, one is most truly oneself and most free to express that self, the words you would have liked to speak earlier, the arguments, the soliloquies, the off-key songs are all permitted. Winter storms in Maine can make for treacherous driving; you develop a certain amount of sang-froid at the wheel. Many people in New York have no car; some have never had a license. I cannot imagine it. A scary prospect, not being able to pick up and go, to explore, to pack one's bag and leave town, to be totally dependent on a municipal transit system. Thankfully, Felinas is not willing to die yet.

In the spring, a semi-formal party is held at school before we are let off for the summer. We sit outdoors at round tables with umbrellas shielding us from late afternoon sun, eating dinner and discussing our summer plans. Later, we will go inside for drinks and I will dance joyfully with the others. I am free of school for the summer. Many of the women, for we are mostly all women in the graduate school creative writing program, will be returning home to other states around the country. Of those who are staying in the city, some have applied for internships with publishing houses or literary agencies, jobs that I have seen posted on the corkboard at Slonim House. These jobs don't pay, and even if they did I can't see myself gaining anything from them. I want to write, not cater to those who write, or to those who serve writers.

I will get a temporary job for the summer to tide me over till the fall, something that will give me the freedom to write. I check the 'Help Wanted' ads in the New York Times for the names of temp agencies where I hope to be hired as an office worker. I have done so much typing I ought to be able to get a word processing job. All of these agencies are midtown, not a place that I normally go to and certainly not during business hours. The tension on the street is so high that if one could find a way to bottle it, it could fuel the transit system of the city. People dash through streets with a look of grim determination on their faces. I know I'm in trouble when I look at the other women who have showed up, like me, looking for temp work. They are dressed in $500 business suits, pinstripes no less, and spike heels. I am wearing a flowing pink satin skirt, a cream-colored blouse and open toed heels. Day after day, I go and take the test for some new agency and fail miserably. I am so slow they don't even have a category for me. It's the pressure, and the clock, and the rules.

So much for a midtown job.

I look for employment with an environmental agency. I'm not too sure what I'm expected to do for them; they are only interested in summer help. When I get to the appointed building, way downtown, I enter a large room full of students, who, like me, just want something to tide them over. I am one of the first ones hired because of a remark I make to their question about environmental pollutants in the city.

"Dogshit on the sidewalks," I reply. My interviewers see this as a sign of originality and are convinced I would do well.

Every morning we gather in the large room and are divided into groups and assigned a lead person, then we are driven to a neighborhood out of the city, some as far as Connecticut, to hustle people with money for some of it to contribute to the agency. I do so well on my first day, somewhere in Bay Ridge, that I am given an award the next morning, and lead people bid to have me on their team. Beginner's luck, it is downhill after that first day, and since I'm on commission I must start looking for something else.

Leafing through the Village Voice want ads after three weeks with the environmental agency, I come across this --

> Psychics Wanted, set your own hours, work as little or as much as you want in the privacy of your home giving readings over the telephone. Psychic Reader's Network, 1-800-***-****.

I can do that!

Has it crossed my mind that I am desperately grabbing at straws? Definitely, but I'm immediately hired over the telephone by a woman with a brassy voice after I tell her I read Tarot Cards. She faxes me a contract in which I agree not to steal their clients, and should there be problems requiring them to take me to court, it will be in their jurisdiction and not mine. What's more, I will be responsible for their attorney fees, etc. After the contract is signed and faxed to her, she gives me an eight hundred number that I am to call when I want to log on, and my agent number.

"Once you punch these numbers in," she says, "you will start receiving calls for which you'll be paid 30 cents for every minute the client stays on line with you."

"What are the best times to log on?"

"Nighttime is when we're most busy."

That evening I attempt to log on several times, but I am too nervous and keep messing up. Hours go by and I'm still not logged on.

What is happening here?

Something important obviously, or I wouldn't be so rattled. I finally figure things out and get through to the preamble. This is the daily message given most often by the owner of Psychic Reader's Network, a nasty little man named Steven Feder who excoriates me and however many other "psychics," as we are called, to keep our averages up, to make sure we get clients' names, addresses and telephone numbers, etc.

Averages? We are judged by how long we keep clients on the line.

Lord knows how I managed that first night. What I remember is total exhaustion after four hours on line and the relief I feel dialing the magic numbers to get me logged off. I haven't really thought about the job too seriously. The company advertises on TV, has a computer system to channel incoming calls to "psychics" throughout the country. The TV infomercials are hokey dramatizations of exotic women with the ability to tell you things.

Does it work? Can someone actually give a reading over the telephone? The eyes often tell what a person cannot, as does the aura surrounding a person's body, lacking these cues, one learns to adapt others. Getting the name and birth date of a person the client is asking about helps, the name of a business or agency, the street address of an important location, a shoe size, any piece of personal data. Although these cues tell you nothing about the situation, they help to focus both you and the client on the matter at hand. There is an aura that clings to a name; a dog does not understand when you call out Fido that it is its name. It relates to the sound, its power, its energy. This is what one seeks to tap into. As to the birth date, the acknowledgment of one's arrival on this planet, it is seldom when I ask a person about the birth date of someone they inquire about that they don't know it, no matter how short the relationship's duration. If the client thinks it is an important piece of information, obviously it must be, and more so than just to ascertain age and birthday. Words are subject to rational and symbolic interpretation, and they also have a numinous quality. Shamans, medicine people and witches when performing rituals, healing ceremonies, or casting spells, repeat oftentimes indecipherable words, 3 times, 6 times, 9 times in a chanting pattern, the sound carrying them into trance states. Poetry, another form of regeneration, surely had its beginning from early sorcerers and healers.

I'm off to a shaky start, but something seems to be working. What's more, I'm making money, not a lot, but enough to pay my share of the rent, put food on the table and maybe have a few coins jingling in my pocket. My shift is from midnight to four in the morning and then afternoons from four to eight -- the prime busy hours. I haven't seen any of the money I'm earning yet, which causes me some concern. What little I know of Psychic Readers' Network, I learn from the daily preamble I listen to when logging in. Bizarre is the word I would use to describe it. Apparently, someone in the company has run off with all of our names and telephone numbers, planning to start their own operation. Steven tells us not to take seriously anyone calling to offer us a better deal, as the person is a weasel and a double dealer.

Hmm, a better deal, more money? But no one ever contacts me.

Brassy woman calls in the middle of my shift, "Psychic Readers' Network!" I respond.

"Why aren't you logged on?" she snaps. "You agreed to work these hours."

"I am logged on."

"Oh," then she hangs up.

I imagine a boiler room somewhere in Florida where these people conduct business on the verge of hysteria, a fly-by-night organization.

Trusting them for a couple of weeks until payday rolls around takes a supreme act of faith, or foolhardiness. It comes and goes and I do not receive my check. Brassy woman is apologetic, tells me she'll cancel the check already sent to me which probably got lost in the mail and send me another one via overnight delivery. I do receive my money the next day, which goes a ways to restoring my faith in PRN.

My friend Kesel is a colonist at The Farm this summer and I go up to visit as many weekends as I am able to get away. Kate asks me to join them for the yearly celebration of Bastille Day on July

14th, a grand holiday in which everyone dresses as noted or infamous French women. An attempt is made at dinner to speak French. In my season as colonist, I had chosen to portray Jeanne d'Arc with tights and a sword.

I arrive in late afternoon, a bit tired from my workweek and long drive. Kate, in costume, walks me over to the verandah where all have gathered. Although I know everyone, I'm at a loss to figure out who is who. Coco Chanel in her little boxy suit and pocketbook greets me; I take guesses at some of the others, Madame de Staël holding court with George Eliot and Colette? Madame de Pompadour? The émigré Gertrude Stein? Our French dinner, (conducted mostly in the English language) served on the Lavender House deck at long picnic tables embellished with wild flowers, lasts late into the night with lots of red wine, a few joints, and the recorded music of French chanteuses.

The Farm is where it all began for me, the commitment to leave Maine and enter a larger world. With Kate and the others in the fields shearing trees in weather that reached 100° and more, out in the pouring rain, poison ivy, deer tics, mosquitoes, then a quick dip in the pond while lunch was laid out on tables in back of the farmhouse. It was a pleasure after the hard physical work to be welcomed with plates of fresh vegetables from the garden, fruits, casseroles whose fanciful colors, along with the glassware, dishes and silverware, gleamed in the sunlight coming through tree branches, the conversation, slow and easy as I relaxed into my other body. Soon I would go up to my yellow room, close the door and get to work on my novel. At that time I felt a true child of earth. Returning to Maine that fall, I had been transformed into a bronzed and muscular woman.

The start of my last year at Sarah Lawrence opens in September with a barbecue in Marshall Field. Running late, I scurry down the stairs of my building in Manhattan and open the front door to find a bird's nest with eggs splattered on the stoop.

It must have toppled from the roof, probably pigeon eggs. That night when I get back from school my roommate tells me he will be giving up the apartment. I will have to leave.

Walking the streets of Manhattan looking for a home, I decide no more roommates. I walk and walk, and I meet many real estate brokers who see me as a bad bet, a student, a phone psychic; I am ripped off, lose money investing in $50 credit checks for apartments I will never get. I don't understand how the system works, so often arrive at sites that have already been leased. As the weeks roll by I begin to recognize my fellow searchers. A pack of us wait outdoors in front of buildings looking for the agent to arrive; we commiserate about the dives we have seen that are renting for outrageous amounts, a desperate bunch spouting gallows humor on the curb. I lose $90 to a manager who keeps my deposit but won't rent me the apartment because he says I am only a roommate not the lessee of my present rent. Information I had clearly spelled out on the application he had me fill out. What to do? There is no time to bother. After two months without any luck, most apartments are simply out of my price range, or totally inappropriate, I put my things in storage in the Bronx. An interesting arrangement in which I drive over with a rented van, two Latino boys come over unload it on the makings of a big crate that is then sealed with the help of forklift trucks. Desks, bed frame, sound system, computer, dishes, clothes all in a crate; it means that I can't come over and get my little black dress, or some of my books if I need them.

Kate comes to the rescue once again and offers to let me stay in her loft on the Bowery till I find a place. I arrive on the last day of November with a small bag, Hermine and my plants to find two of her ex-girlfriends already ensconced in the loft. Warned of my arrival, they are not pleased to see me and make it clear they will do whatever is necessary to get me out, two cats on Dexedrine, claws distended, ready to pounce. Hermine is not impressed. This is not the Farm; I decide to leave my plants in the windowless hall. The recent ex-girlfriend and I are enemies who will never find common ground because she fears I'm about to replace her in Kate's affections. Not to worry, but why should I tell her? It's been so long, I don't even know if I could remember how to do it. The other ex-girlfriend, of many years past, a talented artist, is not concerned about anybody replacing her, she's irreplaceable. A bitch. She pulls in her claws once she understands I don't mean her any trouble.

Living on the interest of a trust fund, she is tight with money but has a generous spirit. In her way, she helps familiarize me with the neighborhood that is the East Village, quite a departure from the middle class neighborhood I just left. The beat is funky, downtown, the food on the street is exotic, lots of cafés and bars; something happening all the time, whether it be in music, art, writing, politics. Students, gays, bohemians walk around with bizarre outfits, spiked and multicolored hair, and lots of attitude. We go to art gallery openings where entry is free and so is the wine. She favors Indian restaurants that serve $3.00 lunches and she takes me to the Buddhist center where I am made to endure a very long zazen meditation sitting in a position that could be used as a form of torture. Afterward, she browbeats the monks and monopolizes the conversation. Her topic? Herself of course. What to make of this enfant gaté?

I was wise enough when I left the sublet on the Upper East Side not to have my phone line disconnected. I merely took my phone and wiring out. In this manner I'm able to make calls and charge them to the still live telephone line. It is a great help to me in my quest for an apartment. My search has taken on a manic tone since moving in with the girlfriends, their little yappy dogs, their music and their screaming fights. It is not much better when they are gone as the long open loft is about as intimate as a row of basketball courts.

I bribe one real estate agent an extra $500 beside his commission which will run him a couple of thousands if he can find me something reasonable. He calls the next morning, after I've left on another search, with what sounds like a decent apartment on the Upper East Side. The agent whose ad I've answered is an Israeli. Morit has come to make her fortune in America. Smart, confident, she has obviously focused on the right profession. The apartment turns out to be a dump. We walk all over the neighborhood looking at other situations just as depressing. She's a cheerful girl, and we get on even though she can't seem to find me an apartment.

"Let's get on the bus, I know a place," she motions toward the corner.

Just when we get to the building someone is walking out. She makes a run for the door before it closes and locks. Once inside, she knocks at the manager's apartment. A buxom, disheveled blonde answers in housecoat and slippers, none too pleased to see us.

"I told you not to come here before noontime!" she says. "I made it very clear; I am up all night working. You have awakened me!"

She is one angry woman and Morit mumbles and stammers about being in the neighborhood and the door being open, etc., etc. The blonde, a middle-aged Slavic woman, whose hair piled on top of her head looks like the aftermath of an explosion, apologizes to me for the scene and decides I am a nice girl that she would like to have as a tenant if things work out.

If things work out: It's an old walk-up building; the hall painted a garish oxblood, but the apartment on the second floor is not too bad. There are tall, old-fashioned windows in the main room looking out on the square below and the park beyond it, another smaller room with a bookcase, and then the kitchen. I note the fire escape overlooking the park has two director's chairs and a wind chime on it.

She wants more money than I can afford.

Out on the street, Morit tells me, "You'll be safe here. This is a pretty good neighborhood."

It never crossed my mind.

"Make her a counter offer," I say.

"She'll never go for it. She can easily get that price from someone else."

"Try."

Back at the loft, having talked to the Upper East Side agent about the apartment he wants to show me, same price as the one I just saw. I'm in a quandary.

"I've got two possibilities for apartments I could see myself living in," I tell l'enfant gaté. "One's on the Upper East Side and the other's on the Lower East Side. I don't know what direction I should go in. Am I an uptown girl, or downtown?"

She is definitely downtown, but wise enough not to advise me. I am left to figure it out on my own. By morning I have decided to take the apartment on the Lower East Side. How I'm going to find the money to pay for it has been put aside for the moment. As Scarlett says in "Gone With The Wind," "I'll think about it tomorrow."

My first task is to show the real estate agency that I can afford the apartment. I call brassy woman at PRN (I have not been able to work for the past several weeks since moving to Kate's loft,) and explain my situation. She faxes a letter for me to the corner bodega with the company letterhead stating that I am one of her star psychics and that the company is offering me a managerial position which will double my income. On December 15th Morit and I travel back to the apartment and are met by my landlady who is sister to the buxom blonde. Her name is Zinaida, but everyone calls her Zinni. The blonde, obviously the younger sister, is named Antonia. Both wear dresses midway up their thighs, high heels and fantastic hairdos. They look like a couple of hookers. Zinni, who is also a bottle blonde, has none of her sister's voluptuousness, straight as a pole and wiry, her face is tough and mistrustful. She leads me through the saloon situated somewhat below ground level beneath the first floor of the apartment building. A couple of Chinese men drinking beer at the bar never look up as our entourage walks past them to a storeroom at the back. On a small card table amidst cases of liquor, I sign the contract for a rent-stabilized apartment, my lease to start on the first day of the new year. I give her two months' rent, and a check to Morit, which is 15% of the total for my first year's rent.

I now have a home. Out on the street, I tell Morit I couldn't have chosen a better person to bring me to my first Manhattan apartment. I feel she will bring me luck. We shake hands and head off in separate directions to make our fortunes.

THE HIEROPHANT

-V-

Demeter, whose daughter was taken away by Hades, made the earth pay for her loss. Crops failed, cattle died and famine spread until a bargain could be struck in which the fair Persephone could spend a season in the upper world with her mother. In Eleusis where it took place the Greeks put up a Temple of Initiation where rites took place in honor of the Gods. Even Bacchus as purveyor of the grape was feted. But no drunken orgies here with nubile maidens and choice delicacies.

Initiates were schooled in the Mysteries by the Hierophant who was master. He sits before us dressed like a pope with a triple crown and a triple crossed staff. A silver and a gold key crossed in front of him open the doors to the upper and lower world. Around his neck is a crescent moon indicating his rites take place in the night. For the chosen few, he will communicate mystic knowledge and a revelation. And so it is when temples are erected and the spirit world is mapped and sounded.

Beware; Gods also speak to bewildered fools. They tease, bedevil and frighten a person into an awakening never sought or wanted.

Upright: Mystic knowledge, spiritual awareness.

Reversed: Rebelliousness, false freedom.

The Hierophant

> One can have an apartment in Manhattan, or a social life, but you cannot afford both.
> Anon.

By the time I have settled my affairs and moved my things in, it is late and the surrounding stores are boarded up. I walk to the next block and can see a neon sign further up. *Hong Kong Supermarket* flashes in rippled red on the deserted rainy streets this New Year's Eve. I enter a world most of whose products advertised in Chinese characters I know nothing about. There, I choose for my breakfast the next morning a teapot, some green tea, a plate, some buns and a saucepan to boil water. The apartment is empty save for a pad on the floor to lie on, my struggling plants, the few clothes I had brought to Kate's loft, several plastic milk crates picked up on the street to function as makeshift furniture. I've put two fat pine boards on some to make my desk; others serve as seats till I get my things out of storage. On my desk, I place Tarot cards, and next to them my plum and white marble composition dream book. The new life starts with these simple tasks. Tomorrow or perhaps the next day the phone company will come to install service.

It has taken me one year and three months to find a home in New York City, on the favored isle of Manhattan in a neighborhood where most immigrant groups started out, and still do. The Lower East Side is populated by Chinese, Jews, Hasidic, orthodox and reform; a battery of low income projects houses African Americans, Latinos, people from Senegal, Ethiopia, India, the Dominican Republic, Colombia, Jamaica, etc., etc. Everyone sticks to their own folk, their own quarters, their own ways and food.

I am in mild shock. It's come to this: I am living in a New York City ghetto. But another part of me is fascinated. It is truly the best place to start my acquaintance with the City. A walk in my neighborhood is like taking a whirlwind tour of four or five countries, sampling the food they eat, their style of clothing, their aesthetic, their music, their cool.

On New Year's Day I head for a party at Linda's (a Farm friend) in Kingston, a good two-hour drive. It's an open house gathering with lots of food, wine, liquor on the buffet, and people milling about. Linda, being in the antique business, the old restored house is furnished with early Americana pieces. I roam past the fire crackling in the living room fireplace, traipsing from room to room, glass of wine in hand. I remember this, the big kitchen where everyone gathers, the aroma wafting from wood burning stoves, the old pieces of furniture, the chilly outer rooms, women with long dresses and soft curls in their hair, they who make pies and decorate birthday cakes, who maintain summer gardens. I am transported back to Maine where I have attended many such open house parties, and been host of, in the country where the ambiance is easy and company is welcome.

But I'm no longer there. I stand in the kitchen of an acquaintance on New Year's Day in my *de riguer* black city outfit thinking, *Who am I now?*

An awkward boy-child, a geeky kid scrubbed raw, standing naked before others.

The person from Maine is learning to live a different life, out in the streets surrounded by stone and steel, the verities of stoic New Englanders from the stone coast of Maine no longer apply.

Who am I? I am a person who is finishing a novel that will serve as my thesis at Sarah Lawrence; I am a woman who counsels people on spiritual matters; I am a woman who lives on the Lower East Side of Manhattan.

I get my stuff out of storage and still the apartment is bare. All I've got is office furniture. My first week is spent sleeping, eating and getting stoned. I need time to develop new dreams, create new scenarios. That I stumbled on the perfect way to make a living (I love my work and am good at it,) I consider a piece of luck. Primarily, I think myself a writer.

At the end of my week's sabbatical, I log in to the psychic network and get back in harness. Having to come up with the rent money every month is going to be a challenge. I begin a pattern of being logged on whenever I am at home. I am on call till four in the morning when clients are most apt to call. They want to know about the husband, the wife, the lover; *is she faithful? Why hasn't he called? Is she seeing someone else? What's he doing tonight? Is this a good person? Is it my soulmate?*

The word feels like a wire brush rubbing against my skin. What, pray tell is a soulmate? Someone connected to one's soul? If that is the case, then every person that comes into one's ken is a soulmate as there is a psychic connection in each relationship one has, otherwise there would be nothing to talk about.

I think of "soulmate", not exclusively in terms of romantic relationship. The essayist Michel de Montaigne writes of his relationship with Estienne de la Boetie in his essay on friendship as one that I would consider soulmates. In ordinary friendships one has to be attentive, thoughtful, careful not to offend or hurt because there is always the possibility of losing that tie. Not so in the soulmate relationship. Montaigne writes,

> [T]he union of such friends, being truly perfect, deprives them of all ideas of such duties, and makes them loathe and banish from their

conversation these words of division and distinction, benefits, obligations, acknowledgment, entreaty, thanks, and the like. All things, wills, thoughts, opinions, goods, wives, children, honours, and lives being in effect common betwixt them, and that absolute concurrence of affections being no other than one soul in two bodies . . . they can neither lend nor give anything to one another.

Such relationships although rare, do occur. It is not something one can will into existence, or go searching for, place an ad in the paper, *I am a slinky blonde career woman who likes the theater, good conversation and walks in the park. Please be elegant, successful, a nonsmoker. Lawyers A+.*

Assuredly, if one has to ask, *Is this my soulmate*, it is not. The relationship between men and women makes up 85% of the questions asked of me. Behind the question is the one that is never asked. *How do I live with my fear and anxiety, with the knowledge of my aloneness in life, with my utter alienation in a world of stone and mortar?* How indeed?

A school colleague recounts the story of a woman who came to her house, "I just mentioned in the course or our conversation of having lost my watch. She led me up the stairs to the hamper, this from someone who had never been to my house before, and showed me where the watch was located in the pocket of a pair of jeans. Now that's a psychic!"

Is she trying to tell me I'm passing myself off as something I'm not? I cannot tell how, or where to retrieve someone's lost billfold, or her diamond ring, and more important, I don't care to. Am I a psychic in the sense that my grad school colleague understands? No, nor do I care to bend spoons, make objects move seemingly of their own volition, or channel past lives. The questions beyond why you have chosen to lose the billfold, the diamond ring, it's symbolic value to you, are more to the point. If the motive is not found, the situation will re-occur in another form. And it is often the case that when the underlying reason for a situation is uncovered, the whereabouts of the lost billfold, the diamond ring, are discovered.

There are roaches in my apartment! Horrible, silvery, brown-backed bugs that move with the speed of an eye blink. And in the park across the street are junkies, nodding, falling from their benches, hookers plying their trade and desperate addicts with their household goods splayed out on the ground, old shoes, frying pans, lamps, sports jackets, dresses, hoping to raise some cash so they can score and ride that horse out of this rotten world. The ground is littered with needles and crack pipes.

I learn, through trial and error, that Raid products really work to eliminate roaches and I scatter those little black packets throughout the apartment, that Chinese vegetables, once I master their art of preparation, are cheap, fresh and plentiful, that the best bagels in all of New York City are made in my neighborhood at an honest-to-goodness, no frills bakery called Kossar's Bialys (the bialys are pretty good too,) that I can go try out some of my prose and poems at ABC No Rio, a venue that supports artists, musicians, writers, actors, performance artists.

It's on Rivington Street, in the gutted first story of a tenement building. With the ad I cut out from the Village Voice in hand, I make my way through the seamy neighborhood. Inside are seven or eight people sitting on various folding chairs and benches which are arranged horse-shoe style around a cleared area with a lonesome stool at center; wires hang from the gutted ceiling, some twirled around sprinkler pipes, and at the far end of the room, boxes, assorted pieces of furniture piled crazily. The toilet door is open exposing a graffiti smeared interior that I would approach only under the direst of emergencies. I take a seat close to the exit and survey my fellow artists, a somber group clutching their artwork close to heart.

A middle aged bleach-blonde with the bloated body and skinny legs of an alcoholic gets up and moves towards the lonesome stool, the kind of person who probably spends most nights at the corner bar scoring dope and bad mouthing the bartender. Her arms are covered with old, faded blue and red tattoos. Her get-up can best be described as Goth, black fishnet stockings full of holes, short straggly black dress, high heel boots and red, red lipstick.

"Anyone who wants to perform can take their turn up here. We have only one requirement: that you not bore the audience," she says. Then she reads from her oeuvre, a novel in progress about a tough cookie who lures men into situations where she murders them in horrific ways. She finds her victims through personal ads in the newspaper and they all sound like they deserve their fate. After this reading there is a pause and a shuffling of feet then someone else gets up and takes the stage. There seems to be no order, you just get up when the spirit moves you. A very mixed group, the uptown lady in fine clothes and spike heel boots has brought poetry to read, and her poems are exquisitely crafted jewels. She gets good applause and acknowledges the group like an old trouper. More people come; the room is so, down in the marrow of the bones, cold that my teeth chatter. I notice some men are passing a flask of whiskey amongst themselves and others are smoking reefer. The afternoon light is gone, the streets are dark and the gathering is just starting to unwind, I'd say warm up but that's not possible in this icebox. A Russian man, obviously mad, reads some of his writing that is riddled with explicit, aggressive, kinky sex. *In your face!* The writing itself is fascinating, a freaked-on-acid rambling with its own inner rhythm and sense, a type of cubist prose. Everyone listens intently, trying to capture the secret in his writing that makes it art.

What a group! And it goes on; a young handsome black guy in studded leather recites some of his funny and caustic rap. I have stumbled onto the heart of creativity. We are all a little mad when compared with society at large, folks who toil silently for no one but ourselves, focused on a mystery we have no hope of unraveling, for reasons that escape us.

Having given a lot of public readings, I am usually at ease on stage, and no matter how many times I return and get to know the regulars at ABC No Rio, I am always nervous before taking the floor in front of such a sophisticated group of fellow artists waiting to take their turn on the lonesome stool.

One semester left before I graduate and my work is going well on the novel, "53." I will be able to have it completed in time. Now that I have my own place, the idea of school is not as appealing. I have listened to everybody's ideas and taken what was helpful to heart and I feel that I am simply fulfilling my obligations to get the degree. I can only remain just so long in an institution before I begin to feel, well, institutionalized. And then I start to rebel and behave badly, but my life is too complicated to indulge in such luxury at this time. Last semester during one of my homeless periods, I broke down and sobbed at a meeting with a teacher. Not one of my best moments at Sarah Lawrence.

As a girl brought up in a Catholic convent from the age of 6 till I was 14, I have an acute sense of what institutions can do to the spirit. I ran away from the convent one night never to return. The feelings I had at the time are similar to my present thoughts about school. It wasn't so much anything the nuns said or did, but the understanding that it was time to move on. I had gotten what I needed and there was no more to be had. The primary purpose of an institution, any institution, be it corporate, academic, or service-oriented, is its own empowerment. The very techniques used to provide a smooth and efficient running system, the hierarchical chain of command, its predictable, consistent practices and rules discourage any attempt at individuality or creativity in its adherents. The novel "53" is based on those experiences. One becomes a 53, a 46, a 32, the class of 95. I didn't care for it at the convent and through the novel the child labeled 53 is individualized and the number becomes a grander symbol than what its original intent and purpose served. *Let me tell you who 53 is*, is the focus of the novel. A motherless child making her way in a world whose primary focus is abnegation. *I will not be buried*, the child says, *I will not be denied.*

A lot of girls upon leaving the convent become sluts, ladies of easy virtue. One in particular developed a much-celebrated reputation for giving blowjobs in my hometown. What you are denied, in your rebellion you will gorge on. I gorge on sovereignty.

I have picked up my first private client, a man in California who plays the market, invests in futures, soybeans. I've spoken to him several times on the network and he's developed confidence in my capabilities so we've set up times that he can call me privately. He is a Hollywood playboy who has many questions about whether the women in his life are seducible. I charge him half what the networks get and he pays me by check, a smart, quick-witted guy whose patter amuses me. How he ever got in the futures market I have no idea, but he is an expert. I have no knowledge of soybean crops and base my predictions to his questions on the layout of cards. One creates an image of the person on the other end of the line. I see him as stylish in his dress and comportment, hair coifed, his nails buffed.

An angel, who remains nameless, as she does not want her generosity exposed, hears of my penurious condition and surreptitiously sends me a thousand dollars. I am dumbfounded at the generosity of a total stranger. I walk the cold, mean streets of lower Manhattan with this secret in my heart, and it is a secret, as the woman (or man) does not care to be known, thinking, *I am blessed.* How else am I to ponder such a gift? *Someone believes in me.* Another part of me is paranoid that somehow it will be taken away.

Of the many things I could do with the money, I choose to fly back to Maine, pack the rest of my things and bring them back in a U-Haul truck. Thankfully, I don't have to go back a pauper.

"You have that New York look and style," my old friend Carlene says when I visit her.

Hmm. What I do notice is the frowzy clothes, the lack of polish in appearance and comportment in most of the people I see on the street. Do I feel sad or lonely being back home? Mostly I feel numb. I don't think I am quite in one world or the other yet. I know the score in Maine, what's permissible and what's not, the ease in which one can conduct one's life, make a living, the large supermarkets, the malls, the spacious houses, but that is not enough. It is not comfort I seek, but stimulation, a greater outlet for my talent.

When I arrive back in the City and park the U-Haul truck in front of my building, Zinni and Antonia come out to greet me.

"You drove that big truck all that way by yourself?" says Zinni.

I get the impression she thinks I'm a powder puff, a silly woman who should have finished with school long ago. Some Chinese guys from inside the bar come out and offer to give a hand unloading the truck. They, along with the two sisters and a couple of other tenants all pitch in. We get the truck unloaded in less than a half hour.

"Hey," says the rock musician from the first floor apartment when he sees my album collection. "You've got some cool sounds here."

I am tired from my long journey and head to bed surrounded by my earthly goods. With this move I've abandoned many things which I simply do not have room for in my small studio: the bedroom set, the elegant Duchess Atlantic wood burning stove, lamps, tables, fully two thirds of my book collection, books on science, psychology, history, philosophy, music, art. It felt like cutting off my right arm, but it had to be done. I chose to keep mostly literature, poetry, some reference books on birds, trees, flowers, mythology, opera, the great ages of mankind and my collection of cookbooks.

Truly, I have brought what is most important to me, good sounds, good reading, great recipes, and my grandmother's Singer sewing machine.

I'm carrying on the tradition, Mémère, doing my work, taking it seriously as obviously you did to invest in such a fine piece of furniture.

The cabinet is made of oak with scrolled woodwork at the front of its drawers. When opened it reveals a sewing machine head with golden griffins painted on each side of it. These mythical animals, part eagle, part lion are an appropriate symbol, as they are known to build their nests of gold and are guardians of treasure. The treasure of course is creativity.

On my birthday, I choose to celebrate by treating myself to brunch at the Cotton Club in Harlem. I ride the number 1 train all the way up to 125th Street where it travels above ground. Looking forward to the Club, soul food, and gospel music.

Once I find the place, in a 'warehouse, filling-station' kind of area, I join the group out front waiting for the doors to open. There's a Lewiston, Maine feel to Harlem. The group around me is composed entirely of blacks. I am taken aback when I realize I will be the only white person at this brunch. The ladies are elegant in huge flowery hats and silk dresses.

We are let in by a hostess who opens her hand in front of me and mouths the word, "Ticket."

"I don't have a ticket. I have a reservation."

"No, this is a private party."

"I made reservations earlier this week. I want to see the manager."

"He's over there," she points to a fiftyish stocky man sitting at a table with the books. He hears my story and says, "No, you didn't make a reservation. This party has been booked for this day long ago."

"Are you calling me a liar?"

A younger man approaches and confirms that he took my reservation earlier in the week assuming he could squeeze me in somehow. After some back and forth about price and seating, I am brought upstairs where he decides to place me away from the others. No table or napkins. I sit down in a completely black world segregated from everyone else. Tears begin to flow. I try to hide it, nevertheless, I have to wipe them as they run down my cheeks.

The younger man brings me a drink, sees that a small table is available among the others and asks if I'd like it. I move down next to a black family much happier about my situation. Still, the tears do not stop. I think about prejudice and about the burden of it, how my mother abandoned me to death and my father topped that by saying that I am unlovable and unwanted. The wound from these two events never heals. I am the outsider, the unwanted. I sit in my darkened corner of the room listening to women sing gospel music. They join hands in the end and people hug. I wait to be invited, and I am. I surreptitiously wipe the tears from my face.

After the show is over I want to slowly slink out. As I leave my table the younger man asks if I liked the show. Yes, I did, and the food. A hand reaches out for my arm as I descend the spiraling staircase to support me. It is the manager who wishes me happy birthday and he holds on to my arm too long, asks why I am spending my birthday alone, how long have I been in NYC? Where do I come from? I respond whichever way, compliment him on the food and want to get away as fast as possible from his question about my aloneness on this day. My tears are so close to surface now I can barely control them. Out on the sidewalk, I realize I've left my jacket in the club. The tears continue to fall on my train ride downtown; I am wearing shades to protect me.

Happy birthday, Lorraine.

Later, I feel transformed by my encounter with the Cotton Club manager. It's as if I've been seduced and I'm now a different person. Perhaps I focus too much on him. The Club brought back memories of going to church, ladies dressed in their fineries, people reaching for a higher plane, for the sublime, family gatherings, ethnic food and, *the family secrets.*

The manager's role was that of hierophant.

THE LOVERS

-VI-

There is a clearing amidst thick foliage where a naked couple stands wrapped in each other's arms, surrounded by calla lilies. The sun is a glowing corona at the back of their heads; the sky, clear blue tinged with green, reflects the color of lush vegetation of the Eden below. As they look directly into each other's eyes, a form of communication over which they have no control occurs, a secret language that more than sex, excites and titillates them.

They seek an unveiling into a state of nature where all is accepted, and the self is perceived beyond the circle of naming. This release floods the soul with beauty and profound knowledge of life. The man's head is inclined slightly, a look of gentleness on him. He has strong, muscular arms that reach round her waist. Her left hand rests at the back of his neck caressing shoulder-length chestnut hair.

The fleece covered cheeks of his ass come to view; it's a tawny body and makes a fine contrast to her peach colored skin, her flame red hair and the pink aureoles round her nipples. She gazes at him, a look of serenity on her face as she purses her lips to accept the kiss she's waited so long for.

Upright: Unity, love, at peace with self and the universe.

Reversed: Outside interference, union aborted.

I stumble out of the apartment wearing the nearest thing at hand, sweatpants, sneakers and a windbreaker, heading for Henry Street where Felinas is parked. The street sweeper will be here in 15 minutes.

Where's the car? Did I really park it on Henry; maybe it was Rutgers? I look and look, walk up one street, and another.

Then the light comes on in my head -- *The car's been stolen!* The officer who comes to take my report knows my story before I put it to words; someone new to the city, barely making it, uninsured car, etc.

But he is sympathetic, "I'll write up a report. It could turn up."

Three days later I get a call from the police informing me that my car has been found. It was illegally parked and got towed to Inwood where I can go pick it up. *Thank god!* It takes me half the night to reach Inwood, which is at the very apex of Manhattan. The battery is dead when I get it and I have to pay several hundred dollars in towing charges, but I've got her back.

Three days later, Felinas is missing again. This time I don't waste energy calling the police. Walking the neighborhood, I spot it, illegally parked, on Monroe Street next to the projects. The man listens to rap music on my radio, and likes cruising around with the sunroof open. This happens several more times until one day when I go out searching for it, I find the clutch no longer works. That is the end of Felinas and she is hauled off for parts.

This is it Manhattan! I can no longer escape you. No more fantasies of loading up the car and moving on. I'm relieved. Moving the car every other day at 9 in the morning after working till 4 am the night before, the expense, the tickets. It's over; I'm here to stay.

The summer before I embark on my vision quest is perfect. I have begun writing in a committed way. My body, through good exercise, is slim and muscular. I am beautiful, happy, generous.

I get an invitation to a party in Casco Bay given by a couple of artists, a great annual 24 hour celebration of the arts in their many guises, good food, lots of booze and music. Some people do theatre, others read some of their work, and I share some of my poems.

While others play touch football, I sit by the floor to ceiling windows in the house watching, a shady view, laughter, loud calls, people moving about. I turn and see two men enter. The big guy wants to know if I've seen so and so. No. A pause. We look at each other. I wink; he winks back.

Three weeks later, I see him at the Gulf of Maine Bookstore. I do not remember him as the person I winked at, but he remembers me, an attractive man, virile. There is something about him. We have both brought friends along, mine is a radical lesbian, obviously not a time to talk. He's back at the bookstore the following week and this time I approach him. There is such a strong psychic connection between us; surely he must feel it. Philip and I leave the store to go for drinks with a couple of friends. He slides his foot up and down the back of my calf under the table. Out on the street after the others leave, we grope at each other and embrace.

I've rented a house perched on a rock wall with a deck reaching out over the Atlantic. My view is of the sea crashing against the profoundly beautiful stone coast of Maine. The only neighbors, beside the great blue heron and an occasional dolphin, are to my left and up on a small hill, another house similar to mine with a tenant like myself, and to our right, a two-car garage with a little apartment on top where our 80 year old landlady, Alice lives.

My place is named the Doll House for reasons I am never told, (Ibsen's play?). Unfortunately, I can't remember the other house's name that is just as picturesque. Alice, a former actress, lived in the Doll House at one time with her husband who taught drama at Harvard. These properties were summer homes for the couple and their friends and family. But that was long ago before Alice's husband developed Alzheimer's disease and had to be placed in a nursing home. The expensive care ate up all her money before he died and she's been reduced to living on a pension and the income from her summer houses.

Philip and I make an interesting match. Both of us have powerful dreams about the importance of our relationship. Strange, inexplicable things keep happening to bring us together. He lives in the shell of a huge house, just a frame, the floors, a central fireplace made of fieldstone, window openings that invite birds to nest inside, and the roof. His tent is pitched upstairs in the back with the window openings to the woods. We fuck all the time and we talk. He has the ability to disarm the devil with his talk, and he talks to anyone. A lot of rich people on the island pay him money to build them fireplaces, he's also a jack of all trades, does everything, has even fished for a living.

He is the quintessential Demon Lover. You know, the kind of guy who's a shithead and a brute, but who also has the power to charm the underpants right off you, the guy who finally forces you to grow up once and for all. He lives in the same area as Alice, and now me. It's by accident (or so I think) that on the evening I bring my things to the Doll House I run into him. He offers to help me unload my van and afterward Alice invites us up to her studio for a celebratory glass of wine to welcome me. She tells of a dream she's had of the three of us in which she foresees Philip and I getting on board a train for a very long journey, but she will not be boarding it. He sees that train ride as commitment and responsibility and wants no part of it.

Yet Alice is serious and asserts her dream had been profound. I don't know what to make of it. Afterward, Philip and I go down to the Doll House and out to the deck. We sit quietly in the dark night with a few stars above and the sound of the ocean lapping against the rock wall beneath us. Then we look at each other . . . *Oh god, what a frightening sight!* I am able to see into the very depths of his and my being and I do not like what I behold. Our stance in life is needy and pathetic. I feel shame. Something similar happens to him. What he sees is an incredibly ugly, vile old woman looking back at him. We go in to the house and hold each other, swaying back and forth to calm us.

The Doll House is a bit strange too with its many mirrors strewn throughout, placed at odd angles and arranged in such a fashion that they reflect the ocean over and over again. I am seeing myself reflected in all my actions. There is no escape. I have brought a little dream to fit my Doll House and it is exploding in my face. Much bigger things are expected of me. I have first to leave the Doll House and Alice, whose concerns over money far outweigh her ability to assist in maintaining and repairing the property. Then I have to leave the Demon Lover; that takes longer.

Philip built the shell of his house in hopes of enticing his ex-wife and children to come back to him, and when he saw it wasn't going to happen he gave up on the project. The unfinished house is a symbol that broadcasts Philip's stance in life. He's an unfinished man because some woman has done him wrong, and he's arranged his financial life such that he doesn't have to pay her any child support. No payroll checks, all earnings paid him in cash, even the house is in a friend's name.

He's a man's man and with him I go hunting, fishing, camping very deep in the backwoods of Maine. We're competitive with each other. I'm jealous of his strength, of his ability to drive his van in places where he could never be rescued. We sink three feet in some marshy woods. No problem, he can practically lift the thing up by himself. A lot of adventures are open to him that I can never have. We fight.

On a mountain climb, we arrive at a very dangerous pass in which the only way for me to save myself is to throw myself at him, about 3 feet separating us, and trust that he has the strength to hold me from the sheer drop into rocks and trees below. Trust. He, when given that same opportunity turns it down. It's a difficult relationship from beginning to end. Philip's a bully. And I have my own ideas.

I figure the only way to bring about a writing life is to get out of the workaday world and go off and do it somewhere by myself. I will sell my house and use the proceeds to live on while I set about creating something. Philip, having met most of my friends and family, sets about to seduce them. And he's successful, even procuring my cousin for one of his buddies. People I thought were loyal to me turn out to be nothing of the kind. But also, I no longer have anything in common with them. The guy's a two-timer, not only to me, but also to the world at large. He's really not what he's portraying himself to be. Sometimes we hate each other.

There is also in each of us a parent talking to the other, an older self guiding. We shake each other up. Wake up; wake up! In the midst of one of our breakups, when Philip comes for a visit, his dog talks to me . . . . . !?

A strange thing happens then, since I have no point of reference for such an occurrence, it is immediately erased from my mind. It has not happened. Only after 5 or 10 minutes does it come back to me. Has the dog mouthed words? No, but information has been transmitted to me. The information is that Philip, who is staying with friends, is unhappy with his situation.

Perhaps it's a projection on my part.

It happens another time towards the end of our relationship. I am walking on Philip's property with the dog following behind, as we approach an area where Philip has strewn garbage, the dog communicates, "Look at the mess he's making!" What's more, the information is transmitted in the Yankee dialect of the region. The message does not concern me; it is not something I would project.

Do I have an explanation for this?

No.

I invite Philip to a weekend conference for French artists. Feeling ignored while friends and associates gather round me, he casts his eyes on other women. Then I don't see him anymore; we're no longer sharing meals.

This is it, I say to myself. *No more of this.*

That evening when I return to our camping van I tell him, "Look, this isn't working. You're hustling my friends. I want to break it off."

I'm sitting in the driver's seat, stripped down to bra and panties getting ready for bed.

He is furious. "Your so-called friends in the hall, go to them," he says and he pushes me.

The door's not properly closed and I fall to the ground and break the elbow. I would rather die than suffer the humiliation of going to ask for help in such a condition. I fight the bastard and get back in the truck.

I have a scary moment at a city hospital 600 miles from home, when he almost abandons me. But we make it back. And there's only one thing left to do, sell my house and get out. I'm a stranger now. Doors are closing and I'm about to embark on a journey. Leaving the area, in the car I make myself a promise, *I will never again embark on a relationship with a man until I am able to stand my ground with him.*

What about Philip? He goes straight, takes possession of his house, gets squared away with the state about his child support payments, in business with another guy. Last I hear he's using that silver tongue of his to produce videos, interviews of local characters that are shown on the public station.

Alice had been right about the train ride. We three had come together at the moment before departure. She had too much at stake in her worldly possessions and was too old to take any risk and she was going nowhere. He balked and behaved badly but eventually got on the train. Thankfully, we were not traveling in the same direction.

* * *

At my cabin after the vision quest, I began to intuit a change. Whereas in the past, I took it as faith that I shaped my life through determination and will, I could now see that there was a certain energy pervading the world, and undoubtedly the universe, that presented me with the needed opportunities if I maintained the right path, and by "right" I mean appropriate to my direction.

Once that was understood, I had to be willing to risk all, to place myself in the most hopeless situation if the circumstance called for it, accepting that I would achieve my goal. I had to be prepared to stake my life on what I believed.

I was lonely at first. My thoughts revolved around Philip and the misery of our relationship. The hardest part of my day was the end of my work period when I left the writing room.

This is life without the ersatz amusements society provides. The mind stops panicking after a while and I learn to inhabit the stillness, the quiet.

People had surrounded me throughout my life and now there was no one. If I was hurt or sick, there was no one I could call on; that ubiquitous box in medical questionnaires requesting the name of a person to contact in case of emergency would have to remain empty. If I needed a hand there was naught but my own two hands to rely on. I was responsible for myself. The fact that I didn't have to interact with anyone through work, that I was taking two years off to write a novel, left me free to design my life as I saw fit. I fell into a pattern quite similar to the one held by nuns of the Catholic convent where I was raised. I meditated, took long walks in the woods, worked in the garden, exercised my body and I wrote.

My neighbor and landlady came over to befriend me, a middle-aged woman with grown kids. She talked about the people in the village, her kids, her cantankerous husband, rattling on for a half hour; I nodded appropriately, but it was as if an inhabitant from Mars had stopped by to chat about the happenings on her planet. This feeling extended to others; I had lost common ground with the human race. I could listen and empathize with their fate, most of which was self-induced, but I could not relate, as it had nothing to do with my present life.

At some point in our relationship the landlord and his wife perceived I would not go along with their program, as I demanded my rights. They decided to get rid of me by trying to make my life unpleasant. This coincidentally occurred at a time when my funds were running low. I asked for two weeks forbearance. They interpreted this as a sign that I was preparing to run out on them and not pay my bill. Their first action was to send me a written notice raising my rent. I refused to pay the extra money. They came to the cabin with the constable to serve me with an eviction notice.

I have spent many hours in courtrooms battling cheaters and crooks through Housing Court, or Small Claims. Court is an interesting affair; it's something one should seek out as a learning experience in and of itself. I was called to court many times by these two. At my first hearing a man from Legal Services took one look at the Notice to Quit they had served me and said, *it's no good.*

What's more, the judge agreed. Apparently the couple had done this on the cheap, hadn't consulted a lawyer; the Notice to Quit was flawed. They refused to accept my rent checks on the false notion that they couldn't evict me if they did. I deposited the rent money, minus the extra they were demanding in an escrow account. I won that hearing and went back to the cabin.

One of the things I learned from my vision quest is that one has to behave in an ethical way; taking on a battle with another individual means putting all my effort into achieving *right* outcome.

"*All of my effort*," means I'm prepared to risk my very life to achieve my goal. There is no pulling out once I've committed myself, therefore I must choose my battles carefully and avoid situations that involve ego and pride, keeping in mind that one's ethics don't always correspond with jurisprudence and the enforcement of its laws. I may have to act in ways that could be interpreted as illegal.

If I'm on the right path, doing what I must to maintain selfhood, doors open for me. If I falter, deceive myself about the nature of my engagement, I'm defeated. I can make the law work for me if I enter that domain with respect. Anything can happen in a courtroom, and does. After my third appearance in district court, I am out of tricks, the landlords have hired a lawyer and I lose.

A bit of serendipity comes to my rescue. The law is changed at this time allowing me to appeal the matter to a higher power. Superior court is overwhelming; I will have to perform a *voir dire* choosing candidates for my jury, a complicated jigsaw puzzle of trying to match up the bits of information the court provides, to the person in the box, and the matter of keeping track of their seating arrangement.

Can I pull this off?

I file the papers and a meeting is set up with the judge who will decide if the case has merit. Everything depends on his decision. I could be packing tomorrow with a 5-day deadline to abandon the cabin if he thinks the matter frivolous.

I'm expending a lot of psychic energy on a matter that cannot arrest the final outcome. It's their cabin. But I cannot allow them to abuse me. Since they're prepared to do me dirty, they naturally assume I will do likewise. I would never cheat them, not because it's the right thing to do, or out of a fear of their revenge, but because to do so would put me in a weakened position vis à vis the ongoing struggle. They don't want to do business with me because I expect them to fulfill their obligations.

Then again, I have no destination in mind either. Where will I go? And to be evicted by others is no way to start on a new path.

"The case has merit," says the judge and he puts it on his schedule.

"Do you want to bother with records from district court?" he asks. "It would take a while to get them here."

"Yes, your Honor. I would like those records."

The process takes months. A clerk could easily run over and get the documents from civil court as the building is just across the street, but the wheels of justice move in an arcane and deliberate manner. My opponents have gotten themselves a new lawyer. Since our last battle in district court, the landlord brags that he's going to make short work of my tactics; this new man is obviously his big gun, someone who has started a line of law offices for the masses, a McAttorney service. The landlord's a fool for challenging Natural Law with his braggadocio. He's asking to be smacked for his impudence.

That the judge decides to accept my appeal infuriates him. His wife accosts me in the stairs, shouting that I'm an evil, crazy woman. That, I conclude is a step up; she had dismissed me as a lowlife when she first entered the courtroom. Though I'm beginning to get respect, I'm a quivering jellyfish inside. Less than ten minutes previously I sat in a courtroom with my future on the line. I could have had 4 days of sweaty packing heading off on the 5th day to an unknown destination.

During this time Yvon Labbé, the director at the Centre Franco-Américain at the University of Maine in Orono contacts me with an invitation to come up to UMO to be artist-in-residence in the fall -- a gift from the Spirit.

My memory of the time is linked to my runs on a hilly country road looking straight at Big Jackson Mountain, my body toned, feeling strong, a raw, cold beginning to spring, and walking through woods on my way back, deep woods with bears, moose, fox, deer. The ground lay under ice from a freakish rainstorm the past winter and deer could not get to the grasses, so I laid out some feed not far from the cabin. In spring, I walk to the area by the clothesline and I find an antler on the ground. They shit perfectly round black balls the size of a big shooter marble. I dry some and use them when creating rituals.

As my time for court draws closer I devise a ritual to protect me against the landlords.

It begins at midnight in an unlit room, save for candles, white ones signifying a pure heart at the start of a new adventure. The room needs to be cleansed of the unhappiness that has occurred in it. Burning sage does the trick. If there is none, improvise. Open a window to the outdoors and pray for the removal of misery and woe. If there is no one to pray to, pray to Spirit, which is the energy surrounding us.

Start by placing and lighting a candle in the direction of the North, from whence comes the cold, snow, and ice, where animals have thick coats and vicious claws. One wants some of that power and protection. Plead for it because, like the hibernating Bear, alone in a vulnerable place at a time of new beginning when the path is yet mapped, one needs defense. Where the road leads, what will be accomplished is unknown.

Turn then and walk East, whose domain is air. There again place and light a candle invoking the residing powers, the great winds that bring change, storms and destruction, the sweet breath of life that supports birds both large and tiny, and the thoughts and ideas that lead to new adventures.

Now to the South, same as before, a lit candle and an invocation to the South's warmth and brilliance, its fire, that which caresses the body, entices it to indolence and passion. Think of the Snake, the biblical tempter, the Armadillo, the cats, Puma, Cheetah, Jaguar, sensuous, powerful, quick. Some of that energy will open doors.

Lastly the West, which is the domain of water, the depths, mystery, the abyss, profundity, a guiding force that can never be quite grasped. Think of the fish that navigate this realm unaware of the world above them except for what lands in their water. They navigate the world's secrets, its great unconscious. Light the candle, invoke this power, and a protective circle has now been cast.

What does one hope to happen? Speak of it. To the powers of the four directions invoked offer a gift that signifies sobriety in pursuing goals, making sure to follow through (a promise, a sacrifice,) on what's been offered.

Look into the flame of a candle until a trance state is achieved. Afterward, open the circle by going in a counter clockwise manner to the four directions thanking the energy residing in each direction for sharing its power.

Good food and wine are appropriate at end of ritual.

In my ritual seeking to curtail landlords' maneuvers, I make a specific request: *I want them to stop telling lies in court; I want their words to trip them up.*

For the occasion, I burn a note they've sent me, handwritten, touched by them, their body oils deposited on the paper. Down to white ash it disintegrates, as I tell my story of harassment, my various court appearances and the upcoming trial in superior court. Once the ritual's complete, I drive to the shop where she works, and where I know her husband joins her daily for lunch, and on the pathway leading to the building's front door where they have to traverse, I deposit the embodiment of my spell, namely the white ashes.

On the appointed day, I approach the courthouse, a brick neo-gothic New England structure, whose design is intended to induce boundless feelings of guilt. My worst fear is of flubbing the voir dire, a rank amateur among the adept.

The judge calls my name and has me approach a stand, then he reads the appeal, "Are you ready to proceed?" he asks.

"Yes I am, Your Honor."

He then turns to the landlords who are sitting in back of me and asks them the same question. A young man with carrot red hair sits next to them.

Have they gotten rid of their top-gun lawyer so soon?

The man stands to speak; I sit facing the judge as I hear sounds coming from the back, floating over my head toward the judge's bench.

"Aaaah . . .Aaaah . . Aaaah . . Uuuugh . . . "

The man is a stutterer!

I sit very still listening to him struggle with his presentation, never once turning to look, afraid the spell will break. His story does eventually come out; top-gun lawyer had a personal emergency and could not be present. He sent his young associate to replace him. The judge asks if we're amenable to try and negotiate a settlement while he attends to other matters.

The lawyer and I, in a passageway leading to the courtroom, come to a resolution. I tell him I will leave the cabin in the fall when I depart for the

University of Maine to begin my year as artist-in-residence.

"They want to be paid."

"Yes, of course, I've kept the money in escrow, and I'll pay them for the upcoming months."

"No," says the couple when they hear what I will pay them. "We want the new rate we had asked for."

The lawyer runs back and forth several times between us; the landlords concede to my desires and we all go home.

I have found that if my cause is right I win in court. Is it that justice prevails? No, it's because I've decided there's no alternative but to act. My courtroom battle is never about my opponent. There is a larger issue at play. It is solely about me. The Spirit has presented me with a challenge. The challenge seems to be connected to my upcoming life once this is over. The nature of the challenge teaches me skills I will need. Am I able to conquer this situation and move on? What is the overriding metaphor at its center? Home, a home.

Without respect, home is not possible, or love. And aren't they the same thing?

What I stand for cannot be about salvaging my bruised ego, my wounded pride, or about moral outrage. After two years of solitude I'm about to re-enter society a different person than when I left it. I will not let others decide my method and time of re-entry. It is Spirit that chooses and one must wait for that sign. I must not be desperate. It's a show of weakness, and whatever is gained from desperation can never be trusted to be the correct choice. What am I willing to pay for my integrity? To re-enter society making compromises with others makes one a compromised person, one who has given some of her power to others, and is therefore weakened by the experience.

Once I made the decision, my energy became focused. I am wary of emotions that tend to run strong in a court of law. It's not about emotions, or logic. It's about power and focus. The closer I am to the *real* me, the more attuned I will be to the energy around me.

This case was an assured victory for the landlord, yet took so long to resolve, and in the tenant's favor that one has to ask, what is happening here? There is a force, an energy that comes to my assistance when I start with a sincere heart, a clear understanding of my purpose, and a ruthless desire to achieve my goal. Meaningful coincidences start occurring, I'm saved in the nick of time, an important message is transmitted, the judge is sick on the appointed day, the law is changed to my advantage midcourse.

I arrive in evening. The building where I'm to be housed is an institutional five story, brick structure that could easily be mistaken for a prison. Coming from my cabin by the woods with its burbling brook, its plentiful animals into this little play world of brick structures clumped together around a carpet of green lawn and carefully manicured trees is a bit of culture shock. I park the van in front of the building, secure the front door open with a brick, and there directly to my left is my new home. The faculty apartment has one large living/study room, a large bedroom and a great bath. I sneak Hermine in rolled in a blanket, as cats are not welcome. It's back to keeping most of my things in storage, traveling light, the desk and chair, the lamp, the filing cabinet, books, house plants and clothes. In and out of the building bringing in boxes, I check out my neighbors who, from the looks of things, are going out for the evening. I can pick up that teenage sense of excitement for the possibilities ahead.

University of Maine at Orono is located in the sparsely populated northern part of the state. Most of its students are from lower middle, to middle class homes in small towns. I arrive during President Bush Senior's crisis over Iraq, and I experience first-hand a sort of mass hysteria taking over students, a crowd mentality that seizes them and they begin to sound exactly like the propaganda coming out of Washington. This, from young people who have the most to lose if war occurs. Flags are draped from every window of student dormitory buildings. There's even a contest set up by dorm managers to see which building will look more patriotic. Students' rooms are invaded without permission to place these flags, and a large message board is installed on the main floor inviting comments about the war. With that many students in the five-story building, it seems peculiar that the board only contains pro-war messages. One day, I include my own comments about the futility of it, and of all the people who will die for reasons that seem dubious at best. On the next morning I find the message has been removed.

Soon newspaper clippings about the war and pictures of boys going into the military are lining the wall leading to the TV room. Fever is spreading through campus and its victims speak in one voice: the archetypal patriarch ready to mete out justice, a strange time and place to come out of hibernation. Pundits write about trying to regain honor lost in Vietnam so many years ago. The world is still crazy. I'm the alien visiting an outer planet.

One is set apart as artist in residence, someone who's come to exhibit her talents, to entertain, to inspire and instruct, the stranger looking in on others' lives, slated to move on at the end of my term. The rosy cheeked teenagers who, from a young age, are taught to respect authority and to obey, are in the majority, a replay of high school, with goody-goodies, rebels, nerds, losers. My interactions with others are often abrupt or rude. It's as if I'm trying to make up for all the years I had been acquiescent. I'm a teenager too. The kids and I are on an adrenaline high. I notice my feet jiggling away just like theirs do.

I take lovers from the faculty, a series of one-night stands with one man, then a short-lived affair with a woman. In both instances, I am hardly present in any meaningful way; the wall of separation is still up, but I do crave the connection, the physical intimacy. My behavior toward others seems selfish, callous to me; I'm focused on myself, my work, my ideas, my energy, in a way that has never occurred before. I'm developing a public voice.

The world of mysticism, the other dimension, is a world inhabited solely by the self. Pieces of this universe can be shared, but sparingly because of society's need to market and package any foreign concept or idea in easily digestible morsels that can be mass-produced, conferenced, workshopped. As such, it gets trivialized till any mention brings skepticism or scorn. Think of words like New Age, A Course in Miracles, EST, Wicca, Angels, tune in, drop out, get high, get in touch with your inner self, find a guru. Every one of those agencies can be of help, but ultimately each individual must, by herself, find the door that opens to the world of mysticism. It can be found through revelations presented in dreams, through symbols, omens; keeping in mind that one's primary interaction is as an animal of the earth, a part of a living universe.

I give Tarot readings, form women and men's groups and give readings of my novel COMICS, my poetry, essays, I speak out against the war and learn to use a computer, to write fiction in one of the library carrels with students all around. *I just need a warm corner.* I fall in love at first sight when I'm introduced to the Apple. I marvel at the word processor with its never-ending supply of page fronts. Into eternity! And, oh god, I can move batches of writing from one section to another. I can revise at will without having to retype the whole thing! I spend a month scanning all my writing, poems, essays, the first novel and the one I am presently working on.

Midway through my year at University I'm approached by Eric Peterson, the Chairman of the Speech/Communication Department who expresses a desire to stage a play based on my novel, COMICS.

The main character, Theresa is a woman with an American head and a French heart. Eric chooses to highlight this dichotomy by splitting Theresa's divided nature and having a different woman act each part in the play. It's a great success and I'm quite satisfied with Eric's adaptation. Sitting in the dark watching the performance of characters I've created, I realize they are not mine and have never truly been mine. The story doesn't emanate from my subconscious. Rather it comes from the same place the visions came from. In a way, the visions taught me where to go to get stories. When I sit at the computer to write fiction, I travel to a nether world where individuals who have something of value to say approach me. If you call that my subconscious, I say you lack imagination.

The story of Theresa in the novel COMICS is about a divorced woman who returns to the home she lived in as wife after being away at college. She gets a job in a mental health center working on the emergency team. Every day people come into her office, or are dragged in by family or police, some drugged into a stupor, others on the edge of hysteria, and in the evening she goes back to the house that is not a home. The crazy people beckon her into their world. They can sense she is one of them.

From Theresa's perspective, her colleagues and superiors seem in as bad, if not worse, shape as the patients. They seem dead to her with their tight, controlled lives, their TV shows, their bills, their little circle, their mates, all neat and tidy in a box. They have been assigned roles, like the roles she and her husband played in the dead house.

What is the proper role for a human being who lives on planet earth? Should she be a psychologist assigning labels to those who come to see her? This one is neurotic, that one is schizophrenic, and the other has a character disorder?

Theresa seems to be falling apart. She lives on the sofa that is piled with blankets, pillows, magazines, pad and pen, books, chocolates. She never goes in the bedroom and she never cooks for herself. The living room floor is covered with the detritus of her takeout meals, save for paths leading to the bathroom and one leading out of the building. She is swimming in the world of the "mentally ill," a euphemism employed in the profession. What does it mean to be mentally ill, and who should be considered a candidate for that label? She no longer has clear answers to those questions. What she knows is that the "mentally ill" behave in ways that upset others; the "mentally ill" cannot be easily controlled. That seems to upset most people. The mentally ill, she has also noticed, have a knack of picking up fairly rapidly the role they are supposed to play vis à vis the mental health professional.

Like a vision, the act of creating fiction is similar in that one enters into another way of perceiving, another way of interpreting, like the crazy people do. I prefer the word crazy to mentally ill. What occurs during those instances is diminished with the euphemistic term, and by extension, so is the person experiencing those special states of awareness. Crazy is a powerful word that encompasses the unknown and expresses something mysterious and fearful about life and the human condition.

My year at Orono helps me to focus on my talents by presenting me with abundant opportunity to read some of my work and share my ideas. I have the luxury of completely free afternoons to write, a wonderful little library at my command, intelligent people to converse with. It becomes obvious to me that I'm a spiritual person now, someone with a strong and vibrant inner life, a clear direction of where my path lies and, I am now also a loner. Perhaps I have always been and never acknowledged it.

THE CHARIOT

-VII-

The Prince stands firmly grasping the reins of his steeds, blue curtains on the canopy of his Chariot billowing in the wind as he travels the open road for this journey he calls life. Two horses, one black, the other white, pull in opposite directions, their spirited natures locked in by the yoke that fuses them into a single force.

The Prince's only connection to this furious power is through the leather thongs that travel from his hands to the bit at their teeth. He's aware of each tug pulling at the reins, wrenching him in one direction then another, to experience the dark terrors that control him, the sunny security which envelops him in a shroud of certainty. He's barely aware of the scenery as it speedily unfolds, imperceptibly changing as the years advance.

Occasionally there are fleeting moments at breaks along the journey when the Prince finds himself alone in the deep-forested night, the voice in his head having lost its power over him. These moments are his only connection with a life that quickly dissipates behind him as he enters deeper into it. He longs to possess it, to hold it in his hand and examine it at leisure, but he cannot and must satisfy himself with glimpses and these only because he behaves like a warrior and holds fast the reins of carelessness and fear.

Upright: The joining of opposing forces united to work in concert.

Reversed: Controversy, imbalance, defeat.

Hell llooo! New York Citt ttay!!! Off comes the plastic from the porch window and the tape sealing its seams, then I lift up the storm panel and she slides right in. The sultry bitch enters with fire alarms screaming, horns tooting, Chinese men in the street below talking back and forth in high pitched, whining voices. Her parfum on this muggy day is Street Tar & Earth. The woman likes to make a dramatic entrance.
I wouldn't have it any other way.

I love my fire escape. Since the last tenants left behind two deck chairs, and someone before them left Chinese wind chimes, I contribute a bird feeder, a hanging plant and some potted flowers. Saturday and Sunday mornings, I have breakfast on my balcony, and read the Times. Sitting on my front porch overlooking NYC, above the tumult of commerce in the street, I am perched like the birds that come to my feeder.

It's a busy day for Zhen Wong and his gang of boys. Half the city's restaurants along with a good portion of New Jersey's get their supplies from his storefront warehouse. Latino boys scurry back and forth on the street below, their dollies packed high with boxes of delicacies for the elegant Chinese men who come with shopping lists in hand. Trunks are popped, back doors opened and all manner of bok choy, lichee nuts and plump shitake mushrooms are packed into their vehicles. Even the men from the firehouse come shop for their supplies at Zhen's.

A woman in the next building, same floor as mine, also out on her fire escape, gives me the nod. In my building, beside the rock musician, there is the actress, two dancers, a writer like myself, and a software developer. Most everyone I meet downtown is an artist of one sort or another. I brought my bike with me and go tooling up to the East Village where "the *scene*" is happening, bars, clubs, cafés, restaurants, and artists. East Village hasn't completely sold out, still hungry, looking to score. A lot of little shops owned by single individuals display funky, original storefronts. The Village's character is punk with gothic undertones and has great sleazy bars with interesting characters, terrific bookstores and a lot of teenage kids hanging around. They sport weird, raccoon kohl eyes, purple or fuchsia hair, extensive, morbid tattoos and pierced lips, noses, eye brows, runaways most of them, living on the street, crashing wherever they can. And they beg.

These self-dramatized kids dress creatively and I look twice because I know that what I see them wearing will be taken up by the fashion world next year. I ride my bike to the KGB Bar on Sunday night for their Reading Series where recently published writers are invited to share their stories. The bar is so packed there is literally no place to stand with others craning to hear in the hall and stairs. The crowd is mixed, artists, writers, grad students from Columbia and NYU, teachers. I come early, take a seat at the bar and order a vodka gimlet, straight up. The bar's decor is blood red walls with black trim, covered with big pictures of famous communists, their posters, their slogans, their military, and a big, red hammer and sickle flag.

The establishment owners, who are neither Russian, nor communist, appear to make their money elsewhere; they seem particularly uninterested in turning a profit at KGB. The Writing Series is what they rightly pride themselves on.

It was during my stay at Kate's loft that I first became acquainted with this neighborhood. She tends to emotional fragility, gets into a major set-to with the Dexedrine cats on Christmas morning. Full force. One of them tries to drag me into the argument.

"I have to leave now. This is upsetting and I don't want to be here," I say and I walk out. Kate's got an *I've behaved badly* look on her face.

Out on the street Christmas morning, cold, gunmetal sky, a few flurries, who knows how long I'll be out? Kate's supposed to be leaving to visit a friend for a couple of days. But she's worked herself into such a state, it's going to take her a while to come down. I walk the streets reviewing my current situation.

On my walk, I meet solitary souls like myself. Maybe there is a small army of us in Manhattan. And with that uplifting thought I stumble upon a cheery coffee and pastries shop. The front doors and windows are wide open; I am practically sitting outdoors at my little table. The cold air and fat, lazy snowflakes, the hot chocolate being served by a handsome Latino man, great pastries, I sit back and watch folks walk by.

Merry Christmas! I'm going to be OK.

I try to get as much out of school as I can, seeing that my time at Sarah Lawrence is coming to an end shortly. My teachers are encouraging, and I have been told that I am producing the most finished work of my class. My goal is to review every chapter of 53 in classes with fellow writers whose judgments I trust, and present it as my thesis. I am also taking a poetry course. What a luxury to have all this individual attention paid to my writing, in a school whose focus is on what I have to say, as opposed to what they can teach me.

Money is tight. What few, occasional telephone clients of my own that I do have, hardly contribute enough to cover my laundry bill. Some things have worked out; the bike especially saves me the expense of subway fares. I get a little crazy worrying about survival at times, but mostly I know I will be OK. The door opens when you're ready. I'm supposed to be here doing my work, on a path that is indisputable.

I earn $20,000 my first year, $10,000 goes to my landlady, $5,000 to the federal and state governments and the rest is mine. Home sweet home. That I survive on $5,000 is nothing short of amazing to me, and I feel justifiable pride being able to pay my bills, having achieved the goal of a quiet time to write, to speak with people about spirit matters. Yes, I do love New York City.

One can learn craft at Sarah Lawrence, but no one can teach you the art of writing. I have about me a bit of the messianic, and turned loose on an essay, I blossom. I never took this talent seriously until my last college year. Studying psychology at the time, I became depressed about my situation, the meaninglessness of what I was studying; psychology then was going through its Skinnerian rat phase. The silliest course I ever took was in social psychology and its field of research. Suffice it to say that human beings in all their complexity can never be fully captured by laboratory experiments. The sham and corruption in most fields of endeavor, and the direction my life was to take overwhelmed me.

I contacted a therapist who I had taken a course with, a Jungian psychologist. From the start, he set me the task of writing my dreams; he expected a dream from me every time I saw him. I, who dreamt vividly and often, could not remember any for several weeks. Out of a sense of embarrassment, I wrote him a story to make up for my dreamless state. It was a story about Alice in Wonderland.

"You're a writer," he said after I read him my tale.

The man is absurd.

The story of Alice was no doubt my story, and still is. I see my life as an adventure, some of it delightful, some of it a conundrum. The therapist's comment stayed with me. I remembered teachers who sought me out to tell me how they enjoyed my essays. I assumed that the subject itself was what they found interesting, not my thoughts on it, or my writing.

I was experiencing great changes in my life. Every day traveling to the university from my sheltered life in a rural home in Sabattus to Maine's only city to speak of. I have many fond memories of Portland, especially its Old Port section by the sea. We would congregate at the Seamen's Tavern with its sculptured whale door handle, highly burnished by the many hands that grasped it, and talk politics and world affair, trying to articulate for ourselves the tenets of a just society, a true democracy.

I was then Director of the University Women's Forum. The subject of power was very much on the table. Who has power and who doesn't, how to get power; is power corrupting? It is a subject that women find difficult to come to terms with. And society, contrary to its posturing on the subject, is not comfortable with strong, independent women. The writer in our group was someone that I grew fond of. To be a poet in a feminist organization is of no great consequence, but Tracy wisely understood differently. Because her writing was such an integral part of her, she was more centered than other women. We talked about her work and about the writers she was studying with.

I sent a letter to the editor at the Maine Times about one of his editorials. *If the letter is published, I'm on the right track.* It was my test of the Spirit; I wanted a sign.

The Spirit's reply?

My letter was published.

And then I graduated. Driving home, my heart sank at the loss my intellectual community. I was cast adrift in a world of drudgery and ignorance where the dreaded phrase, *earning a living,* comes into play.

Writing was a luxury I could not economically, or psychologically, afford at the time. I applied for a job in a mental health clinic. As part of my interview, I was asked to read several pages of a patient's story, his problem, his past treatment, his family history, etc., then condense the story, and write a report about the patient. I gained invaluable training from all the reports I wrote about individuals, their problems, strengths, capturing the one detail that brings the person and their situation into sharp focus. But I did not write outside the clinic. I tried keeping a journal and my first few entries were of such poor quality that I gave it up.

Later, I had a dream:

> I am accompanying my boyfriend on a train. He is there to visit the Old Man. My friend seeks him out for advice and direction. I remain in the adjoining car while they talk. When my friend

rejoins me he says that the Old Man has, for a long time, taken an interest in me and whenever we pay him a visit, he writes notes about me.

I think my friend flatters himself to imagine the Old Man would be interested in his girlfriend. As we leave the car, he shows me as the Old Man takes notes on my behavior, writing on a small piece of white paper that he shoves between his legs.

He's a sorcerer, a brujo with power for both good and evil. He can also transcend logic, reality, time and space. I am overwhelmed by his presence and experience a great many feelings, awe, fear, yet attraction, and somehow at ease in his presence.

In bed that night, as I slowly drift off to sleep, I am suddenly awakened by the presence of someone on top of me. It's the brujo! Alongside of him is a huge cat, perhaps a tiger or leopard. I remain very still, frightened for my life. The brujo caresses my entire body; the cat makes lewd approaches with its tail between my legs.

Suddenly, he sits on top of me and points to the piano on his left,

"I haven't been able to play for 5 years," he says. I reach up and gently stroke his steel gray hair.

Then he was gone and I awoke. Terrified, hysterical, I jumped out of bed; *nothing I could do would protect me!* I put the light on, still very frightened, pacing the floor from one end of the room to the other.

What does it mean? Why am I so frightened?

The only way I could calm and soothe myself was to run some warm water in the tub and get in. *It was real, a visit. From where? Oh god! What did it all mean?*

A guide. I had imagined guides to be an inner spirit. Not so. It is out there and it is real. I reviewed everything that occurred between us. He signified sexual potency with the notes about my life that he shoved between his legs, the very data he collected of my behavior and my utterances. The steel in his hair is what I reach for, his strength, his power. I was afraid he would destroy me when he was on top of me in the bed. A clear sign of dominance, but he did not hurt me, choosing instead to stroke my body, but not in a sexual, penetrating manner. It was the big cat that was trying to seduce me, who would eventually embody me. I belonged to the brujo now.

That he was unable to play the piano indicated to me that something was missing. I would have to do something, I didn't know what, but something was expected of me.

His act of caressing my body brings another message: love yourself, it tells me, because his caresses touched the very core of me. I was taught shame and humility in the convent, and in my community, so that truly loving myself was foreign to me. And by truly loving oneself, I mean respecting and trusting one's actions, ideas, beliefs. Assuredness. I also understood from the dream that my life would not follow a conventional pattern.

STRENGTH

-VIII-

Tall, thick palms grace the distance, and beyond, jagged mountains against a bright yellow sky; one questions the validity of what appears in foreground. Amid incipient jungle growth a blond woman with a crown of flowers in her hair is bent to a full-maned lion. She's got its head tucked under her left arm like a clutch purse, her hand grasping its lower jaw.

The cat's bright red tongue curls out of its mouth, as if seeking to lick the hand resting on top of its nose. Is she stroking the animal's snout, or attempting to clamp shut its maw? A lighthearted note is evident in the woman's crown of peonies, her lovely white gown and the lion's kittenish appearance. Yet the jungle's riotous growth, and the animal's jaws embody a strong potential for danger. The beast could easily lurch for her throat, sinking its teeth into pink flesh and deftly sever the spinal cord.

One is aware of its potential in the dark night, or in the approach of the unfamiliar. How to deal with it? What of this woman gamboling in Eden with the animals? There are no answers here, there is only the animal's faith in its prowess, the woman's belief in the power of her tender feeling.

Upright: Trust and belief in one's power.

Reversed: Weakness, cowardice; not trusting one's strength

On my way to Barnes & Nobles on Astor Place, I run into a guy who sells reefer in Washington Square Park. I see him all the time plying his trade.

He is the Buddha. So named he says, "Because I shaved my hair off once and my buddies thought I looked the part."

I find him and his story charming. He comes from Mount Vernon, a nondescript, working-class town I drive through on my way to Sarah Lawrence. Buddha lives on the street, hangs in the park with his friends. He crashes wherever he can and is having a pretty good time of it, an innocent in a world whose machinations barely register in his mind. Buddha is a big black man. His skin is dusky, the color of dark bittersweet chocolate. On our first meeting, he wears dark slacks, a knit shirt, and he sports a saucy white golfer's cap.

"You look very nice," I comment on his outfit.

"You like that?" he says with the look of a Cheshire cat being stroked. He talks about how he would like to open a clothing store, a little boutique.

A fantasy that I don't think he truly believes is possible, or maybe he does.

"You got no polish on your nails." he says as he picks up my hand to examine it.

He's probably thinking of black and Latino girls' nails that are meticulously maintained, designed, painted, polished, and long. I slip off my shoe and show him blackberry painted toenails against white, white skin. Not knowing yet that Buddha has a toe fetish, I've definitely made a good first impression.

We eat Chinese, listen to music and hang in the park. I show him a bathroom he can use at Barnes & Nobles, an important bit of information for a street person. He is not comfortable in my neighborhood. I point out that the smaller Chinese and Latinos undoubtedly perceive the Buddha as a threat, and that may explain their strange behavior in his presence.

He is leery of Seward Park, which I view from my windows. Mostly it is covered with tar and cement, but has beautiful old, full-headed deciduous trees. Not a place where he cares to sit and pass time. I don't either, but I like to walk through it under the cover of its leafy umbrella. A homeless man lived under one of its benches all winter. With cardboard and blankets, he fashioned a makeshift tent covering the bench which he crawled under at night. Becoming accustomed to seeing people in desperate straits with nothing I can do about it is a slow process. I look out my window in the dead of night with the temperature below freezing, snow on the ground, and see him crawl into his cocoon. At first, I feel obliged to witness this, as if pulling away is somehow callous. I leave a roasted chicken for him on Christmas day, but I never speak to him. A young guy, late twenties, the cops come by a few months later while he is gone, tear his camp down and haul everything away.

The park with its magic show of hard drugs is brought about courtesy of the dealers, an underworld of grim, young street corner hustlers who are all business; the only thing lacking from their attire is an accountant's green visor. It is they, perhaps that Buddha fears.

I had doubts that I would be able to get it completed and hand it in on time, but on the last day I turn in my thesis. It's down to the wire as I print up the last chapters at the computer center, minutes before it's about to close. The officious man in charge goes out of his way to be obstructive. Thankfully, another guy comes to my rescue and helps resolve the problem of getting the font *courier* to print italics. Afterward, I march up the hill to the bursar's office and get cards so they can make two copies (on acid free paper) to be housed at the Esther Raushenbush Library of which I am quite proud and satisfied. Up and down that horrible Sarah Lawrence hill I travel four or five times, at the end carrying three scripts of 53 and a ream of paper plus my handbag with a book in it. I arrive at Slonim, the graduate house, just as Alba, our secretary is walking out.

"Leave the scripts on my desk with a twenty dollar check," she says.

I'm exhausted, but I've made it!

With the names of a few agents to whom I can send my manuscript, a job working for the psychic networks, whose officials are no more than small time hustlers and crooks, and the beginnings of a freelance career as a "psychic," I'm venturing forth into the world. The mail is interesting on this momentous day. I get a flyer for a thousand dollar discount on a burial plot in Brooklyn. My little message from the Spirit letting me know that the clock is ticking. That evening in a new, flowered summer skirt I walk over to Little Italy and treat myself to a lobster dinner at an outdoor cafe.

Fourth of July on the Lower East Side: Boom! Bam! Pouf! Sowwwwwwwwwwwwwwiii! Hermine takes a few steps in the livingroom and it's back to the very end of the apartment on the bathroom mat to escape all the noise. The polite little explosions of the Upper East Side simply won't do. All corners of the neighborhood send up their sparklers. There are so many explosions it sounds like a military offensive. Are we celebrating the birth of this country or the Chinese genius for creating exquisite firecrackers? They, of course, are the ones who've supplied the neighborhood.

My first 4th of July living on the edge of Chinatown is memorable. I am now a citizen of New York City, struggling to be sure, but nevertheless an *Immigrant of the Hear*t, appropriately living on the Lower East Side where it all began. I am deep in the true heart of America surrounded by a good part of the world's people in their varied shades, and many cultures. We've all come with our hopes and dreams.

My scheme is to fix myself a steak that I plan to barbecue on the fire escape. Out comes the old Hibachi and some charcoal that I fire up with lighter fluid. VOOM! Flames shoot halfway up to the next landing. People in the street below look up.

Oh my god! I'll be arrested on the Fourth of July!

Only a rube from Maine would do such a thing. The fire quickly dies down and the coals are red. With an eye peeled on the streets below, I place the steak on the grill and continue with my barbecue.

In Maine, people are eating shore dinners with lobster. The best Fourths I remember were served with hot dogs and burgers, walking down to the river afterward to watch the fireworks. I've also celebrated some very elegant Fourths. One with steak and champagne at the then attorney general's country home.

"I wonder what the poor people are doing tonight?" he toasted as we sat at our well-laden table.

On another occasion, I spent the fourth with a woman who played harp with the Portland Symphony and her lawyer husband (I was dating his brother.) We spent the day at the beach, and then stopped to shop for our dinner at a farmer's market. I remember the strawberries were delicious and the harpist was elegant. We all got drunk and rowdy at the fireworks.

Hermine, who is now blind, does not care for the noise and remains in the bathroom that evening. She is an old woman who has lost patience with the shenanigans of the world. She wants her tuna fish in the evening, likes her water from the piece of pottery that she can tip to feed herself. It's near the plants and the altar where she likes to roam. Mostly, she spends her time in the office with me sitting on the arm of the love seat underneath a lamp I've hooked up for her.

Living in NYC for an artistic person is the equivalent of a kid moving into the candy shop. My first ventures into the art world are visiting galleries with some women from The Farm; and then Kate's a member of an artistic co-operative with its own gallery in Soho that exhibits members' work. For many years, Kate has focused her energy both in her writing and her art on the question of victimhood, especially in books like "The Basement" and "The Politics of Cruelty." At one of her exhibits, which I help to set up, is a large glass tub full of water in which she inserts the mannequin head of a woman with long brown hair, stroking it intimately before plunging it in. We place a large thick sheet of glass on top of the tub thus enclosing the head. I step away from the exhibit to get some perspective, and to my horror see that the bobbing head is a depiction of Kate!

I go to museums as much as possible and am on the lookout for new exhibitions coming to town. One that especially moves me is the Edward Hopper exhibit at the Whitney. I am close to tears viewing its power and beauty. Bleak, the very word my don at Sarah Lawrence used to describe my novel. I was put off by the word at first. His canvasses are so powerful, I need to sit down and digest what I'm seeing. I, like he, try to render each character I write about in the full complexity of their existential situation.

The Whitney also incorporates quotes from some of Hopper's contemporaries alongside the paintings, "Solitude gives birth to the original in us," says Thomas Mann, "to beauty unfamiliar and perilous -- to poetry." Since I made a commitment to writing, my life has been solitary. I can see there's no getting out of it.

I leave the exhibit thinking, *I am not alone. I have a strong bond with this artist.* An incredible thought considering the nature of alienation and solitude of the scenes in his paintings.

I meet Bijou (an endearment, I've christened him with as I consider him my fine jewel) at a French Film presentation at the Alliance Française. I don't remember the offering that night, but I'm sure he can, the date and time too. Bijou remembers all the details of our relationship, the anniversary of our meeting, and my birthday. He sits across the aisle from me, way at the front of the theater. The row is empty save for Bijou at one end, and me at the other. He looks across and smiles. After the movie, we go to eat at a restaurant by the park.

He reaches out to touch my arm during the meal, and then hesitates.

"It's OK to touch," I say.

We have a bottle of Pouilly Fuissé with our meal (he's both an eonophile and Francophile.) Afterward, he walks me to my train station and, not wanting to part, decides to get on it with me. An old man standing by us keeps interfering in our conversation. He comments on my relationship with Bijou, about it not being right. By this point, I already know that the relationship is destined. We are going to be lovers, and the old man's warnings merely confirm that fact. An omen.

Bijou was raised in the suburbs of Brooklyn, in a middle class German Jewish home. I wasn't sophisticated enough to differentiate between the myriad New York accents at first, but I now recognize the Brooklyn/Jewish lilt to his voice. We meet at a restaurant of his choosing in the East Village on our first date. Roethele A. G., a French-Alsatian place, greets us with Edith Piaf over the sound system, singing the National Anthem of the Heart for many French girls in Maine. He is nervous and tells me corny jokes as "La Vie en Rose" wafts down to our candlelit table. There is an innocence and a sweetness to him, a *Petit Prince* from a far planet who's stumbled upon me and finds me truly irresistible. He dresses like a nerdy kid too, in polo shirts, chino pants, a baseball cap and tennis shoes.

A golden moment, the world is reduced to a cozy table with Bijou and I, and the occasional visit from our server. I have steak and red wine. He orders choucroute, pulls out a pillbox and takes a handful of vitamins.

I don't think either one of us tastes any of the food. Walking through the East Village after the meal, arms entwined around each other's waist, he pulls me to him at a street corner and we embrace passionately. His sexual-intercourse-of-the-mouth kisses leave me hungry for more.

THE HERMIT

-IX-

The boy displayed a propensity for drawing back, a need for solitude. He did not join others in their games for he sensed already that he would counsel these very children from the wisdom of the silence he inhabits. At maturity, he avoids family activity, allegiances, keeps his own counsel.

They say he is shy, bookish. But he is not timid. Challenging life to deliver on its sweet promise of enlightenment, he wants the honey taste of experience lolling on his tongue, filling his intestines. The Hermit seeks to penetrate, to examine every shard of the prism, the magnificent, bizarre, even the horrific. In the quiet world he inhabits, Beauty is the path that entices and leads him to the summit.

On this dark night, he stands amid snowy mountain peaks, staff in hand, wearing a monk's hooded cloak and habit. A simple man, old now, his long hair and beard as pure as the snow at his feet. He holds a ship's lantern aloft with a radiant, six pointed star inside. Although the pentacle casts an inviting glow, think not the Hermit beckons. Alone, one must realize the void, and then seek him out.

Upright: Travel to the mountain where wisdom abides.
A need to become quiet, to reflect; seeking one's own path.

Reversed: Remaining in unfulfilling situation.

Psychic networks have hit the big time and money is rolling in -- for the owners that is. Mr. Feder, who records the day's preamble for us and tends to hysteria and abuse becomes more and more erratic, cutting our rate of pay; we are told we must maintain a 20 minute average, i.e. client conversations must last that long, or we will be terminated. He also institutes a program in which calls are funneled according to call averages. The big talkers get most of the calls. This part of my work is uncomfortable and I question the ethics of it.

If I can, in 5 minutes, be of assistance, I don't see the point of continuing the exchange. The person got what they wanted and needed, and I am satisfied that I could be of service. I continue to work nights because the riskier people come out at that time and have a story to tell, at least 20 minutes long.

There are many reasons why one would call a psychic hotline: most important is the desire to connect with someone who is in touch with other realms of seeing and being. You can tell a psychic anything; she will not judge you: *I'm having an affair; I've embezzled the company; my child is dying; I'm being hit by arrows on all sides and I have questions about why I'm attracting this negative energy to myself; Is my lover abandoning me? In a tight spot, wondering if I'll make it till the end of the month when the check comes in? Two job offers, which is the best choice? Will I make it as a rap artist? Are associates trustworthy? Running from the law, in Kansas now, should the next direction be Texas, or New York?*

I handle these questions, and many more from individuals as varied as clerics, to men with particular sexual habits they would not care to discuss with acquaintances or with on-line sex workers. A retarded woman somewhere in the Midwest, who lives in a room with the help of government assistance, calls the psychic network because she is alone and confused in a world that makes no sense to her, but she has been able to figure out that with her government allowance providing telephone service, she can call the psychic network and have someone to talk with. The box she lives in is a recent change, before that she was at school with others.

But she's been discovered. When the state finds that she's running up major telephone bills, they reach an agreement with the phone company to cut her off after 3 minutes with the network. This retarded girl circumvents their efforts by calling 50 times a day.

Some may say the network is taking from a girl hardly able to give knowledgeable consent, but that is a trifling compared to what is happening to her in our society. Her life is like a Kafka novel, the box, furtive looks in the streets hoping for some bit of human kindness, and the TV. Our technological world does not exist for her. She has a hard time buying food at the market or the diners because she can't figure out the money system and she gets cheated. What she hopes is that some agency will find her a factory job where she will do boring, repetitive work, 8 hours a day. There, she stands a chance of meeting other retarded people. But for now, she is in her box on the phone seeking human kindness.

There are few questions I would not answer of a person seeking help. I will not predict a person's death; I will not predict an unborn child's sex, and I don't care to hear of projects that are illegal. But I will answer questions of someone who is in trouble with the police as long as those questions pertain to the person's well-being and safety. If I know of someone about to commit an act of violence, I will contact the police.

A woman calls at 2 in the morning. I give her a general reading and then she asks me a question about her boyfriend. Typical call, but then she starts talking about the guy standing by her at a terrible time, and that meant a lot to her. So I ask about this terrible time. The floodgates open and she talks for 30 minutes straight about what is really on her mind.

I was raped a year ago by 5 guys in a hotel room. When I told my mom she called me a slut, and my family didn't want to have anything to do with me.

She was alone, lost everything and became homeless, sleeping in her car and showering at the shelter. Working nights as a cocktail waitress, she made her way out of that dilemma and now has her own place and is doing OK. She even has enough money to call a psychic.

I'm still scared though, and I sometimes feel anxious for no reason."

"Why did you call me tonight? It wasn't about the boyfriend, was it?"

My car's in the garage; it needs a ring job, and it's too old to invest any more money in it.

The very car she lived in, home to her when everything around her was falling apart; she is afraid to lose her safe place.

Perhaps part of the price for starting over with relationship is giving up that safe place. Those months living in the car, alone for the first time in her life, the vehicle became a cocoon where she transformed herself from family child to a responsible adult. Those months are vivid to her because she had to survive by her wits. She was most alive because most alert, and also most open.

I recommend a ritual, a private affair between her and the car.

"As part of the ritual, you need to tell the story of your life in the car, all of it, and also mourn the girl who died in it, the girl who became a woman, successful in her work, in a deepening relationship and financially stable."

Why call a "psychic" about her car? She understands that it's a question of power. The car has been with her through thick and thin, has nurtured and protected her; will she lose her power, her confidence, now that her talisman has died?

"Your childhood self is still in the car. The matter needs to be resolved. Telling the story in the middle of the ritual will allow you to reclaim it as your own."

A Hasidic Jew from Brooklyn, who calls me frequently through the network, soon becomes a personal client. I will call him Hershel. My talks with him start with questions about his wife (an arranged marriage) who interferes in his business, shows no interest in sex (they have 12 children,) and opposes his wishes with a mulish stubbornness that drives him to despair.

When oh when, says Hershel, *will this woman start behaving like a mature adult?*

Indeed.

Questions about his wife aside, what he really wants to talk about is G-d, how people through time have envisioned G-d. What should our relationship to G-d be? A spiritual life? My understanding of "God" is as far from Hershel's understanding as Santa is to Yahweh. Is Santa a god? He is as godly as any in the panoply of Greek or Roman gods. What he brings in his sac is Generosity of Spirit and the possibility of magic. Hershel and I are able to communicate about these matters because, although we may not agree on the specifics, we have the same basic understanding of what the *essence* of God is.

Behind this talk of God, Hershel has a sense that something's up in his life and that is why he has contacted me. But he's not ready to hear what I have to tell him. He skirts around the subject, or will offer offhand remarks. I do not push him. He will tell me when he's ready. It is often also the case that a person will ask the very question they least want to have answered.

The hardest part of my work is counseling the many people who are in psychologically, and even physically, abusive relationships. They know very well that they are being abused, but they do not abandon the partner. Were I to expect them to leave the relationship within a reasonable time, I would be sorely disappointed. What is the impelling force driving the bond? What is the person seeking to achieve? What role does power play? How much power does the client have? It becomes hard to tell who is the abuser and who is the abused. Has someone unknowingly, or deliberately cast a spell on the person, draining him of his energy? That can easily happen. The power that connects one to another human being (of the millions of people, why connect with a particular one over another?) is an energy force. It can empower or weaken.

A person may choose to be weakened. Or it may be that a force that cannot be mastered traps one. As any torturer will tell you, every human being has a weakness that if tapped, has the capacity to destroy him or her. Some cannot perform their duties in life without the help of alcohol, or drugs, others cannot stop over-eating, or smoking after they've been told it is injuring them. There is a force between lovers that is easily corruptible through fear, distrust, or need. Ethics are tossed aside and the worst characteristics of each partner are allowed free play. One is absolved of responsibility, becoming a prisoner to the lover in this type of relationship.

I can't trust him; is she seeing that guy at the office? It's 6 o'clock, where the hell is he? I looked through his e-mail and . . I park by her house and watch who's coming and going; he's cruising porn sites on the internet! It's as if the devil himself in his big black limo opened the door and said, *Hop in honey, we're going for a ride.*

There is a devil out there waiting; it is possible to come to terms with it, if one chooses to face it. The devil can't be beat; what he has to offer will always look enticing, but one can learn to be a good warrior assessing both one's strengths and weaknesses and using them to plan strategy.

A personal client tells me stories about how he was beaten severely by his stepfather when he was a child. His nose was broken a number of times. He is a handsome man, virile, intelligent.

"It seems to me, you would want to have your nose fixed to erase your stepfather's mark."

"It's a mark of distinction. A man with a broken nose," he says, "signifies a tough guy, someone you don't want to mess with."

It is his badge of courage, his protective shield. I would think it signifies an abused person, someone who, for whatever reason, took a beating. It may also be that my client, on a subliminal level, wants to show the wounds he has suffered, how he has been battered and beaten by life.

When I look at the face of boxer Mike Tyson I see a bully to be sure, but I also see a wounded human being. He has become a metaphor of the cruelty and battering he endured in childhood. He's incorporated the duality of the situation. My client is not pleased with my assessment, because in truth he has become both the cruel stepfather and the wounded boy, understanding or accepting neither. None of us want to see that other side of ourselves. But the world sees it, clearly.

The problem with duality is that it restricts one from acknowledging and expressing one's complexity. Duality, I once assumed, was created by Christianity with its ideals of good and evil (I'm not so sure of that now. It seems an inborn trait.) The worst depravities, cruelties, barbarities are always *other*, monsters -- Hitler, Mussolini, Saddam Hussein. Yet they were human, a part of us, and, given their situation and the tremendous power they held, who knows how any of us would act?

If a wild animal comes charging, one doesn't judge whether it is good or evil, or whether it is being unfair; one gets out of its way. A cat toying with a half dead mouse it has captured is merely manifesting its intrinsic nature. Why then turn a blind eye to our own viciousness or victimization? It becomes difficult to see these two sides of the same coin in other than value-laden terms, but truly they are not. Aggression and viciousness serve a necessary role in the evolution of Homo sapiens. Mike Tyson is not evil, he's just a stupid guy who keeps sabotaging himself, and messing up every opportunity he has to get himself out of trouble. Hitler and Mussolini were truly stupid men who self-destructed in short time. And their pathetic, egotistical ideas! What possible chance did they have of succeeding? That duality, the inability to see one's dark side condemns one to glorify it, to create a larger than life persona for it, to assert righteousness about it. Take it as a given, whatever someone tells you is most offensive, most deplorable to them is what they will surely do to you given the right set of circumstances.

When my work session is over, I get out for some air. The night is crisp. I take my stroll up Division Street, and then back down East Broadway. A lot of shops, fish markets and vegetable stalls are still open. I do not look into the eyes of passersby, rather I am in tune with the stillness of the evening, this absolute quiet where I can hear the big trees breathe and sigh.

So much noise every day, droning noise trying to muffle the sound of the ticking clock; in the stillness, there is no ticking clock, only the breathing of the earth, the water, the trees. A group of Chinese businessmen, crisp and polished, step out the back door of a restaurant. It looks as if they've had a meeting as they are serious and speak respectfully to one another. I walk by them, a white woman on a dark back alley street, unnoticed.

WHEEL OF FORTUNE

-X-

Success arrives with the bubbles in a glass of champagne, the good beluga, and frosting on the cake. It's a heady exhilaration experienced solely by the audacious, the defiant. But the brass ring glitters for all without favor, and fools are content with the trappings.

The Wheel of Fortune looks like a meat grinder with a giant hand appearing out of the clouds, turning its handle to rotate the wheel. As befits a king, he sits at its summit, heavy booted, one leg crossed over the other, his arms extended, a wine cup in one hand, the other clasping the hand of his queen. She is turned from him facing a precipitous future while he peers back at his achievements.

The couple looks as if they are dancing a tango. She grasps her dress that has been caught by a man falling off the pinnacle of the spinning wheel. His obdurate hold drags the queen down. And so the tango continues and fortune grinds on. With patience, one learns what falls inevitably ascends. The wise woman sets greater goals; success is rarely more than a measure of what can be achieved or bought.

Upright: Fate brings prosperity. Success is at hand; choose wisely.

Reversed: Locked into pessimism and doubt.
Do not be fooled by the trappings of success.

At the staging of my novel, COMICS, I was interviewed by a reporter for the Bangor Daily News. She commented that I was "lucky," somehow a golden person favored by fate. I can see how it could appear that way, but what she called "luck" is a more complicated affair than she imagined.

Good fortune is a daunting responsibility. We would all be rich if we were not so afraid of money. Sad stories abound of those who win the lotto. Many end up acknowledging they were better off before they had money. Their stories are enlightening. One man spoke of his wife leaving him after he won because, as a rich person, she now felt entitled to put on airs. He thought she was becoming false.

He couldn't hang out with his friends anymore because they were always asking him for money, and when he refused, they were insulted that he, who was now rich, was being miserly with them. They had always been generous with him. Lotto winners are not satisfied with receiving $10,000 a week, or whatever amount is doled out to them. They want the whole bundle, and they sell their financial package to a broker for a fraction of what it's worth. Living on $10,000 has become too demeaning.

Some would say, *Those people lack fortitude to deal with their changed circumstances; I'm a lot stronger and wiser. Believe me, I'd have no problem enjoying it.*

A TV show comes to mind, "The Jeffersons," about an African American couple who are "moving on up to the East Side to a deluxe apartment . . ." He has struck it rich in the dry cleaning business. If the premise of the show were taken seriously it would be a tragedy rather than a sitcom. A fairy tale, the kind of tale we tell ourselves so as not to face the reality of money and our own convoluted relationship with it.

Money is the primary relationship in one's life. It puts food on the table and a roof over one's head. How a person relates to money is not different from the way he/she relates to a lover, to work, to friends and family. The link between the overuse of credit cards and obesity is overindulgence. It is the act of relating which remains constant in all situations, one's way of dealing with the giving and receiving of life.

Take the case of thieves: without them our economy would collapse. The majority of rich thieves far from being stopped are lauded for their acumen, while it's a commonplace that small time hustlers are arrested. Are they more stupid than the rich guys? I don't think so. So why are they getting caught?

The common thread in these examples is the complete changeover in a person's life that must occur if wealth is to be accrued. The price is high. Long held values are exposed for the self-deceptive sham they truly are. Unprofitable allegiances must be eliminated, as they become a barrier. One becomes a traitor to all that has been held close to heart, a freak, who having crossed that boundary has only the community of self to fall back on.

The wife who was putting on airs may indeed have been the one making a better adjustment to affluence than her husband. She accepted her separation from others and looked to the new privileges she had gained. It is naive to think one will, or should remain unchanged by wealth. The most egregious fantasy we hold dear in the U.S. is the belief that it is our right to be treated equally no matter our station in life.

The rich are in the same predicament. Losing their wealth would be as devastating as the poor gaining it. Being poor is also an intimidating responsibility. The business of money is not for the timid.

Most clients consult me about relationship, affairs of the heart mostly, concerns are about matters of trust, questions of disloyalty, unfaithfulness, base cruelty, indifference and finally, abandonment. It is a surprise to some that in choosing to leave a relationship they are not immune from feelings of abandonment. In truth, the partner left spiritually some time ago. Widowhood, divorce, loss of a child are difficult, painful experiences that try one's ability to cope, to endure. One becomes lost in the world, spiritually homeless, and inconsolable.

A year goes by, then two and the pain is just as sharp. A woman, I will call her Beverly, seeks my counsel about the boyfriend she's had a passionate affair with after a 20-year loveless marriage. The affair was the one piece of perfect sunshine in her dreary life and she would not let go of him. He made it clear that he was no longer interested in maintaining a romantic relationship -- *just friends.*

Her questions to me are directed at trying to control the events, change the outcome. *Where is he tonight? Is he seeing that blond secretary? Are they having sex? Is he going to show up; follow up on his word?* She is not completely deluded. Although the man is brusque and rude to her about his independence from her, he also encourages her, in subtle ways, to believe otherwise.

Why did this happen? What went wrong? What can I do to put it back together? She keeps asking. She wants an explanation, something that makes sense. Unwilling to gamble, call his bluff, she is too fearful to cut him off.

Some may choose to try and outrun this negative energy by plunging into one thing or another, a new relationship, a time-consuming business venture. One ignores negative energy at one's peril. It becomes a wound that never heals, psychically and eventually, physically. Tell me what part of your body hurts and I will tell you what is making you ill. The body responds metaphorically.

You have heartburn and your stomach is tied in a knot?

You are ingesting something, or someone that is poisoning you.

Backache?

You're carrying more than your share of the load in some relationship and resenting it.

And yes, people do die of a broken heart.

Science will offer up its explanations for the backache, heartburn, cancer, syphilis, and they are all to an extent true, but one is not separate from one's body. Rather one is an active, if somewhat unconscious, participant in its functioning. I am not espousing a Christian notion of disease being punishment for one's sins. Living in 21st century society is not conducive to a stable, meaningful life in community with one's neighbors. Stress is as common and deadly as cancer; it eventually becomes cancer or cardiac infarction.

At the shipyard where I once worked, the boilermakers on our ship went for their regular check-up and it was discovered that, out of a crew of 25, fifteen had spots on their lungs from the asbestos in the fireboxes where they work.

I asked a friend, and thankfully not one of the 15, "Why do you work at this job? It will kill you."

What about the work you performed at the mental health center? That'll kill you too.

Remembering the 20 pounds I gained during the time, the return of my two packs a day smoking habit, the turmoil, frustrations, the loss of faith. He had a point. The body does not punish, it adapts.

Why didn't he get sick, is the more interesting question, he was as exposed as the other guys. Probably because he didn't want to. He was playing a game with fate. And aren't we all, if we care to acknowledge it.

We are closest to the wolf, deadly hunters, hungry, nasty, brutish. The skills needed to survive are not taught in schools, but on the street. Children exhibit the gamut of human behavior in pure, un-adult-erated form. It is on the street that one learns to play ball so to speak, to stand apart, and still be part of the group. One learns that allies can turn into enemies, hatred simmers on the back burner, and eternal enmity awaits some first encounters. One learns how to assess threat, how to deal with it, and how to read the nuances of social behavior. Family cannot protect one from danger and harm. Depending on one's character and psychological complex, a role is chosen. This role will be different than the one exhibited at home.

The social role gets revised, honed and polished with time, but basically it is a variation of the one adopted in the schoolyard. In a world of hunter and hunted, overpowering force gets accommodated. Mom and Dad, schools, the Church, the Police, the Internal Revenue Service, the government, courts, laws, the boss, illness, death, but mostly the bank balance will not be defied. One is made to obey others, cater to their wishes, follow their rules. To each of these individuals and institutions, one gives away a bit of power, whether for good or ill. Often, the obedience demanded runs counter to one's best interests, or even to one's safety. The rules have become so arbitrary that their enforcers are quick to tell you, *I don't make the rules.* There is a price to be paid for each of these accommodations.

And that price is a loss of virility, potency -- "luck". Beverly, who has spent her life accommodating others with little power left to take care of her own needs, is unable to fend in relationship, nor does she want to. Fending for herself would surely drive him away is what she believes, and she is right. He chose her because she accommodated his needs. If she were to start being more demanding, he would see it as unfair, not part of their unstated agreement.

Go along and get along is easier for her. She's more comfortable being the prey of others. A hunter needs a victim for reasons, inspired or mundane. She is needed.

We have all played both roles depending on the nature of circumstances. The officer writes a ticket that he deposits on your windshield as you approach. "They" hunted you down, had it all planned, and sent this officer out looking for you. A true connoisseur of the hunted role will extend the ticket incident to excessive proportions, milking it for whatever attention it garners her or him. A man in my hometown, during the time that I worked at the mental health center on the Emergency Services team, climbed up a tree and was alight one of its upper branches, dangling precariously. He needed attention; life was not treating him kindly and it had reached a point where he couldn't handle it anymore, so he was giving it to us.

This situation exemplifies the complexity of the hunter/hunted relationship. Who is prey and who is the hunter is open to debate. A large crowd gathered in the street to give him audience, the police got a truck with a bucket to get up there and fetch him, an officer with specialized training was summoned to talk him down peacefully. For one sparkling moment, the man was king. A hunter. He used up most of his sparse energy in the performance and will not easily regain it.

His plea to our common humanity could not readily be rendered; his money problems, his departed wife, his hopeless situation will remain. Truth be told, humanity has mixed feelings about those in crisis. High on the list is a desire for a dramatic show -- like the movies. The man in the tree presents himself as a victim, chooses to address us as someone put upon. He's going to jump off his perch in a death dive. With that threat, he dominates us. We stop and listen to him, and fetch help.

Our humanity is exhibited in being able to identify with him, to understand that this too is part of human existence. One can reach states of desperation and lose control. This guy is no different than us, a neighbor; and he exhibits courage taking charge and speaking his mind.

Human beings are not purposeless, surely there must be some gain in this situation, otherwise why pursue it? The man in the tree gets hospitalized in the psych unit of the local hospital where attention is paid to him and his situation. He is made to join in a group with other patients. There is time to reflect, recharge, then he is released back to his situation, with pills no doubt, and a story. He is now worthy of attention in his community, "the man in the tree." For a single moment he made us all see the fragility of human existence.

Beverly may not see her man more than once every other year or so, (he moved away) at which time he will have sexual intercourse with her, play the part of hunter, adamantly denying any possibility for relationship. They e-mail, and there is the occasional phone call, mostly initiated by her. This sham relationship with its pathos is preferable to her than taking her chances being alone. Not only is it preferable, she can't get out of it. No matter what he says or does, how abusive he becomes, she will not abandon him.

The psychologists Rubin, Burgess and Coplan in a report titled "Social Withdrawal and Shyness" noted from research done, that some babies, when placed on the floor with a group of others will not approach other babies, or any of the nearby toys, but rather cling to their mothers. In group after group, a third of the infants exhibit this timid behavior with no *discernible outward cause* for it. These babies "come to view the world as unpredictable, comfortless and unresponsive." (Srofe 1983.) There is ample evidence that these are inborn traits. One questions the ethics of demanding more aggressive behavior from such children, of labeling them deficient, emotionally disturbed.

What happens to these babies when they grow up in an aggressive nation like ours? Timidity is not an admired trait. A timid woman can make herself into a man's image of what he wants. She will fit herself into his world, serve him. A timid man will have a harder time of it, especially with women. Some overcome this by being nasty to their mates, who being smaller, can be physically threatened with impunity.

To condemn a person for her timidity makes about as much sense as condemning the tiger for its ferociousness. Since there are more followers than leaders, I would say the percentage of timid people is fairly high. Being timid in an aggressive world tends to bring out overcompensating traits, foolhardy attempts at being macho, or ruthless, climbing trees and threatening to jump.

How do I counsel someone like Beverly? What do I have to offer to someone who is seemingly so unhappy and with so few resources to cope? What I've come to realize is that the benefit outweighs the abuse for those who remain in such relationships. I answer her questions concerning the boyfriend, *Where is he tonight? Why didn't he return my call? Will he remain at his new location, or will he come back to my city?*

I am direct and honest in what I see, and I tell it as such. In some instances, I may couch it in a softer light where I see that a client does not want to hear what I will say, but I will say it. This is what I have to offer: I give my clients a look at themselves and their situation in as much light as possible so they can then make correct decisions for themselves. Beverly's choices are not my choices, but that is what she deems important in her life, and she is undoubtedly right.

Power=luck, and one acquires both by fulfilling the first responsibility in life which is to care for oneself. It means loving, nurturing and respecting oneself and one's self-truth so that one is not at the mercy of others. All of the goodness, beauty, creativity, strength, virility, *luck* and good fortune one possesses comes from fulfilling that first responsibility.

JUSTICE

-XI-

Justice wears a wimple round her throat like a nun's habit covering head, neck and wrists. Only her face and hands are visible. On her head is a golden crown with a red jewel at its center similar to the clasp that holds her green cape. Her dress is red; its underside is blue like her wimple. Behind her, a purple veil jars hideously.

These colors do not blend or contrast well. Like emotions, they scream for attention. The stern looking woman holds a sword upright with one hand, and with the other, the Scales of Justice weighted to one side. She is not blindfolded like her modern sister, but gazes directly into the matter. Justice begins from the premise that the human realm is freighted with logic. How to correct this imbalance, to allow for the irrational?

Think of woman and man in their circling dance of power, each bound to the other by their singularity. A tangle of cryptic rules keeps them in this gracious pattern. Otherwise, she would gladly crush his heart to a fine powder, demand his head on a platter; he'd brutalize and rape her. Justice demands balance. Keen, unyielding, with sword at ready, she cuts through the cloak of logic to expose the heart of the matter.

Upright: Creating balance in one's life; resolving a situation; going to the source.

Reversed: An imbalance. Intolerance. Unfair judgment.

At best this business is like the lotto, but you cannot win if you do not play.
Phil Raia
B. A. Literary Agency

After sending twenty-five queries along with my resumé to editors seeking a position, I get one reply, from Victor Navasky at Nation Magazine. He speaks in terms of writing a political column. I send him a couple of reviews and an essay.

"Perhaps you're better suited to the literary portion of the magazine," he suggests and he puts me in contact with an editor who, it turns out has so many applicants that there is no need to hire anyone. A small army of interns does the work for the exposure, and in hopes that the company will eventually hire them.

What does it mean to be a writer? Is it a role that one takes on? Does one work in the business? Is that how one gets ahead, makes connections, gets one's work looked at? I, who have an aversion to institutions, hierarchical systems, either in the role of top dog or underdog, being in an office 8 to 10 hours a day, under someone's command, the commute; it probably comes through in my job queries.

I suspect that out of the 8 million people in New York, 6 million probably have a book they want published. I have my own work to accomplish, and part of it involves counseling people. Getting 53 published is another task; the two leads I got from my don at Sarah Lawrence were a bust. One agent was pregnant and not taking on new work, the other was snippy in her rejection of 53.

I now send out query letters, along with a dozen pages of 53 and a synopsis to literary agents whose names and addresses I get from books like Writer's Market, Literary Marketplace, etc. At first, innocent that I was, I approached the task with slow deliberation, sending out four queries and then waiting till they replied before sending out another batch. The rejections run the gamut. Quite a few agents like my writing, but are not interested in representing me. They look to markets, trends, whether they will make any money from this, what editor would be interested, of which I know nothing. Some rejections are form letters of the Dear Author variety. Some just send back your query letter with nothing on it except your very own words mocking you. Thankfully, professional that I am, I place their name and address in the top left-hand corner of my index, which I now cross off the list. I've got the drill down pat. I even keep a file of the names of people I send queries to and the date they were sent. This busy work saves me from having to think of the demoralizing aspect of what I am doing. I am paying to be treated disrespectfully. In the packet I send agents is a self-addressed stamped envelope for them to reply, the query letter, on good bond paper, the manuscript's cover page, the content page with chapter headings and pagination, a piece of writing from the first chapter, one from the middle of the book, and a synopsis (which is not high on my list of things I like doing.)

I realize that quite a few of my queries for 53 are going to the wrong agents, but that cannot be avoided. Agents develop expertise and valuable connections in certain niche areas of the publishing world, and although they list themselves in trade publications as accepting books from almost all fields, save poetry and short stories, they do not. They're just keeping their options open.

Getting rejection letters, I don't care how decent and supportive they are, is upsetting. Most of the letters give me no clue as to why my script is being rejected. I am groping in the dark with no idea how the publishing/agenting world works. I need them more than they need me. Not an advantageous position to be in. Sending out queries is not a task I enjoy, but one that I do religiously. I will find someone out there to connect with, someone who appreciates my novel and wants to see it published.

Midtown getting my driver's license renewed, at the License Express Office. It's the pedestrian version of a drive-through window. Zip, zip, you're supposed to be out of there in no time. Chromium poles with ribbons connecting them together in a maze pattern, narrow tables along the way to fill out the necessary papers and zip, I'm at a woman's desk that sends me over to have my photo taken. I push my luck and ask the photographer if he would take another shot when I see the dazed, dealing-with-the-system look on my face. Lord knows how many pictures he takes a day.

"Sure," he says.

When I go back to the lady at the desk she sifts through my paper work and asks which photographer took my picture.

"It was the Oriental," I say. The moment it slips out of my mouth, I realize I have said a boo-boo. The operative word is *Asian*; Oriental is now seen as pejorative. I leave with bittersweet feelings about losing my Maine driver's license. Later, I head over to Rizzoli Bookstore to hear André Dubus read. I met him at Stonecoast Writer's Conference where I first began to write. A delightful man, dark hair, chunky, short, wearing jeans, well-worn cowboy boots; he looked like a bantam cock, but with a soulful heart. His stories, which are full of passion, speak to the secret heart of a person. André, up close, is vulnerable, open, generous. He taught me an important lesson about ethics.

After his reading one evening, I walk outdoors and run into him and his girlfriend, "What did you think of the story?" he asks about his reading.

The story was completed a short time ago, and he's still too close to it, has not completely understood or resolved its denouement.

"It was wonderful," I say. A lie and we both know it. I have missed an opportunity to have an honest conversation about writing. We bid each other good evening and I walk away with my silent lesson.

It's been a few years since I've seen him, and I've read about the car accident, how he almost died, and is now crippled. I don't know what to expect; the place is packed and the only seat I can find is way in the back. I would've liked to have a few words with him, but with this crowd it won't be possible. He is cosseted by an entourage that helps him and his wheelchair up on the stage. His sweaty face is bloated and red; he speaks slowly, the same message about the human heart and the ways we love each other, or not. André will die soon; I can see it emanating from him. Although his hold on life is tenuous, he is still the storyteller with a last fabulous tale for us. No one coughs, fidgets, or makes noise, as we take in a story written in hell.

Walking home afterward, I think of my own situation. André Dubus, who's writing was much appreciated within the writing community back at Stonecoast, but unknown to most of the country, is now a star in the firmament of writers. Through dark, blighted commercial streets, closed up tight for the night, I walk past graffiti splattered walls, iron gates, an occasional rat scurrying along.

He was always a star, for Christ's sake. Do you have to get run over by a truck going 70 miles an hour on the highway to get someone's attention?

I have introduced Bijou to my landladies. I tend to think of them as my maiden aunts; obviously my assessment is not based on the outward appearance of the bouffant blondes in their skimpy outfits, the black Lexus parked out front, and the sisters hanging in the bar chatting up the customers. Neither has a man. They are proprietary toward me, and offer me tips on how to survive in the big city, where the bargains are, how to deal with the system from the phone company on down to city offices.

I offer to go out and get us some pizza one night at the bar.

"Leave the pocketbook here," Zinni, the ever practical businesswoman stops me before I go. "You don't go out with a pocketbook after 9 pm."

Sound advice that I still adhere to.

Antonia, her manager and the building's superintendent, is a romantic, embittered to be sure, but vulnerable too. She presents herself to the world as a voluptuous, Botero seductress. Zinni is tough as nails, and wary of people, like a thief about to rob you.

I stop by the bar and have a glass of wine with them occasionally. On graduation night from Sarah Lawrence I dropped in after dinner and treated the bar, mostly Chinese men, to a drink. They chivalrously toasted my Master's of Fine Arts degree in Creative Writing.

Bringing Bijou to meet them is like having the family look him over. What they must think of him, I can only imagine. He is the picture of a courteous gentleman, with baseball cap and tennis shoes, not someone either of these women would find attractive or manly. And he is married. I see him several times a week and he takes me to dinner in the East Village or Greenwich on the weekend, small restaurants with interesting food and good wines. It is such a treat to dress up, wear heels, jewelry, and play the lady.

I guess you could say I'm in love with Bijou, but it's a peculiar situation. I find that we don't have much in common and he can be annoyingly competitive. Love's metaphor of a putti shooting its arrow through one's heart is apt, an unfathomable mystery not without its agony. I love Bijou because there is a lot of child in him; he has a certain elegance in his interactions with others and the world around him. And then there's the sex. Something about this man drives me wild. As a lover, I've had better, but none as potent. And what I love best is that he is physically affectionate. He loves to kiss, hold hands, an arm round the shoulder.

His wife is ill, has been for quite a while and will continue to be. Her medication has made her fat and unattractive. They are family rather than lovers, and he lives a fairly independent life. But nevertheless, he is married and that makes for complicated arrangements. When he first told me about it and explained his situation I thought, *I don't have much free time to give to a relationship myself.* I find I need a lot of quiet periods alone.

I cherish the solitude of roaming the streets of New York, exploring the different neighborhoods; alone I sit at a dingy, 2-table hole-the-wall restaurant where I am served the most mouth-wateringly delicious Chinese food prepared and served graciously by a family that speaks not a word of English. My neighborhood, which was formerly immigrant Jewish, is being swallowed up by the Chinese who are also expanding their horizon into Little Italy. In narrow, cobbled streets immigrant Chinese, back doors open to their business establishments, smoke cigarettes in the quiet night. I feel the intruder on their private ruminations, but they pay me no heed.

Bulkas, byalis, bagels, onion wheels, at the Jewish bakery on Grand Street, I inhale deeply of the yeasty dough, the toasted onion, garlic and sesame. The old Spanish woman eats shelled peanuts behind the counter, while men to the side of us busily shape risen dough into byalis and place them on long palettes which they will slide into the institutional ovens. Behind me are the products of their labor this day, mountains of large brown paper bags filled with bread to be delivered to restaurants, cafés, specialty shops. Brown bags keep the bread crisp and fresh.

The old woman doesn't like me. I'm offended at first that she waits on another who has arrived after me and I create a scene. One of the bakers comes and waits on me apologizing for her rudeness. Again tonight, she waits on another before me, but I do not fuss anymore. Fussing takes too much energy and what does it accomplish? Not much, obviously. I choose six onion bagels that she places in a small brown bag and she asks if there is something else I want. I do not reply, rather I hand her the $2.70 it will cost and head out with my week's supply of bread.

When news services report the shooting by police of the innocent African American, Amadou Diallo standing on his stoop, showered with 41 bullets, I react to the injustice one night at the bakery when a Hasidic Jew calls her nasty names, making comment about her Hispanic origins.

I point to him and shout, "You are a bigot!" visibly upset.

The woman is stunned that I have come to her defense and treats me respectfully when ringing up my order. This thankfully, doesn't last and she is back in form the following week.

Up the street, lights are on all night in the big lofts above the stores. These are factories in which clothes are fabricated for corporations. Undoubtedly sweat shops where immigrants work long hours and get less than minimum wage. The detritus of their handiwork, urban hay bales, fabric scraps compressed into squares and strapped with wire, sit on the curb in front of their shops. One can tell what colors will be popular next season from the scraps. I think about the women, (they surely must be women, save the boss and the mechanic,) working the night away, exchanging glances, maybe flirting, thinking of the lunch they've brought to eat later, seeing the night grow darker from the large loft windows. They dream of love I'm sure, the love that makes a trifling of their misery, a necessary trial to test their worthiness, their commitment.

I walk down East Broadway and come upon a white woman, middle-aged, weather beaten, flat out on the ground, the drink she still holds in her hand splattered all over her blouse. She looks drunk, probably drugs. Business is proceeding as usual at the nearby outdoor stalls while her body lies unconscious at the intersection. People walk by unconcerned. No crowd gathers; it's not happening. I walk by too. I am sure the inscrutable Chinese do not want a drunk white woman sprawled in front of their establishments, so I assume they have called 911. I too have business to attend.

I have started a new novel, “Alice in the World”; it's about a teenage girl who has lost a part of her childhood in a Catholic convent for girls, a follow-up to "53." She leaves at 14 and goes out to explore a world she knows little of. Her sexuality blossoms among chums who've dropped out of society, or been rejected by it. And then there's Dad, who's drunk a lot, and doesn't talk much when he's sober. But I trust the girl to make something out of her situation.

I'm still revising my Tarot poems. I feel something off-balance about them, but I don't know what I should do. So I revise. Writing poems requires an attitude, a reflective, deliberative frame of mind, which is a luxury I seldom have now. The world that I live in takes up most of my attention. Is that a good thing? I don't know.

I have a new client. Dora (pseudonym, also different but similar situation) tells me about a relationship she is having with a married doctor. From the moment they meet over drinks at a mutual friend's cocktail party, it's a *coup de foudre,* straight to the heart. Both are in loveless marriages. The relationship starts innocently; she sends him little notes. He makes a point of being at gatherings where he knows she will be, bringing his wife along. They phone; she sends gifts at Easter, Thanksgiving.

Pictures and cards begin arriving at her home with no forwarding address, and no note or signature. Their theme seems unrelated to any outward event, rather they appear to contain secret coded messages.

The couple flirt and talk sex, but don't acknowledge that there is anything between them, or that he's the card sender. She spends hours trying to decipher his code. The pictures come almost every day, and her question to me is,

"What's he trying to say in this message, what does it mean?"

The pictures come in series. He sent her Mexican muralists cards, followed by photocopied pictures of Albrecht Durer's macabre woodcuts, pictures of animals, horses, elephants, raccoons, whatever he finds of interest. In their dance around each other, they are playing a game of ego-building.

Someone desires me; I can do this for a while and no one need know. If I don't have sex, then I'm not really being unfaithful.

What's behind this for my client? She is a childless (her choice) woman in her forties, married 20 years to a successful businessman. Perhaps it was not her choice to make. I'm reminded of Jung's words "The psychological rule says that when an inner situation is not made conscious, it happens on the outside as fate."

She wants to believe in love again. The hated mother, a working-class woman with no appreciation of her daughter's uniqueness, or the girl's aspirations, has come to live with Dora in her old age. She has Alzheimer's disease and no one else will care for her. My client hates this vegetable her mother has become more than the woman she despised before her illness. The husband and third member of the household, likes to golf. They haven't had sex in years.

She will not leave the upper-middle class life he provides her with. It has never occurred to her to make a life for herself, a career. She has never worked. But she's smart and quick, a woman who lives by her wits socially, a charmer, used to having people make a fuss over her. In my mental picture, she is petite, stylish, has short bouncy, dark hair, creamy skin, long slender fingers and good jewelry.

She calls me in the morning when I'm awake, but still in bed. A good time for a consultation, as I'm still close to the dream world and am most "psychic." Morning coffee on the end table, Tarot cards on the blanket close to me, Hermine at my feet, I look into the conundrum she presents for us to decipher. I have seen from the start that her life is about to rupture and that the relationship will end badly.

"I know," she says when I point this out. It is not what she chooses to focus on. I hear her mother whining in the background. She's by the bedroom door and wants her daughter to get off the phone and pay her some attention.

"Just a little bit longer Mom, just a little bit longer."

Not soon enough for mother who starts whining again. Dora gets up and shuts her mother out of the room. The old woman needs constant attention, or she makes trouble, putting her feces in the refrigerator, throwing her clothes out the window, wandering outdoors.

And then it happens. Mother falls down the stairs and is badly hurt, several broken bones, ribs, a hip.

"I can't handle her anymore," says Dora. "I'm going to put her in a nursing home." She wants to know how her mother will adapt to that environment.

The old woman does not recover from her fall and dies less than a month later at the nursing home. Dora had expected relief. Instead, the loss of the hated mother deals her a blow. As an only child, mother is the last of her family. She is now alone in the world, save for her husband, and he doesn't count. She wants to have an affair with the doctor, have some adventure before she dies.

He's got trouble of his own. Her call reaches him shortly after his wife has abandoned him and he is distraught.

"You don't have any feelings for me. You don't even know me!" he says. "I get this kind of thing from patients all the time. They're having an imaginary relationship with me, and they create scenarios that will never happen."

A bucket of cold water thrown straight at her face! She quietly puts down the receiver and never speaks of him afterward. Not only is she alone, she's been seen as ridiculous, pathetic, by a man she was prepared to open her heart to.

We've come full circle. The life she has lived before the doctor, before mother's death, when the three of them lived in the house, is gone. The unknowing person she had been will not come back. Only through such a blow, will she awaken to life again.

It's her rite of passage.

THE HANGED MAN

-XII-

Clouds rising in the background encroach on a small triangle of deep purple sky. Before us, two parallel trees stand denuded of boughs, their tops cut in branched V notches from which a pole intersects. It looks like an arrangement where a motor hangs suspended in the back yard while the gutted automobile waits nearby for its rebuilt engine.

There's a raw expectancy in the misty air as someone is being hanged for the world to note. Like a chicken ready for bleeding, an impish figure is strung up by his left leg; a quick slit of the jugular, blood splatters in all directions and the pot is set to boil. Yet there's something incongruous about this man in light of his predicament. He looks like a harlequin dressed in red tights, pointy yellow slippers and a blue tunic tied in front by a row of ten tiny buttons. His arms and one free leg are akimbo forming three symmetrical triangles.

Reflected in the peaceful face, is the untroubled heart of a person who's given himself over to the will of the infinite. The inverted body is a symbol for the reversal in his way of life. There'll be no blood letting here, no futile thrashing while the revision is in progress.

Upright: Giving oneself over to the will of the infinite.

Reversed: One who is bound by established, traditional ways, unable to see beyond them.

There are times when it seems as if I'm on a roller coaster, at the top, coming down at break neck speed, and it feels like it too. But this is not the heart of the situation. Like the Hanged Man, one is suspended while internal work readies a person for upcoming change, a time when one is quiet and observant.

Going out with a married man leaves much to be desired. Although we have understood that the relationship cannot lead to deeper feelings, the heart makes no such distinctions. *Feed me*, it says, *feed me*. The deeper I get into it the worse it gets. Our social life revolves on the question of whether he is able to sneak out of the house. Forget about making plans.

"I feel I'm at your beck and call -- Oops, *my wife fell asleep; want to get together?* -- I never know when I'll see you; I don't even have a way of contacting you."

"I have obligations. I'm married; you knew that coming in," he says, more to the floor where he gazes, than to me.

Although strongly attracted, we aren't able to connect in a meaningful way, "I don't have those feelings for you," he says when it's clearly evident he does.

We are caught in a trap of our own making. I can only attract what is mine. If he keeps me at bay, I do likewise to him. We are safe with each other. This false safety with its closed doors, its shackles, chafes at us. I become rebellious and demanding, he chooses pettiness and avoidance. Then again there are still some good times, affection and lovemaking. But it's not enough and we break up by mutual agreement.

Having recently discovered the internet and being impressed with its possibilities, I get to work setting up a web site where I can put some of my writing, and essentially become my own publisher. *I like that idea!* I get a web master to help me create 4 sections representing the four-petalled flower of knowledge each of which is introduced by an animal icon.

The Snake tempts with a glimpse into future possibilities. Here I write weekly predictions based on Native Americans Jamie Sams & David Carson's book, "Medicine Cards" with its accompanying deck of animal, bird and insect archetypes. Tribes and clans have their own individual animal totem and consider themselves psychically connected to that animal, i.e. Bison Nation. Both the animal and the tribes people living on the same land, sharing the same food and water sources, exposed to its climate, its extremes in weather, are intimately connected with each other at the most basic survival level. Our siblings, the animals have much to teach us if we care to pay attention to how they conduct their lives. An animal's "medicine" is the traits that one admires and wants to incorporate in one's life. That animal needs to be studied in its hunting, mating and predatory habits. What are its strengths and weaknesses? A picture of it in a private corner strengthens that bond. Obviously there is a reason one admires this particular animal as opposed to all others. It may also be that the animal chose someone because it has an affinity to it. That animal is one's guide, and needs to be emulated.

When I was an eighteen year old, unhappily married girl with a baby, I had a strange, incomprehensible dream:

> An eagle appears at the top of my refrigerator. It does not speak to me, but somehow transmits the information that I belong to It, and It is the ruler of my life.

I was a headstrong girl and did not appreciate learning that another ruled me. I didn't fully understand the dream, but I knew it was significant.

As a girl raised in a Catholic convent, although a non-believer from an early age, surely I could not help but incorporate the Church's philosophy, its ethical system, its doctrines, its very icons of divinity into my perspective. Jesus, The Holy Ghost and the angels were not eagles. And why did it appear on a mundane thing like the top of the refrigerator? Why not perched on a tree branch, or in flight? The message from this strange divinity that controlled my life was that it also controlled my nourishment. There was nothing to be done about my unhappy predicament except to mature and learn from it. I was trapped. The dream was my first encounter with the Spirit. On my web site, the Eagle is the psychopomp of my journal.

When counseling someone, I seek to communicate with a hidden or disguised part of them, the one that observes, has been doing so from the beginning, lives on a different plane, and has other needs; this persona is alone in life, knows death is coming and will be faced; loving friends, challenging foes, a family, a network of acquaintances are but a diversion, the persona is alone experiencing life.

It makes decisions, attracts people and situations to help one along, or to shake things up when needed. It has been given many names, the soul, the Ancient One, the id, vital force, psyche, the unconscious. It is part of what I call Spirit, a power, or energy that permeates the cosmos. This energy is not interested in saving mankind, or whether one is good or bad. It does not differentiate or value one phenomenon from another, or one species from another. But it does value impeccability about one's person and in one's life. If one is a thief than one must be the very best, the cleverest thief one can be, definitely more clever than the community that would seek the thief's imprisonment. And if one is a teacher, then one must be open to every facet of knowledge.

I start the journal with a few Lakota words, which are part of the spiritual teachings of the Sioux people, most especially the ritual of the Inipi ceremony, the sweat lodge ritual. These aspects of their teachings from Chief Archie Fire Lame Deer and Helene Sarkis' book, "The Lakota Sweat Lodge Cards" which I choose at random without thought to what will follow always reflect what I'm about to write on. They serve as a door into the essay. I want the journal to be spontaneous. Being read by a public audience, it is of necessity not as intimate as a private journal, but that does not influence what I'm going to write about, just how I'm going to present it.

My Inipi ritual:

The gathering place is an hour and a half trip to northern New Jersey, in a jerrybuilt house that sits up on a hill, and has no parking accommodations for crowds. Upon entry, a sign informs me that I must remove my shoes before entering the living spaces. I am shocked to find an old woman in the living room sporting a Vandyke beard; another young woman sits with her. We nod and I ask about the ritual. It seems the first one is being performed as we speak. My group's rite will occur in a half hour. Apparently, the Medicine person has been scheduled to perform four such rituals this weekend, two yesterday and two today.

I go for a walk to check a nearby sanctuary. Coming back I head for the sweat lodge. The first group has emerged and the only person left in the lodge is a big fat Indian woman who comes rambling out barefooted with only a towel wrapped around her in icy winter weather. I am wearing thermal underwear, a sweater, a pullover, an ankle length skirt with a slip and two pairs of tights underneath. Topping it all with my navy pea coat and a long woolen scarf that I have wrapped around my head and neck.

The woman, a Lakota Indian, has a little rose tattoo above her left breast. The fleshy body and tattoo, the thick black hair, her mud caked bare feet and her sang-froid somehow add up to sensuality for me. A young blond woman, who's been smooching with her girlfriend, goes off and gets the Indian woman, whose name is Beverly, some blood oranges and strawberries. I watch her eat the fruit with gusto, its red juices running down her chin, all the while maintaining a running patter with some of the women who have gathered.

The first group of celebrants have gone back to the house and are feasting. Turns out, the blond is the fire keeper. Since early morning, she has been burning wood on top of the rocks that are used in the ritual. More women gather around the fire. Beverly gives instructions on how we are to proceed; and each of us has her body anointed with smoke from burning sage. Since I have never taken part in a Sweat Lodge Ritual I am to be one of the first ones to enter.

"You must now take your clothes off," says Priestess Beverly. I lean against a pole to remove my tights.

The fire keeper approaches and says, "I use that pole to lean my shovel and pitch fork on, and I need it. You should not stand in my way."

I look steadily at her as I stand half naked and vulnerable among a group of strangers on a cold winter morning, "It will take a second for me to remove my tights and I intend to lean on that pole to do so."

"I can't be responsible for what happens if you are in my way," she says.

The tights are quickly removed and I am off the pole with no bother. The ground, although still frozen, has a thin layer, maybe a quarter inch, of thawed mud from people walking on it. With Beverly leading us and chanting, we circle the lodge, a group of thirteen naked women, wrapped in towels, some barefooted waiting to be invited in. I have kept my clogs on and will not remove them till I enter the lodge. It looks like a geodesic dome piled with lots of blankets, quilts and tarps. I am shivering and a bit humiliated by my nakedness and the mud. Finally, after some chanting we are invited into the lodge one at a time. Rather than dreading the heat that I had obsessed about all weekend, I now am looking forward to it. Thankfully, I had the foresight to bring two towels, one of which I place on the frozen muddy ground below me, the other wrapped around me, as the lodge is still cold. We are told it is not a shame to leave if a person becomes ill from the heat.

There will be four rounds to the ceremony. At the end of each round the lodge entry flap is opened to allow light and air to enter. More hot rocks are added to the pit and the next round begins. I am aware of the peculiarities of my naked body. The old woman with the Vandyke beard sits to my left, skinny body, healthy looking and spry. The beard throws me off and I cannot see beyond it. She, or it, repulses me and I have no desire to communicate with someone whose sex is so indeterminate. We are packed in close and there is no comfortable way to sit what with the shape of the dome preventing one from leaning back against it.

The fire keeper starts handing in hot rocks on a pitchfork. Beverly places them in certain positions, maneuvering them with a deer antler, and the woman to her left drops sage on each one. A bucket of water is brought in and the flap is closed. Beverly drops water on the rocks and Grandfather's Breath is gladly received. She prays for all of creation, and she chants.

At the second round, we each offer a prayer. Beverly speaks of a woman who once asked for a million dollars.

"At the time, I wondered how a million dollars could possibly come to the woman. Through the lottery or somebody's death? I did not think this was a good request. The woman got her wish; she was in a car accident where all of her family died, but she came out of it unscathed and a million dollars richer.

"You will get what you ask for in a Sweat Lodge," she tells us, "so choose wisely."

I ask the elders for wisdom in guiding the people who come to me for assistance so that I may direct them on the right path. It occurs to me that I am not asking about my novel. With wisdom I will have it all.

We smoke the peace pipe and drink water. My body is dirty with mud. I can feel the grit on my inner thighs and I imagine that my makeup is running down my cheeks. Some perversity made me paint my fingernails and toenails blood red for this event. A middle-aged woman across from me pours water over her head, her red blotchy face and body.

It looks gross, but I understand we are down to the basics, heat, water, shelter, and when the ladle comes my way I see it as a golden elixir able to save my life. Later, we are given sage tea to cleanse the impurities from our bodies. The heat at no time overwhelms me. What I find hardest is the discomfort of my seating arrangement. By the third and fourth round I lie on the ground to relieve my cramped body.

Beverly asks us to hold hands and sing along with her the holy songs of her people. The old woman grasps my hand. I find that body-to-body we are able to communicate in spite of my squeamishness. Once out of the lodge, I quickly grab my clothes and head for the house to dress.

To hell with this outdoor business!

Inside, a table laden with food that the participants have brought awaits. We form another circle, the old Vandyke woman prays for us, and then we dive into the food.

This part of the ceremony is anticlimactic. Are we still in the ritual? People line up and load their plates with food, two and three times. And they eat, and they eat, and they eat. The talk is chitchat. Some people have come in small groups and they form cliques. I am bored and would like to sleep. One wall is covered with tee shirts for sale and there is some Indian jewelry. As soon as I can get away I say good-bye to Beverly, giving her a good hug, thank the hostess who owns the house and am back on the road.

* * *

In my shamanic journeys Eagle is often my guide. When I was feeling most alone, most abandoned, I journeyed to the upper world to seek healing and Eagle came and took me flying; I lay on its back, holding on to its wings with both hands. This touched me most deeply and I cried like a child. I was in the Eagle's care. It would support me.

On another journey, I sat at counsel with eagles in a cave, all of them perched on the rock walls, and so was I. Why Eagle brought me there I can only surmise, but I felt honored and privileged, considering it an acknowledgment of my serious intent.

To the poems I post on my site and the stories of how I came to my path, only one animal could be guardian to such a section and that is Bear, the guardian of my writing. From the moment I took my craft seriously Bear began to appear in my dreams counseling me about commitment and what was required of me. For whatever reason this animal chose to guide me I am eternally grateful. When Bear appears, which is not often, its intelligence is profound. It is also a hard taskmaster. Such a dream is not ordinary. A powerful bear on its hind legs coming at me with claws swinging and foam at the mouth has caused me a few times to reassess my actions, my future plans, and to see the error of my ways.

The last site section, Mes Apprentissages, is the tale of my ramblings; what has inspired and caused me to pursue my course. I have chosen the Crow as hierophant of this section, as Crow is the representative of great change, death of an old life, and a walk in the dark before one sees the road ahead illuminating new possibilities. That is how Crow speaks to me. It will hunt me down no matter where I live. My building on the Lower East Side has three floors above mine, yet Crow perched on the rooftop vent leading to my bathroom gave me its distinctive caw as I sat in the tub. I welcome these greetings as they signify a debouching of psychic energy that will lead me to new adventure. Whereas the path was blocked, it now unfolds before me.

Writing on my site is the centering pole in my life. Once a week I organize my thoughts on one true image, or as true as I am capable of. I want to invite the readers inside of me, to feel my emotions, to know in their gut what it is to walk that line between the two worlds; the path of Spirit where I look to my natural environment for direction, a world where doors open when I follow certain rules. Maintaining balance between that and the "rational" world of NYC is not always easy; one gets sucked in and is corrupted. Doesn't take long to get off balance; I catch myself behaving like a moron, doing things that have no possible meaning for my life.

While perusing the basement zoology stacks at the Colby College Library in Waterville Maine, I saw the light one day and concluded that all the books in the library on science, biology, philosophy, politics, etc., were specious documents, that except for the stories and the poems, none of it could possibly be accurate as we have such a propensity for self-delusion, for only seeing what we want, and explaining matter in ways that serve our purposes. The sole writing one can trust is fiction.

The only truth I have to share is my story, keeping in mind that its fabrication is what's true, not its facts.

DEATH

-XIII-

Death is a skeleton in a black cloak that neither beckons, nor entices. For Reaper has already crawled inside, imbedded itself into the womb; a feral energy that in due course expands like a mushroom. The rooted fungus, passed from parent to child, waits patiently to sprout and decay from within. A body exudes subtle odors to indicate that fungi have begun its work of turning matter to soil.

Also rooted in humans is the belief that stasis is attainable. Laying claim to the land, to the children, even the deceitful body, one learns through pain that very little can be grasped firmly. In the distance a red sun bleeds into the stream, reflecting its vivid color at zenith then washing out to pink like the skies above. It's the shadowy time of evening when the mind is oppressed with foreboding. Skeletal hands maneuver the long bladed sickle towards what's been cherished, leaving behind a void.

The awkward body tries to hide from this emptiness and the knowledge of its complicity in unleashing Death. Ready to join in the dance of dying, a silent heart bleeds into the night, the hand opens releasing its grip at life. Overshadowing the grim figure with sickle is a large, perfectly formed white rose; it signals the path of transcendence.

Upright: Releasing present hold on life, transcendence;
an end to old ways.

Reversed: The end of a political arrangement, the death of self-defeating behavior. Giving up control of situation.

Death

> But why should I mourn at the untimely fate of my people? Tribe follows tribe, and nation follows nation, like the waves of the sea. It is the order of nature, and regret is useless. Your time of decay may be distant -- but it will surely come.
>
> Chief Seattle,
> Duwamish Tribe.

Halloween weekend and I haven't gone to the New Moon/New York Pagan Ritual at the Gay Center, nor have I chosen to attend the West Village parade. On such a day, I have to do something. In the Voice listings, I find there is a celebration at the American Indian Community House; they are celebrating the Mexican Day of the Dead. Before leaving the apartment, I cut out the listing thinking to check it out.

Walking on Houston not far from Broadway where the Community House is supposed to be located, I'm not sure what to do with myself. I get the Times and a baguette. No umbrella, and it's pouring; *I gotta make a decision.* I check my pockets for the clipping. Not there. Just ahead on a newsstand is a copy of the Voice opened at the listings. An omen.

I get to the building, a pretty ritzy joint, and am ushered into a small waiting room where a group of people sits waiting for the show to begin. The Voice listing spoke of traditional Mexican food, dance, music, artists making sugar skulls, altars, and paper decorations. Our host, a big Native American man with long hair and a chiseled face comes to tell us the elevator is broken and there will be a 15 minute delay while they regroup. I am the only white person in the room, the rest are mostly Mexican Indians, and lots of noisy children. In my Manhattan outfit of black tights, black sweater, black jacket and shoes with my copy of the Sunday Times, I feel like an apple among the avocados. I'm also getting ambivalent feelings about ethnic America, the squalling babies and long suffering women, the macho men strutting about.

Our small waiting room becomes overcrowded. I don't know what I expected, but this is a bit more intimacy than I care to indulge in. Finally our host comes and brings us through a door down a long hallway past many cubicles with computers. Somebody in this organization obviously has formidable grant writing skills. The Centre Franco-Américain at the University of Maine with its paucity of funds could learn a few tricks here. When we get to our destination the room opens on a huge altar with decorations, lots of tall candles, fruit, bread, carnations, yellow, red and white, plastic skeletons, skulls, yellow flower petals on the floor in front of the altar.

But nothing is ready for us. Some people are still arranging tables. We sit at chairs placed in two rows at the edge of the room. The kids, some in Halloween costumes, have taken over the floor and are scurrying back and forth, one baby over to my left is shrieking. We sit and sit and nothing happens. People are still putting up decorations. Some women are making sugar skulls at one table. It is all too sad and tawdry this trying to recapture one's culture on alien soil. The mystery and magic of the Day of the Dead occurs in other lands. Here in America there is a picture of the Frankenstein monster smiling moronically at us in the Rite Aid Drugstore.

Someone makes an announcement in Spanish. The woman next to me figures I'm a gringo and explains what's been said. It's a friendly overture that I don't care to acknowledge. I want to get out of here, sneak away down the long corridor past all the computers with their false promise of authenticity. As I get to the elevator our Native American host asks, "You're not leaving so soon, are you?"

Back home, I fix the traditional pork preserves, créton, a common breakfast toast spread of my childhood (I've replaced the greasy pork with mushrooms,) which I spread on my baguette and I listen to 12th century hymns on the radio program "St. Paul Sunday Morning," the very hymns I heard as a child in the French Catholic convent I boarded.

I remember in early spring some men came and set fire to the surrounding fields. The nuns told us they were doing it to make the new grass healthier, greener come spring. It made an impression on my young mind seeing whole fields charred and black. I watched how the men set about doing it, trying to control the flames from going out of bounds. They would, depending on the wind, travel very fast or die and had to be resparked.

I can still see it to this day. How well I remember the smell of dry grass burning, and very green shoots growing from the charred rubble afterward. It seemed a miracle. Did I grasp the concept that after death comes renewal? It was a time in which I was much attuned to nature. Breughel could have painted the scene described above: peasants in early spring out in the fields preparing them for their flocks. I was viewing a primal scene. The convent nuns who came from Canada and France knew how to manage land.

Breughel's peasants undoubtedly performed rituals of fertility and congress invoking the gods at this time of death and renewal. But nuns had no such ceremonies. This was the twentieth century and we all lived in our heads. Our prayers were focused on saving our sinful souls from eternal damnation. Death was seen as the day of reckoning not a time of renewal. Today I, like witches the world over, perform rituals to celebrate the solstices, the Equinoxes, the turning of the wheel. I use the word witch for myself, not in the Wiccan religious sense with its adoration of the female deity, but in the archaic meaning of wise woman, a woman of power. My pagan spirituality began to take root in a Catholic convent.

The earth's first rule is not broken: everything dies, whether one wishes it or not. The trick is in learning to accept these losses, both major and minor, with grace. A client, I'll call him Tom, telephones for a reading. His life is a reproduction from a Norman Rockwell painting of a middle class American white man. Tom lives in a small town somewhere in the Midwest. His father owns the town's only hardware store, which provides a comfortable and secure life for him and his family. It is understood that Tom who works in the store will inherit it. His parents plan to retire soon.

Tom's been to an Ivy League college and his voice is that of a man at ease in the world, intelligent, and in charge of his situation. He wants a home, a wife, and a family. And he loves Sarah, has done so from the beginning.

"We've been together since our freshman year in high school," he says.

A pause then, "She wants to break up."

"What's her reason?"

"I presented her with a diamond and I asked to marry her. She said she was going to grad school and she wants to be free."

After we talk for a few minutes, I can see that Sarah doesn't want him anymore, will never want him again. She sees him as responsible for not pursuing her own interests, her career. She's going to grad school and he's not going to stop her.

But Tom does not want to stop her; he's agreed to wait till she graduates to get married. Something happened to Sarah and her worldview changed. She doesn't want this man anymore, or the life he offers. A part of her has died, and now a change of direction is needed.

How did I know so quickly that she would never come back to him? I heard it in his voice. It was that of a person who has suffered a loss, a bit of mild shock, incredulity, and anger. We speak on the phone at least once a week for months. She comes to spend an afternoon with him before she goes off to school. They speak on the phone a few times, and once, while he's in her city, he drops by her apartment to say hello. A bald, fleshy, older man is with her. It never occurs to Tom that the professor might be Sarah's lover.

She drops out of grad school, moves in with the professor and they become engaged, all in less than two months. Tom's life during this time is pretty much the same as it has always been. He has a group of friends from college who invite him to parties; the guys go off to their college football games (he's tried dating, but isn't ready for it,) he goes fishing and he works in the store with his father, but he lives alone in a house he has purchased. He never asks me if she's coming back. He wants to know how she feels about him. He wants to know what her telephone calls to him mean. He wants to know if she's happy. Is she having an affair with the professor? Will she marry him? It's a protracted death.

Losing someone is a painful process. One is angry, sad, feels despair, and one is alone. Some choose to be the leavers, that is, they initiate the break-up, while others prefer to be abandoned. The fact is both parties are equally involved. Obviously, Tom stopped listening to Sarah way before she broke up with him. He pulled away from the relationship on an intimate level, preferring the security of a picture-perfect semblance of the real thing. Attending social functions, family dinners, church rituals, they ignored their growing boredom and unmet needs until Sarah forced the issue and acknowledged that the relationship was no longer viable.

After Tom comes to accept that Sarah isn't coming back, he becomes critical and judgmental when speaking of her. He finds a girl friend that he sees as a better person, more mature. Will the relationship work out? Probably not, nor will Sarah's.

Losing someone one has had a ten to twelve year relationship with is a major blow. As a child, I remember women wearing black clothes, black shoes, black stockings, which they kept up for a year after a beloved, or family member's death; men wore black armbands. The French word deuil, which indicates the state of mourning, also defines the act of wearing mourning clothes, (porter le deuil.) The sight of people on the street wearing mourning clothes made of the facts of suffering and dying an everyday reality. Unfortunately, we have lost the custom of wearing mourning clothes. The ritual of identifying oneself as a person who has suffered a loss serves the purpose of focalizing one, making a public acknowledgment of the loss, and working through the process of coming to terms with it. Within the community, persons in mourning clothes illustrate death and loss as inevitable parts of the cycle of life, not something to hide or pretend away.

Tom and Sarah believe their relationship ended because of the other's shortcomings. I never agree with that assessment. Relationships end because the conversation is over. The couple has come to differing assessments of themselves and their respective journeys. Clients often talk about a specific moment of clarity where all was understood about the nature of the relationship. A process of untangling oneself follows. Blaming the lover is a form of holding on, and especially a need to have power over, to control. But death will have its way.

The new relationships will not work because Sarah and Tom never properly acknowledged, or took the time to mourn their long-term relationship. Unable to come to a resolution about the break-up, they left it with a taste of bitterness on the tongue. Hence, one acquires "baggage." After four such break-ups, the load on one's back is horrendous, and others slink away.

Hermine is sick, very sick. Five o'clock yesterday morning, I found her with one of her nails caught in the fabric of the easy chair. She was hanging over the side flailing about, trying to free herself. I lifted her up and put her on the chair, then worked to free her paw. Normally she would never allow me to do that. Not a peep. The floor is wet and so is her fur. *She must have been hanging and struggling a long time.* All of a sudden, her body starts convulsing. I hold on to her and she quiets down. Afterward, I pick her up and put her on the bed with me. I notice she's not moving. Her position is awkward but she makes no effort to straighten herself out.

She stays on the bed all morning. After I come back from my run in the afternoon, she's up and I feed her some tuna. Appetite's fairly good.

She'll come out of this.

I notice she's not climbing on anything, staying on the floor. It's going to take a while for her to get over this. I doubt she ever climbs up that chair again. In the evening, I get her a little rug that I put in a corner of the closet she likes to go to. She stays for a while then she comes out and settles on the floor.

Around 1 o'clock in the morning I hear her flailing. At first it appears as if she is chasing something, and then her body starts going crazy flip-flopping all over the floor. *A seizure.* Blood comes out of her mouth, and she has again lost control of her bladder. I'm becoming worried and frightened. It takes 10, 15 minutes for her to regain some control. There is no awareness yet. I take her and place her on her rug, her mouth all bloody, her fur soaked with urine. I place my hands on each side of her body and I speak to her, nonsense stuff.

"Lorraine is here; the world is still here; I love you. You are home." I can see she is soothed.

I get back in bed.

She's not going to survive another seizure.

Then I get up, light the candle on my altar and I pray for Hermine, I want whatever is best for her. If this is her time to die, she is 17 years old, make it a good death. And if she is to live, give her strength.

I don't know what to expect when I wake up in the morning. She's up and about. I feed her and watch for a bit, again, no climbing. I place her on the love seat across from my desk. She starts having another seizure; I hold her body and it quiets down, but she's still going through hell internally. It takes her two hours to come back to where I see she is peaceful. How am I dealing with this? I'm trying to make her as comfortable as possible. But I don't want to start crying. With her sensitivity to energy, I want to project a strong and confident mien, the person she cares for. I clean the house; it's a cool day I can shut the NYC noise out by closing windows, and I put on a long dress and some makeup. I do this for myself because Hermine is blind. It will help me feel more at ease and she'll pick up on it. I will also cook something later so the aroma of good food permeates the apartment. If this is the end, I want it to be peaceful.

Hermine was with me when I broke up my home, followed me to the cabin by the lake, then the house in the mountains, living on the beach, hiding her from the officials (with their "no pets" policy) at the faculty apartment at the University of

Maine at Orono, then the Farm and the move to NYC. We were even homeless for a few minutes together, a couple of wanderers traveling the highway in a Ford van. She has never been my "pet", and anyone who treated her like a cuddly little thing was attacked for it. She taught me and continues to teach me the true test of strength, how to be proud and to maintain independence no matter how vulnerable I am. She has also taught me to be still and to read energy rather than sound. Many times, she informed me through reading their energy that the person or group I was dealing with was untrustworthy. She was right every time. This little cat positions itself three feet to the front of me in a proprietary way; *nobody's gonna mess with me while she's around.*

Another seizure . . . a bad one.

I'm falling apart. She's quiet now, stretched out under the lamp. I don't think she's fully conscious. The heart is beating wildly. All I do is sit and look at her. There is nothing to be done except look for signs, any sign. Her body is calm and her eyes are closed, but her heart is still beating violently. She has always been incredibly strong, even in her blindness no one ever suspected it.

On Saturday, Hermine has a small seizure around 5 in the morning, and another one a short while after. She is disoriented and cannot get her bearings, walks into walls, etc. Yet, these seizures are shorter; she hasn't lost control of her bladder and she doesn't become comatose afterward.

There may yet be hope.

Sunday afternoon, seizures continue. In her confusion, I call out for her tuna fish feeding to see if she will understand. She picks up immediately, finds her way to her dish, eats well and keeps her food down. *Good signs.* And she's more alert between seizures too. It's been a long sleepless weekend and it's not over yet.

Hermine and I visit the vet and she does not have good news for me. There are tests that could be done, keeping Hermine overnight, but she doesn't recommend it. From the smell of urine on the cat she can pick up a telltale odor of ammonia; the kidneys are no longer functioning.

"Can you give her something to stop the seizures?"

"No, there is nothing."

She then suggests putting the cat away. "We have the facility to do that." She doesn't try to force the decision on me; it's an option.

I shake my head.

"It will be easier for her if she has plenty of water and she eats well, some vitamin B12," are the vet's last words.

When I get home I take a warm bath, see to Hermine's comfort, and then off to bed. The next day, Tuesday is not too bad, she has two big seizures, but she also eats well and is able to stroll around. She is my responsibility; I'm not going to have her killed by strangers in an institution. As long as she has some quality left to her life, I'll see to her care. I also solve the problem of urine on the floors with newspaper covering all of them.

Wednesday: There have been three seizures today and it's only 7 PM. Hermine has not cleaned herself, hasn't moved most of the day. She's becoming feral, ready to pounce at the least disturbance. I walk around considering murder. How am I going to do this? To see someone you love so ill, in such misery and knowing there is absolutely nothing you can do to ease their suffering causes one to think seriously about life's meaninglessness. I take her on my lap in the afternoon. We sit on what I've always considered to be her easy chair; she immediately laid claim to it the first day it arrived. She's able to relax with me and we have a nice exchange. At some point, I become distracted and probably move my body. She growls at me in her old way.

Hermine is a bitch; she does not like to be disrespected. A bitch lets you know her boundaries. And in that way you are free to set your own. After this particular growl I get really pissed at her.

"You're abandoning me and breaking my heart!" I lash out.

In the evening she has several more seizures. I will have to do something in the morning.

I'm still awake at 5 am, and from then on every hour on the hour I wake up to the sound of the clock chiming out its number. I give it up 8 and get up just as Hermine's having a seizure under the bed.

I have recently read the story of Sammy (the Bull) Gravano. Sammy was the Cosa Nostra gangster who blew the whistle on the organization.

I was curious about his work as a hit man. Gravano, who is no dummy, said the very first time he killed someone he was frightened and jumpy, but he was also elated afterward, saw the event in terms of an acquisition of personal power. I can appreciate that. Anytime a person breaks a social taboo, power is acquired. One has dared to take personal responsibility for one's actions, regardless of what the world thinks. To be sure, there are different reasons for killing. Sammy did it for the Cosa Nostra, a world with different rules. It was a sanctioned act in his milieu.

Hermine does not move from her spot next to her feeding dish all morning. Her eyes are crazy and she stands ready to fight. The world as she knows it has come down to food and defense. I sit close to her on the floor and I sing a song I made up about her name that I often entertain her with in our moments of intimacy.

"Her - mine! Hermini, mini, mini."

I can see on her face a relaxation of tension, and her ass gently drops to the floor followed by the rest of her body.

At one in the afternoon, she feebly walks over to the living room and positions herself next to her water supply. Shortly, her body goes through its awful contortions and she is soaked with urine sprawled out on the floor. I pick her up with the bath mat and bring her to the tub that is filled with water. The mat protects me from her flailing body, her claws and teeth. She fights vigorously. When I think it is over she comes back up out of the water. My determination wavers momentarily when I see her sad little face struggling to get free. Afterward, I cleanse her body, wrap it in a towel, put the bundle in a shopping bag, then into my backpack. On the street, I realize that I'm a little crazy, but determined to carry through my plan. Hermine is placed in the East River; quickly because I think what I am doing is probably illegal. There are no parting words.

I've been fragile the past couple of days. I go amongst people, but I'm not really with them. Inside my shell, the feeling is one of being wounded or violated, and of an ancient wisdom about life. All the particulars of Hermine's sudden illness, the seizures, the debility, the loss of contact comes back to me. The mind needs to understand. Most of the day after she dies I keep reliving the scenes of her drowning in the tub, her little face coming out of the water when I think she's already drowned, afraid I will have nightmares. Thankfully, I do not.

Is it true what Sammy the Bull says about a boost in personal power when one commits a murder? I certainly didn't feel any surge like Sammy did, but yes, I think he's right. I cite as evidence the fact that in the past few days people look directly at me in the streets, especially men. I can feel a definite change coming over me with no clear direction yet. In the apartment, I keep thinking she's in the other room, in her easy chair. What's hardest to bear is that there is no longer anyone to greet me when I come home, no little endearments.

TEMPERANCE

-XIV-

With a hermaphroditic body and broad golden wings that would put any eagle to shame, the angel is a truly mysterious being. Standing by a cluster of yellow irises, the spirit wears a white gown trimmed at hem and collar with a gold border. There's a large red triangle on its chest, a symbol one sees on farm equipment denoting a slow moving vehicle.

These fanciful creatures have been with us from the beginning. They are the totem beings that stand by our side and ward off malign forces. With those magnificent wings, they can, at a moment's notice, intervene with any power on our behalf. The angel has one foot on land and the other in a swiftly moving stream. Rooted in both elements, it pours liquid from one cup to another, infusing spirit into matter. A dirt road in the background leads to massive stone mountains.

"Take heed and move cautiously," the spirit warns, "the way is grueling for those who are ignorant of the cost involved in taking such a path. The universe as you know it will cease to exist as the trail unfolds. Every action, every thought and word will be leavened with high purpose. "

Upright: Choosing one's path and acknowledging its responsibilities.
Making correct decisions, being aware of their cost.

Reversed: Scattered forces, conflicting interests;
acting in ignorance, without forethought.

> Living in New York, you're always going to feel a little broke. You're always going to feel like an outsider. And you're always going to feel a little vulnerable.
>
> Jim Gaffigan

An invitation in a pagan journal for witches and pagans to march under their own banner in the Gay Pride parade, apparently the witches have been doing this for years. Should I walk with the pagans or with Kate under the banner "Farm Dykes" as I've done for several years now?

Tina, another colonist from my summer at The Farm sends me a note asking about my plans. I write back with my two options and feel that I should march with Tina and Kate who I owe some fidelity to. Yet, the thought does enter my mind that I truly belong with the witches.

When I call Kate to find out if she's marching, "Too long. Too hot," she says.

"I guess I'll walk with the witches."

"That's good; I'm going upstate."

With the end of that conversation comes the end of my mentoring by Kate. A witch now, not a farm dyke.

It rains throughout the march. I join up with New Moon/New York, a good group that I am glad to be with. Trust a pagan to enjoy a good party, or a march. And then there's the ex-colonist, my buddy Tina. Before starting off, our group forms a large circle, performs a few breathing exercises and we raise a cone of power.

In front of us is a float with seminude bar boys gyrating to hot music. And in the back are the Radical Faeries, and they are indeed radical, fighting with our marshal about where they *goddamn well want to march*. I, and some of the other witches, sluts that we are, at every opportunity, break rank and scurry over to the great music in front of us to boogie. For this occasion, I wear pink hot pants, faintly lavender tinted sheer hosiery, and a black halter with a large pin of a witch. My girly has a wart on her huge green nose, a modern bob of shocking red hair and a black pointy hat with a picture of a purple bat on it. Her eyes move back and forth. The little darling gives us a gap-toothed smile.

We raise Cain in front of St. Patrick's Cathedral for the church's stance against homosexuality, a mortal sin, and its advocacy of abstinence to stop the spread of AIDS. A couple of queens pay homage to Sak's as we walk by, while some of the guys in our group run over and genuflect in front of the bar boys, getting up to put money in their G strings. It is crazy, and wild, and poignant, and very real. Thank god, I left the Farm Dykes!

In the midst of shaking my ass to the music I see a woman, perhaps ten years younger than me, a reporter with camera in hand capturing the crazies. She looks directly at me, but does not take my picture (I don't fit the profile.) The expression on her face is one of wonderment -- *What is going on here?*

At the end of our very long march down into the throbbing heart of perversity that is Greenwich Village, we again form a circle to bring closure to our experience.

Feeling sickly. I look in the mirror and my eyes reflect my weakening spirit. I am exhausted from yesterday's Pride Parade. My knees hurt, (this is becoming a problem that I will have to resolve.) I've had an ear infection for a month and got some Chinese medicine for it hoping it would clear up, but it's much worse.

Occasionally, feeling sad. This exhaustion is a result of the emotional and psychological energy I expended in the parade.

Still sick a month later, the Chinese medicine hasn't worked. I've even stopped running and exercising. The illness is visible in my eyes. Looks like I'm going to have to see a Western doctor. An experience akin to bringing your car to the muffler shop when you start to notice the car's motor pinging. I am sure at some date far into the future, the world will look on our current medical practices much as we view the bizarre leeches and bleeding treatment employed by our forebear. Treating someone without any training into, or understanding of the spiritual aspect of healing, of a person's psychological makeup, one may hit on the correct diagnosis, but then again, someone may end up with a new muffler and the same problem. There has to be more to healing than cold, antiseptic, grey hospitals and doctors' examining rooms.

I approach the profession as a foreigner trying to make myself understood in a land whose language I don't speak. I am expected to discourse on my body as "it." I, who exercise 5 days a week and run a couple miles every other day, *am* my body.

Illness comes at times when there is a need to pay attention to one's life. I've been sick since the Gay Pride parade. I note that I've gotten sicker after the Fourth. These two events speak to me of personal integrity and independence from larger society.

Responsibilities -- *t*hat is what is causing me to be sick, to slow down and pay attention.

A kind of low-grade malaise that I have seen the doctor for, actually, he was a Physician's Assistant at the Gay Center's clinic. Skinny black guy abundantly pierced, courteous, gentle. He looks in my ears. *No, everything looks fine.* Takes my blood pressure; the thing is way, way up there, 150 over a 100; I normally get readings in the mid-90's and 60's. The skyrocketing pressure in my veins explains the pain in my ears, in my face, my eyes, and the pain in my knees.

The descriptive word is *wired.*

I heard recently about a man who was diagnosed H.I.V. positive. He remained thus for some time and then his condition reverted. What I found interesting about his story is that he knew what had happened without any confirming tests. He just sensed it. Spoke about opening the window on a bitter, cold night, breathing the air and knowing, absolutely, that his body was healthy again. Out went the protease inhibitors!

The body speaks. One ignores it at one's peril. While working with dying people, many times, I heard the words, *I'm gonna beat this thing.* But no one on the staff ever took that kind of talk seriously. If you were going to beat it, one, you wouldn't brag about it, and two, the last place you would be is in a hospital. I was naïve at first and had to learn.

I myself have an intimate relationship with my body. Modern medicine would probably call me an hysteric, but that's because Western medicine is a strange system in which mind, body and emotions are not attended to as interrelated. When I see a doctor I expect to tell him/her what is happening in the proper context of my whole being, but they're not interested. I therefore have to exclude the most relevant parts of the story. I prefer a shaman, a medicine man or woman.

My body has a way of warning me when I've received an overload of either sensory or emotional stimuli. My first inkling occurred when I was about 15 in the freak tent of a carnival. Before us on stage was a woman labeled "The Fish Skinned Woman." She wore a bikini and her body was a network of large scaly patches of flaking skin. She would rub or scratch herself as she talked and the ground around her looked like a light snow covering. She removed her turban to indicate it had affected her scalp. A few strands of hair were all that remained at the top of her head. She went on to tell us that she was married and had perfectly normal children. I walked out of the tent and next thing I knew I was looking up at my friends from the ground. My body had said no! This swooning, this sensitivity was a knowing of one's complicity in one's fate.

A woman, I'll call her Mary, I don't remember what was wrong with her, but when I came into the picture she had already been informed she would not go back home, not ever again. The hospital staff was looking to find her nursing home facilities and her family was ransacking her apartment as she lay in the hospital. She was in excruciating pain and medication was no relief. Her doctor, the shift nurses, the physical therapist, myself and members of my team, everyone involved in her care, offered information at a specially called staff meeting about what could be done to help her. Having someone with her seemed to help so we set up shifts to keep her company. I brought her tapes of soothing nature music, read to her, rubbed her body, then I would go home in the evening thoroughly drained and demoralized.

One day, when I went to visit Mary in her hospital room, something unusual happened. I winked. A spontaneous act that she didn't take kindly to. I was being disrespectful to a dying woman. Yet we had arrived at a moment of truth that she was trying to avoid, an intuitive truth that I came to like the resolution of a koan. She was complicit in her method of dying. We both acted a part in a play. The pain was real, there was no denying it; the attention was real too and she was getting lots of it, probably more than she ever had. She might have chosen otherwise, me too. That very day a medication was found that worked for her and shortly thereafter she was transferred to a nursing home.

I pay taxes for the first time in five years. It's down to the wire. I owe the government two thousand seven hundred four dollars. My account holds two thousand six hundred and something. I deposit three checks and mail a personal check to New York State and one to the U.S. government short one hundred dollars in my account, hoping my deposit will clear before my checks are cashed.

Welcome back to the work world, Lorraine!

I'm working for the LaToya Jackson Network lately. The other people let me go. Actually they let most of their psychics go. They are into high finance now and can no longer spare us the time. Mr. Feder decided to sub-contract the work of hiring and supervising psychics. But he kept this to himself. We just couldn't log into the system when we dialed our work number.

I write between calls during the night, in my journal from 10 to 11 pm, then have dinner and start up again at midnight, work for an hour on a poem and a couple of hours on the novel. Before going to bed the other morning at 4:30 I looked out the window and there in the park was a man doing a strenuous variation of T'ai Chi. At first I thought, *a crazy man or a drunk*, but he was serious, a fellow dancer of the night.

"Diana Bontemps" is a teenage girl whose name is my book's title. I am writing it in the first person, a new and more intense experience. I walk around with the soul of a sixteen-year-old girl. Hence, a lot of dating, being into makeup and clothes, having exaggerated mood swings and self-destructive behavior.

Bobby is an example:

He is someone I meet in the park. He gives me a bright smile and *Hello* whenever I cross his path. Drop-dead gorgeous, a Cuban, tall, virile, dark, (*African-American*, I thought at first,) the color of his skin is olive to black. His silver hair, crinkly as opposed to nappy, is cut in a fade, and his outfit of choice is a black leather jacket and jeans. An AIDS awareness ribbon completes his outfit (his sister died of AIDS.)

Bobby used to work construction, but that's not happening anymore, blames it on a back injury from his last job, a long time ago. He's got something cooking though, hanging in the street talking to the guys, all day, every day. I don't think he's a dealer, but there are other negotiations that a person like me might not be aware of. Home is an arrangement he has with a woman in the neighborhood for room and board, and whatever else may be needed.

"Lorena," he calls to me in the park. Without turning, I know it's Bobby as he is the only one who calls me by that name. A diminutive and sign of affection, but all I think of when I hear the name is of a currently infamous woman who cut her husband's penis off because he mistreated her. Her name is also Lorena, Lorena Bobbitt.

The other night, high on peach liquor with beer and heroin (he sniffs it,) he stood on the street in front of my building around 3 AM, directly below my window, bellowing like a bull moose.

"Chulita!"

The clumsy animal in heat is my Romeo. He ingests life from the gut. Every situation is augmented to the 10th power, whether buying a tomato or negotiating a lawsuit. He's currently bringing a claim against a small neighborhood storeowner because he fell in front of the man's premises. Bobby doesn't like the guy so he's setting him up. Gets a lawyer, and a chiropractor.

We hang out at a Latino club on Henry Street. With no outdoor sign, the place indeed has no name, and its entrance looks like any other. Inside, down half a flight of stairs one encounters a cantina with tables and a jukebox encircling a handkerchief dance floor. It is Latin music we dance to, Mongo Santa Maria, Tito Puente, Candido, Celia Cruz and Marc Anthony. The dancing is first rate, from sexy girls, old ladies, little children, studs, and pot-bellied men. Across the dance floor are a couple of pool tables that occupy the hustlers, and then the bar which has only two stools and was probably dragged out of someone's basement rec room. A big bottle of vodka, and one of whiskey on a shelf behind the bar are the only hard liquor.

Most people drink beer. I settle for one of the sodas, ginger ale or coke.

Dancing in our society is generally conducted to arouse sexual feelings and/or intimacy between romantic partners. Some people use it to make a personal statement, to create an artistic presentation. We forget about the real power of dance, why tribal people use its energy for a different purpose than we do. In my teens, I got an indication of that power when I danced the dirty boogie at a local popular club. I had no idea what possessed me, a convent girl, to do such a thing. A crowd gathered round and I could feel the electric energy in the room. Was it sexual? Undoubtedly, but more than that, it tapped some primal chord in me. I like to incorporate drums and dancing in my rituals.

Bobby tells me the place is unlicensed; the owner has a deal with the police to keep it going. As long as there's no trouble they will take his money and look the other way. We choose a table with two of his young friends.

When Bobby gets up to get us a drink, his companions, who do not speak English, look at me, smile, and nod. Having come in from the rain, I feel like a drowned rat. Soaked, clothes cling to my body and my straight hair is all ringlets.

Precioso, they say to each other. *Precioso,* and then they both make a move for me. I would never come to the bar by myself because this sort of thing goes on quite a bit the minute Bobby turns his back. Men stop by and peddle their goods, bomber jackets with team lettering, little rocks and fine powders, reefer in one joint packets. Some women pull me aside to warn me about what a badass Bobby is.

"I know," I tell them. "I know."

He's not my lover. We tried sex once, and it was a bust, so that was the end of it. He's often an older brother, teaching me the ropes about life in the ghetto, introducing me to people. What pleases Bobby to no end is when I fix him some of my New England cuisine. We eat mussel chowder, red flannel hash and boiled dinner from my repertoire of recipes that are as exotic to him, as sushi was to me when I first arrived in the city.

I hadn't seen him for almost a month when he came and threw some pebbles at my window at four in the morning.

"Come for a spin."

He looks good, bedecked in gold; four, five chains around the neck, one with a picture of a saint who performs miracles, several gold chain bracelets, one with gold letters that spell out the name Robert, not Roberto. There is also a big gold watch, new glasses with gold rims and shades clipped on them, aviator shaped and mirror glass.

Bobby got the first installment on his $16,000 lawsuit settlement today and he went shopping, a cellular phone, a golden crucifix, shirts, two *Saturday Night Fever*, John Travolta cream colored suits, And lots of new friends. The next evening he takes me out to dinner, in his new (to him) car, a big Eldorado 86, white with maroon velvet seats set permanently in a slight recline. We are traveling uptown to Victor's Café, the epitome of Cuban haute cuisine.

Being with Bobby is an adventure. I never quite know what to make of it. Towards the end of our extravagantly delicious meal we get into a fight.

I leave. There follows several more such incidents, and he's making trouble on the street, high all the time. The big shot.

I'm concerned about what's happening to him, but I don't like him much lately. He showed up last week asking to take me to brunch. I think he came to see me because the money's running out. Most of it was spent on his image, the suits, the shirts, and the jewelry. We were together approximately one hour and during that period he drank a half a beer and three shots of liquor.

On Monday, one of the guys from the cantina tells me that Bobby started a big brawl at the bar; the cops were called and the cantina is permanently closed. And Bobby? He's packed his John Travolta suits and has decided it's a good time to visit Miami.

THE DEVIL

- XV -

An invitation to descend into the pit is proffered. The offer may be repulsed, choosing safety, or you may plunge into darkness aware you may not have the strength to free yourself of the horror you will encounter; the picture of yourself you will never be able to accept or reject. It's an ethical decision you cannot avoid. Wanting to turn and run, never to look at the lickerish, horned goat, especially not to focus on those sulfurous, bloodshot eyes, you swear you will not be pulled in.

Yet, you wonder, what is it that is so terrible? To question is to begin to lose control, you slowly sink into the pit of madness, experiencing exquisite pleasure, as you taste freedom from pettiness and the narrow life. Fearfully, you acknowledge the green slimy stub of a candle burning above the goat's head, keeping record of your diminishing existence. Below it is the witches' golden pentacle, inverted and placed between the goat's upcurling horns, a blue bottle fly at center.

Recalling the old witches' dictum about power abiding where there is fear, you plunge deeper into the pit and are engulfed by a fiery red circle. Otherwise chaos becomes rampant shattering your psyche. As it is, you see your wanton needs leering at you, an inborn weakness unable to fend off the destructive spiral of fear. *I will survive it,* you declare.

Upright: Temptation, illicit pleasure, fears.
Reversed: Giving up dissolute life. Removing the chains that bind.
Seeking freedom from a self-destructive spiral.

In this winter world of night which is Manhattan, a city made of stone, bricks, cinder blocks, concrete, cobblestone, glass, tar, steel and iron, where the foot rarely touches good earth and the sky is but a scrap peering between buildings, evening descends like the extinction of the human race. People do not tarry on the cold, dark streets as the Jungle returns with its laws and commandments.

"I'm inebriated. That's how I got up the courage to call you. I want to see you. Call me. I'm having an operation, of all things," unspools from my telephone message minder.

Why do I love this goofy guy who thinks having an operation is a vulgar imposition. Bijou has been cosseted from much of life's vicissitude. Perhaps that is what attracts me to him, the innocence and gentle manners.

And then there's Buddha.

This wrenching open of the heart waves needs to be done periodically or I lose innocence and the all-important faith in human beings. It is precisely during such periods as I'm experiencing that magic occurs. Somehow, a door opens to new possibilities.

On the streets, I become aware of people. A Chinese woman, I think that our cultures and background are so dissimilar we would have little to talk about. I see her with my, *I'm just arriving in NYC from Maine,* eyes. A game I play with myself to see if I retain innocence. Not to fear, I am not corrupted. NYC holds all the magic it did when I first arrived.

Having seen the Chinese woman in this inviolate state, a crack develops in the world and I realize I am lost in the middle of a concrete jungle. We, the human inhabitants, dwell in a world as solitary, sentient beings, isolated profoundly from each other, with each individual trapped inside its own world of knowledge and beauty. For a moment the scene feels desolate. I had a vision one night looking out the window at winterworld. I saw myself as lost in the middle of nowhere, a lifeless planet made up of inert materials, a destitute canyon in some foreign planetary system. I became so frightened, I lit the candles and cast a circle to protect me. I not sure what the vision means. Is it predictive of worlds to come?

Buddha calls several nights in a row during the week, wanting to be with me. We plan to meet on the weekend. I also make a date with Bijou (Yes, he's back in my life) for Sunday brunch. Busy, busy!

Come 6 o'clock, no Buddha, no call. I give up at 8:30. Just as I'm walking out the door Bijou calls.

"Are you free for the evening? Would you like to join me for dinner?"

I head for West Fourth to meet him, cross the park and there's Buddha sitting by himself, having a beer.

"I just tried to call you," he offers lamely.

"No, you did not try to call me," I reply, still walking.

"There you go," the hand is in the air sending me on my way. "You're always walking off. Come over," the hand slides down to the rim of the park's elevated center circle inviting me to sit by his side.

But it's all bullshit. I look at his face. He's incredibly sexy and I'm attracted to him even though I know it's impossible between us. Buddha takes in my whole person looking at my body, my style. It's the same look of attraction and acceptance of fate's decision that I give him.

"I can't stop I have other plans," I say.

"Wha, where you going?"

"I'm meeting a friend for dinner."

"It's a guy?"

"Yeah."

"There you go. Who is that guy? I'm gonna kill that bastard. I shoulda known. It never works."

I walk away feeling I have at least saved face and left a deteriorating situation with some pride, thanks to Bijou's invitation. I notice Buddha used the incident to his advantage too. His basic assumptions about human relationships were reinforced one more time.

You can't believe in women; they will let you down every time.

Buddha wanted to be with me, but he couldn't. It was too scary. Still, I would have wanted to hear that phone ring tonight, pick it up to hear his deep rumbling voice, "Hi Baby, what's up?"

Certain things must be said about Buddha. He gives me pleasure. I'm at peace when I'm with him and I'm happy. We don't talk very much; it's a relief not to be constantly "on."

I can see a shocked, offended look in faces on the street when we are out together holding hands or touching. The relationship, in a way, serves as metaphor for some things that need to happen in my life. I must act from my center, regardless of how society judges me for it.

Several months roll by before I hear from him again. A knock at the door in the evening, he's in a black goose down doughboy jacket.

"Hello Buddha."

He slips his arm through mine, teases me about my sexy black leggings. I reach over and touch the little gadget hanging from the zipper of his jacket. He kisses me and I invite him to stay for dinner.

"I was arrested in Georgia," he explains.

"What happened?"

"You'll have to expect this sort of thing with my profession," he says.

My old standby, spinach tortillas, the easiest thing I can throw together at a moment's notice with a bottle of pinot grigio. Afterward, we move over to the living room, Dave Brubeck and then Ottmar Liebert playing on the stereo. We make love, such a long time coming, so passionate and powerful.

I spend the most delightful two days, making love over and over again, each time as passionate if not more than the last. In between, we talk about Al Sharpton, the incongruity of our relationship; we listen to Big Mama Maybelle and Ruth Brown. In the evening, I make us black bean soup which I serve with onion bagels. He gives me a bath and ends up in the tub with me. His body is round and feminine with a good dick and tits like a woman. The colors of his skin range from mahogany to gunmetal grey. In the creases, it is charcoal. All of these shades and tones play off each other and are remarkably beautiful.

Our lovemaking is a healing to me and I think to him too. It had been a while since someone had made, and I mean truly made, love to me. We could not stop stroking each other.

Someone spotted my business card at a candles and oil store and called to get a reading. We talked and I invited him to the apartment. A bit chancy, seeing as I've never met him, but I did it. It went so well that it seemed like the most natural thing in the world to do. I, who had worried about delivering enough information to earn the money he is paying me, ended up having to point him out the door because we could have easily gone on for another hour. There was no strain, yet afterward I was done in.

There has to be a tie where I feel a psychic connection when choosing clients. After telling one man who asked about expanding his investment business out of state, that a smart and wise woman was going to come into his life to help him, I realized that it was I after we hung up.

And then there are the crazies: A woman calls through the network and tells me that she is tape-recording my phone conversation with her.

"It doesn't seem to matter what kind of birth date I give any of you, you all come out with predictions." Her rage and venom are palpable.

"What is *your* name," she asks belligerently when I ask for hers.

A traveling lady calls occasionally, always from a different city and state. She chooses boarding houses to live in and gets into factious relationships with the people. I think she's running a scam that causes her to keep on the move.

Every session is scrutinized for the service I have rendered. I'm giving my clients a lot of thought these days. *Did I provide the necessary wisdom to be of help? Did I fail to interpret the signs correctly? Was there more I could have done?* Having a private client allows me certain freedoms I don't have with the networks. I am not yet using that freedom wisely.

When I lived in the mountains in Maine those two years writing "COMICS," I felt safe. I was living on the proceeds of the sale of my home. Out of the daily hubbub, its rules and limitations no longer applied. I didn't need the world and it certainly was not aware of my departure. I lived like a nun. Every action was imbued with reverence. One could say I had money hence the reason for my feelings of safety and well-being. I'm sure that contributed, but it wasn't always easy, financially and otherwise.

Having lost everything I cared for, my home, my friends, my family, I didn't have anything left to lose. That was more important than my financial situation in shaping my attitude. I lost my fear of death; hence I didn't lean too far forward for anyone or anything. If good fortune came my way I calmly received it, and if not, I accepted misfortune with the same equanimity. My reaction when I ran out of food and money, and couldn't find work, was acceptance. If fate wanted to provide me with an opportunity I would take it, but I was not going to do anything that I thought was inappropriate, such as seeking public assistance. I was prepared to die.

Once you have reached that point all things are possible. Where do I stand now in my different circumstances? Living in the midst of the most important city in the world takes some grit. It's taken me a while to commit myself to it. What I find hard to handle is the social life. I'm afraid it will get out of control, that my needs will overwhelm my common sense. I am also afraid for my financial well being in spite of the fact that one [illegible]s thing after another has happened to save [illegible] afraid I will not succeed. I am afraid I [illegible]d and will blow it. Back then, I was operating from the center of my being, fears did not control me. I'm working very hard to get back to that safe place. I think of the artist and writer, Alex King who died rather than be operated on by a surgeon (the only surgeon who could perform the particular operation he needed.) The doctor did not want to take the time to get to know Alex before the surgery.

What's the sense of getting my life back through the callous actions of a moneygrubber, is what Alex thought.

Just got off the phone with a client, a woman with a degree in education, an MFA in art and a law degree. She has been trying to get work as a lawyer in DC for the past 12 years and has never been hired.

"They all want Harvard degrees and I don't have one," she says.

It's one problem after another that somehow stands in the way of her achieving love and/or meaningful work. She can't get a job teaching because her teaching certificate comes from another state and is not honored in DC. She would have to take a whole bunch of courses in order to be certified. She doesn't have a love life because her husband left her with a small baby to care for and no financial support, therefore she can't get help or childcare to go out and meet people. Etc. . etc. . .

"What about the art degree?"

"There's no money in that," she says.

"Shouldn't you have known that at the beginning."

"I thought I might teach, but that never came about."

You have failed me, she tells the world. And obviously it has, or she has failed it. Regardless, the message becomes the life lived.

And then two young girls: One of them, 17, is living with a 38-year-old woman at the woman's uncle's house. The girl's mother died a few years ago and she was sent to live with her father who molested her. Recently, he's been thrown in jail for dealing drugs and stepmother threw her out. Hence, her present situation with the older woman lover who [illegible] lost her apartment and is living with an [illegible] e woman is unstable and has a mean

The second girl is 18, presently living with her brother and his roommate. She was living with her boyfriend, but they broke up and she can't go home to Mom because Mom's boyfriend doesn't want her there. The situation with brother looks unsteady, but the worst of it is, it looks like she's pregnant. That's what scares her the most.

Will they survive? Of course, it's baptism by fire, going from one world to the next, one way of being to another. My life is a series of such desperate situations propelling me to new rooms, new experiences. Leaving Lincoln Street and my family to enter the convent at 6, running away at 14, pouring rain in the middle of the night to seek freedom and a life, escaping the chaos of my father's home to marry, the divorce followed by the life of the mind, New York and homelessness, entering the nether world of *being*.

One must suffer the shaman's death to cross over into a new existence.

A momentous day, I go down to the Supreme Court building, a serious enough structure where my bag and pockets are checked. *I get a queasy feeling about being in a building terrorists and loonies like to shoot up and bomb.*

The last time city government and I talked, I asked for food stamps and welfare. Today, I approach for an entirely different reason. The building is round. I think of the Pentagon or some such horrible place, lawyers scurrying in and out of doors. Down in the basement, I find room 117B. Shelves and shelves of old books and ledgers, I have walked into Dickens' world. At any moment I'm going to bump into Mr. Micawber. One woman works alone in this huge hall of ancient books.

"I've come to register my business name."

"You'll need to do a title search," she points me to a set of books.

The dreams and hopes of humanity are in those books, all the names of the businesses operating in NYC. I check to see if anyone has my name. No, it's mine.

With that information, I proceed to the next room. Another relic. This one is busier. I'm not the only petitioner. The woman who serves me looks at my business name and asks me what it means.

"What do you mean, 'what does it mean?' The first part is a phonetic pronunciation of my given French name and the second part is the French word for wolf."

"Write that down," she says.

"You did a title search?" Then she corrects herself, "As if there would be another Luhrenloup in the city!" she throws her hands up. But she types it in correctly, Luhrenloup, capping the two L's. A feeling of pride of ownership as I walk out the building.

Oh yeah, Manhattan? You ain't heard nothing yet!

I've also bought myself a credit card processor to accept electronic payments, and a serious sofa and winged-back easy chair for my counseling sessions. Money is good these days!

Buddha spent the night and left this noon with a raging toothache. He again spoke to me about marriage.

"You would have to know what you want for yourself, have some direction, a job, for anything like that to happen." I say.

I'm having woman problems, perhaps a yeast infection. That's never happened before. Derek can't see me, so it's Doctor Jayne at the Gay, Lesbian, Bisexual and Transgender clinic. Another Physician's Assistant, short young dyke, stocky, buzz cut hair dyed blond, but pleasant, soothing.

"Is it a yeast infection?"

"No, I don't think so." Her tentative diagnosis is Chlamydia, a sexually transmitted disease.

If this is true, I have caught it from Buddha. I get home and call an STD hotline to get more information. The counselor gives me the number of a clinic in Chelsea where I can go and be tested to find out if indeed I do have an STD. I am furious with Buddha coming home from my appointment. Once, just once, I let him enter me for less than a minute without a condom.

Just wanted to feel him inside of me.

Turns out the disease I've contracted from Buddha is Trichimoniasis. I've been given some medication along with a penicillin shot in case I have gonorrhea. The next morning my piss is black and my body's in shock from all the strong medication. I took the HIV test while I was at it and they tested me for syphilis and Chlamydia.

Later, I got really scared. What if the HIV test turns out positive? If I contracted trichimoniasis from Buddha who's to say I didn't get HIV? I don't sleep a wink all night.

Three days have gone by since my visit to the clinic and I am now in worst shape than when I went there. I call the STD hotline and the woman tells me most likely it's because of the medication that is very strong, or it could be that the disease has come back which sometimes occurs.

Walking in the streets, very little strength (I had to go out to get toilet paper. Imperative, since I have diarrhea every day.) I see black children with cornrows, *what is this world of strange folk I live amongst*?

I am in a world of foreigners, all of us alienated from each other. And then . . . I realize that New York is beautiful in spring. The trees in the park, the creamy tulips in front of the Jewish building, the patches of grass and the shrubs hugging the surrounding structures, all green and budding. I am serenaded by a song of hope and renewal from the birds in nearby trees.

Maybe I won't leave New York after all.

Buddha calls several days later and I tell him about the disease. He gets upset and hangs up. I don't want to see him and I certainly don't ever want to have sex with him again.

An old white beard Hassid stops in the street and asks if I am Jewish, then he reaches over and tries to kiss me. I recoil so he takes my hand and kisses it instead. An omen.

Back at the clinic I learn that I am not HIV positive and that trichimoniasis has not come back; life has given me a reprieve. The doctor tells me the medication that has made me sick will be out of my system in two weeks. Hopefully, I'll be able to start running again.

Walking out in the street afterward, the smell of clipped grass as a couple of lawn mowers drone on to the side of me; I'm acknowledged by the men who walk by. On the train, a skinny young black woman and her colleague address us. She's in grey tights, a tartan skirt and beret. *What a strong and cocky spirit!* They represent an organization for the homeless. I give a buck. I'm alive and I'm going to be OK; gotta spread the good energy around.

Buddha calls a couple of months later, at 8:30 in the morning. Then he calls several times during the day. He finally reaches me in the evening.

"How you doing?"

"OK."

"Are you still interested in me?"

"I'm not too sure anymore since what happened."

"I never had trichi . . . trichinosis. I went to my private doctor and he didn't find anything."

"That doctor is wrong!"

Oh, but he also saw another doctor who couldn't find anything wrong with him either. I won't buy it so he hangs up on me.

Then Bijou calls . . .

"I've got other plans."

Buddha comes over the next evening with some Chinese take-out and a big smile. He tells me that he loves me.

We are interrupted by a call from a personal client. A long call, but Buddha does not leave, shuffling from room to room, sitting and standing. After I hang up, I tell him to go, I need the sleep before my night on call. The next morning I discover that he has robbed me. My gold chain is gone along with the contents of my billfold, about $17, a couple of tokens, and whatever was in my change purse along with the purse itself. He took my camera too!

On a bathroom shelf is a birthday card I had once given him with my picture inside.

I'm sitting at the lunch counter by the Laundromat as the owner recounts how a teenager robbed him.

"How could you diss me like this when I was a friend to you and helped your family out?" he told the kid.

Another man comes in; apparently he's been robbed too. I feel even sadder after leaving them. I am barely able to get into my building before the heart cracks open.

How could you do this to me Buddha, I was your friend and I loved you?

THE TOWER

-XVI-

A man and woman have been forced to leap from high atop the tower where flames shoot out of turrets and open windows. Like rag dolls, their bodies float oafishly down to sea. Plumes of smoke crisscross their downward spiral, and billowing grey clouds above them swirl against a black sky.

The couple is scarcely out of harm's way when twin shafts of lightening strike at the tower from opposite directions. Years of neglect, debris and trash piled up the staircase, nourish the fat howling flames. Meanwhile, sea swells thrust up and seize our marionettes sucking them into the ocean's womb. Having fallen from such great heights, they will not recover the position of strength afforded by the tower.

Like those who've suffered through nature's disasters, they will be left with a sense of violation. Knowing there's nothing to be done and nothing to protect them, they will search for spiritual guidance. Meanwhile, fire roars through the tower; rings of smoke rise from its top as if the earth, quite humorously, is enjoying an after dinner cigar.

Upright: Losing one's assuredness in a false world; end of road.

Reversed: A change in one's life for the better;
freedom achieved at some cost.

> What a world uptown! Gee, I miss living among "folks." Honest, I do. I miss the energy too, the wolfishness. No wolves on the Lower East Side, mostly we've got prairie dogs, raccoons, possum and weasels. But I got wolf in me and it needs its pack at times.

I journeyed last night traveling to the upper world. At first I was not able to see the Eagle. I kept seeing other birds. Then several things happened. I was taken to view myself on my daily run. Eagle and I stood on a sheer cliff near its nest and together we flew off the cliff into the void. All I could see was sky with nothing under us as far as I looked. I felt tremendous joy flying in the great unknown. The last thing I was shown was a couple of reels of film in a wicker bag. *Make yourself strong* was the message, *learn to enjoy your ability to perform in situations that are unknowable.*

The reels of film? I don't know.

I have not kept you posted on 53's progress in the world. At present a copy of the script is being held and hopefully read by a woman in the West Village who has had it for 2 months. She told me she would not be able to get to it till after the holiday. Another agent midtown has had the script for almost a year, 10 months to be precise. I've given up on him. Four months ago his colleague informed me that the man was truly inundated with scripts and undoubtedly hadn't gotten to mine yet. The way I figure it, if the guy can't keep his affairs in better order than that, how can he properly represent mine? I just sent out query and sample chapter packages to several other agents hoping to seduce them.

At a ritual celebrated by New Moon/New York at the gay center, we were asked to think about our dreams, what we hoped for. I could think of nothing that is seriously out of balance. My life is heading in a good direction and if it continues on that path I'll be quite happy. I find it strange that I didn't think about getting my novel published. I have been lusting after that for so long and it never popped into my head!

Perhaps there is something wrong with that lust. I tell clients that they shouldn't want something (or someone,) more than it wants them. That rule applies in this situation too. If it's meant to be, so be it, and if not, I'll survive. My identity does not rest on it. The door will open when the time comes.

An old Farm friend drops by. I haven't seen Thyme since that summer we sheared trees together. She takes me to dinner at Boca Chica in the East Village, an enlightening encounter. I become aware when she first sits down with me how I've changed since the last time we were together. I have become a sophisticated New Yorker.

This perception of myself as a Manhattanite with its style and appetites creeps into my mind and I become more and more committed to that life. A lot of doors are closing in the process.

Thyme is just back from California having bought herself a $700 car. She's threatening to move up here for good, is talking about moving back to Jersey, out in the country. Sounds like a fairy tale.

When I first met her she was traveling across country in a truck with a camper top on it, going from one feminist or lesbian colony to another. She had left some blood-sucking girlfriend behind in California along with an apartment, a car, and a houseful of furniture. The girl's got a lot of wanderlust in her. She supports her life by the gracious generosity of the federal government through its SSI program.

I had her over for dinner last night -- garlic mussels with pasta. She's had it with lesbians and their Nazi system of bigotry against all things tainted with heterosexuality.

When I was in college one of my professors, whose name I've forgotten, gave us a test, a psychological evaluation that measured the relative levels of femininity to androgyny that one fell on in his scale. The word androgyny at that time could be equated to domineering, power hungry, bull dyke, virago. I scored very high in that category, and the professor who had taken an immediate dislike to me, agreed vociferously with the label.

What did it mean? I certainly didn't think I was unfeminine. My independence had obviously pushed me over the gender barrier. I was thinking and behaving in ways considered leaning towards masculinity. In my femininity there is also the wolf. I look out the window of my apartment and see a beautiful, tall and lithe, black woman walk by. She is sleek like a tiger and I want to possess her, want to feel her long chocolate legs on my back as I kiss the center of her beauty.

Kate invites us to the Farm. Thyme demurs (Kate was mean to her because she wouldn't work or commit herself at the Farm.) We are to celebrate Obon, a Japanese ritual for departed souls. The Farm's colonists have built a quasi-raft/small boat that is piled with wood and twigs to be set aflame at the appropriate moment. At the Friday evening dinner colonists and invited guests (friends of the Farm and former colonists) are asked to scribble their one wish on pieces of paper, and these also will be tucked in between the chunks of wood on the boat.

But first, we have champagne sitting around Kate's bed in her studio in the Blue Barn, champagne and munchies and first introductions. "The kids" as I tend to think of present colonists regardless of their age, are a good bunch this year.

Mellow, know pretty much who they are, a few "I am coming out as a human being" types for whom this is a first experience of living close to nature, working in fields, being part of an artistic community. There's not much outside interference so that one has lots of time to think about oneself in a serious way. These dozen mainliners who are getting a full dose and walk around starry-eyed are the Farm's best crop.

Friday night dinners are the finest. There are new people visiting, new ideas, lots of talk. We eat at a long table on the deck of the Lavender House. Serving dishes travel every which way, red wine flows freely and conversation carries late into the night stoked by after-dinner coffee. On this evening there is a delicious chocolate cake with ice cream and, as the pens and notepaper are passed around for us to write down our wish, I ask for more chocolate in my life, but more than that, I ask for the ability to discern what is chocolate, and what isn't.

The following day, I head for the pond and try out the kayak I've been eyeing the last few times I've been here. It's been a while since I've done any rowing so it's a bit of work maneuvering it, but I manage without crashing into the shore, or the island. Afterward, I head for the fields. I walk and walk and all I see is Christmas trees, no houses or people. Just nature and me, and of course, magic. I gather some wild flowers to place in the houses. In late afternoon we make our own individual boats that will travel alongside the big one. Ours are made with a six-inch plank of wood from which protrudes four little posts one at each corner. A nail has been driven through the center of the boat to hold a votive candle and blue tissue paper is wrapped and stapled round the four posts. When the candle is lit, it casts a blue glow on the water.

After dinner and toasts to the Farm's 19th year and remembrances of those who've contributed to it, we head down to the pond to launch our battalion. As it happens this year, one of the colonists is a competitive swimmer and Kate asks if she will bring out the big boat to the middle of the pond and set it ablaze. The word Charon comes to mind as I watch the swimmer maneuver our funeral pyre, which is alive with darting tongues of fire, to the center of the pond. Across the river Styx did the hideous old Charon ferry the spirits of the dead. I am sitting on the quay when the pond pulls me in and I fall up to my waist while attempting to launch one of the small boats. I take off my wet clothes and jump in, swimming up to the blue boats to help them along toward the pond's center. We sit around for a long time afterward watching flames eat up the big boat surrounded by our glowing blue lanterns. A shearing season has come to an end and this year's colonists will leave one or two at a time in the next few days.

I spend Sunday morning in the recording studio making a tape of some of my poems. Afterward, I take a last walk in the fields where I pick some goldenrod, Queen Anne's lace and loose strife to bring back to the city. Commuters turn to look at the big bouquet of wild flowers peering out of my bag on the jaded subways of Manhattan evening.

Bijou calls and apologizes for the break-up mess. His call interrupts my writing session. I am working on the novel, the part where her father is abandoning Diana and my emotions are raw.

"No, this is no good," I tell him. "I don't want the hiding, the sneaking business," and then I cry.

"I'm sorry that I hurt your feelings," he says, and hangs up.

Two days later at 11:30 at night, he calls from his home, says he misses me terribly, tells me he loves me and doesn't want to lose me. Nothing's resolved. I knew before he called he was coming over. I had presentiments of it all day, putting fresh sheets on the bed, taking out my Chinese-red nightgown. Nothing has changed, except our desire for each other grows stronger. He doesn't want the relationship to end and I don't want it to end either. I can't see continuing it as it stands now. We'll shortly come to the same impasse.

Sitting in the tub mulling over my options -- *He should accept some responsibility in the relationship.*

Over dinner on Friday night at the appropriately named, La Frontière, I bring up the subject, "I want you to take care of me, to provide some financial assistance."

"I'm afraid that I'll be thinking about you all the time and won't be able to be effective at home," he says.

It starts to rain during dinner and afterward we wait underneath the awning for it to clear up. I sit at one of the patio chairs watching fat drops of rain wash away the day's fatigue while Bijou talks to the chef who's joined us. They speak about wines, easy talk between connoisseurs. The chef bids us farewell when the rain lets up and I take a cab home.

The next weekend, he takes me out for a lobster brunch with champagne and he buys me a summer hat I coveted. This is followed by a visit at end of my shift the following night. We immediately fall into making love. Our times together are spent eating in restaurants, or in bed. Oh, and there's music too. Then we talk about what's happening to us in the relationship.

Afterward we break up.

Between the heart and the head, a mighty ocean roars. My relationship with Bijou crumbles by the minute. I'm on edge knowing the final break-up is coming, tearful one moment and off on a jaunt the next. It hurts and I feel like I'm walking around with an open wound. The heart goes through its seasons and there's not much to be done.

I'm moving. Money is good and it's time for an upgrade. I haven't yet found another apartment, but I'm looking. Things have changed dramatically since I did this four years ago. It took me a week to figure out the business where you ran out to the Astor Place Newsstand (the first stand to receive fresh copies of the Village Voice,) at 7 pm on Tuesday, but it's no longer valid. Our desperate bunch would wait in line for the real estate listings so we could be first in the morning to get to the agent. A ruthless bunch determined to get an apartment, no matter what. I was pretty desperate back then, my things in storage, living at Kate's loft with the Dexedrine cats while looking for an apartment. These were my first hard lessons about the real estate business of New York City. My naiveté was such that I assumed I would find a rent in a week or so.

A grad student back then, not a good prospect. What's worse, Sarah Lawrence had messed my financial aid papers so badly that I was reported delinquent to credit bureaus.

Both Kate and the Dexedrine cats were making my life miserable; I wanted out, and they wanted me out. So I found this apartment, which is not without problems, but it has served my purpose well. There are so many horror stories in New York about landlords and their tenants that I do not consider myself misused by mine. Zinni's scam involves fixing nothing until a tenant leaves (she even told me I could leave whenever I wanted in spite of the lease.) That way she's allowed to increase the rent on the stabilized apartment by a sizable chunk every time someone moves out inching it closer to the magic number that deregulates the apartment to free market status. Then Zinni can charge what she wants for it. Things wear out? She buys the cheapest, most inappropriate materials then hires inexperienced immigrants to perform the work.

The hallway is filthy and deteriorating badly; they sweep up 4 times a year. A couple of weeks ago, someone got into the building and waited in the dark; a young woman returning home was assaulted and held up at gunpoint. The following week our front door was busted open with a crowbar by the fire department in order to get to the back of the building next to ours; since there is no buzzer system, they had no choice but to break it. The door remained unfixed for 5 days while Antonia searched the immigrant community for someone to fix it on the cheap. Strange, desperate people came knocking at my door.

But my studio has been nurturing. This is where I started my business, where I came to understand that my writing and spiritual life are not separate, that having combined the two in a formal, professional way has enriched both; here is where I purchased a modem and embarked on a creative journey through the internet; here I connected with other downtown writers. I have walked these streets many nights and crowded days, shared a life with people whose language I don't speak, whose customs and beliefs I don't share. We were never strangers. It was my home.

And now it starts again. You don't have to rush over to the Astor Place Newsstand on Tuesday night anymore. Both the Times and the Voice place their real estate listings on the Internet way before their papers hit the streets. Rent seekers have been turned from warriors filching ads to be ready at the crack of dawn, to nerds at the computer tapping busily away. It looks like what I want, a studio preferably two rooms in a good neighborhood downtown, is going to cost me about $300 dollars more than I can afford, but hey, what's life without a challenge.

To find my dream apartment, I must tune in to the Eagle; enter the realm of magic, bearing in mind that what I want may be different than what the Spirit believes is correct for me, i.e. nourishing, challenging. Never mind the beautiful pre-war buildings I lust after, and my fantasy garden in the backyard. My list of absolute minimum requirements are: 1), a respectable looking building with attractive entry, stairs and landings, 2) on a residential street and 3), sans spray painted decor. Oh, and I forgot, 4) nothing above 14th Street.

Whenever I'm about to make a change, a certain way of being takes over and I become powerfully psychic; I am a warrior, focused on my task. I know immediately when I am with a person I can connect with. Without that connection success is not possible. I can't explain it better than to say it is a bodily energy, as opposed to mental or emotional, that travels between people. I also have this connection with animals and birds. They flock around me, give me the message.

The other morning after cocoa, I put on my robe and flip-flops to go down and get the mail. As I step out of my door something that had been huddling near the crack runs out, grazing my left leg. Aaaagghh! A rat! A huge fucking New York rat! I jump back into the apartment quick as a heartbeat and slam the door; the rat running like its ass is on fire. Of course I can't stay in this place. This is not the first time an animal comes up and huddles near my door; two cats did the same thing. Of all the doors in my building they choose mine. Do not mess with the Spirit. If you make a commitment to move, follow through, is the message Mr. Rat came to deliver. There are some pitfalls to having psychic energy.

Kate's got her own rent problems. City government owns the property where she lives and wants to tear the down building in order to put up housing for middle income and poor people. All the good lefties in City Council voted in favor of this new housing as being good for their community. Kate's building has four gargantuan lofts and a warehouse on the ground floor. She has two of the lofts, an old girlfriend has another and there's the tattoo guy on the floor between them. She got these lofts at some benign time when New York City was kind to artists. I'm sure she cut a few corners to end up with two of them.

Kate thought she could protect her building by having the place named an historic site by the Landmark Preservation Committee. (Apparently, a group of prostitutes inhabited the building long ago. They committed suicide swallowing caustic poison.) That's not going to work. And now she's threatening to chain herself to the front door if all else fails. What is sad about this situation is that she doesn't understand how outrageous her demands are. She expects to get sympathy for her plight, she, who is living in a 2000 square foot loft with exposure on three sides, and great views of the city. What's more, she has another loft just like it where she creates her sculptures. In a city of 8 million, people choose their priorities stringently when it comes to handing out sympathy. Having seen quite a few studios of 120 square feet go for outrageous money, no more than a prisoner's cell, and people jump at these apartments, I can appreciate how the tide is turning against her on this one.

I've been following her troubles in the press as I look for my own apartment. There was a sympathetic piece in the NY Observer written by one of her friends. The Voice was not as generous, juxtaposing Kate's blaming Giuliani's greed for her troubles, in the context of her right to two enormous lofts. Others interviewed for the piece bring up her 67-acre farm in Poughkeepsie and how the city has been subsidizing her for years.

In a curious way Kate's apartment troubles and my quest for a new home is reflective of our relationship. As a woman who's writing career was in its raw beginnings, I was thrilled for the opportunity to expand, to meet someone in the field who could surely show me a few tricks. The Farm was not free. We had to pay board and room and were expected to work 5 days a week in the fields, for five hours each morning. I felt I had gone as far as I could as a writer back home. What's more,

I could see my fellow writers as not being serious about their commitment to their art. Kate impressed me from the first. She worked from morning until night, out in the fields with us, working in her silk screen studio, constant phone ringing, piles of mail to be answered, speaking engagements and the never ending task of keeping her name current in circles of power.

She was insatiable and manipulative. No matter what we did, it was never enough. She always tried to get more out of us than the required 5 hours. Some people began to see the Farm not as an art colony, but Kate's preserve. The colonists were just this year's fodder, or as Kate often called us, "the volunteers" in her life.

I didn't care. If she was using others to maintain her lifestyle, so be it. I worked every day in the fields, brutal, exhausting work, shearing and shaping Christmas trees, my body covered with poison ivy and thousands of needle pricks from tree branches, sun-beating temperatures that very often rose well above 100° before noon, wild flowers all around, hawks circling in the sky. After work a quick, naked jump in the pond, followed by a communal lunch and then an afternoon of writing. I felt I got my money's worth. I went back home finished up whatever needed to be done and the following summer moved to New York.

She admired me and was fond of me so she kept me on the fringes of her circle of "friends." I spent Christmas Eves at her loft having dinner and exchanging gifts. But now, we are moving away from each other. It began when I started to make my own way artistically. I do love Kate and will never forget how she came to my rescue when I needed it. I would do anything to help her if she were in trouble, but as things stand now we are heading for different playing fields. I find my life more interesting than hers.

I wish her good energy in her fight with the city, and by that I mean the energy to do what is correct for all involved.

Up early every morning. Get out there and run, get back in and start on the apartment listings! Three weeks left before I'm out of here and I still haven't found an apartment. Tick, tick, tick, tick . . .

I decide to widen my search and include the Upper East Side (UES), Grammercy Park, etc., lots of studios on the UES. *Dull.* But I see a listing for a nice big studio with lots of sunshine and a private entrance.

Private Entrance? Hmm, good for clients!

The agent makes an appointment for me to see it the next day. Considering how fast these places go, the man seems decidedly laid back. That very day, I am free for a few hours, and go to look at the apartment on my own. From what the agent told me, and my knowledge of the neighborhood, I can pretty well figure out where it is. Riding up on the 3rd Avenue bus to the 40's, 50's, 60's, 70's, I am back in the white world. Chic little boutiques, gourmet markets scattered like small pearls on a brooch throughout the area, top rated New York restaurants, flowering trees in bloom up and down the streets, daffodils, tulips in a profusion of colors. I am close to tears at the beauty and grace. Most of the pre-war buildings are quite elegant with great entrances and huge big windows.

Why, oh why did I ever find this world dull?

The building that houses the apartment I've come to see is an anomaly, a small 2-story structure with a tailor shop on the 1st floor and the door to an upstairs apartment on the left. From the street, I can see the front of it is almost all windows with a small balcony in front.

Once the tailor shop closes at 5 or 6, a person has the building to herself, I presume.

At the end of the street is Carl Schurz Park, one of New York's prettiest, bordering the East River, its valleys and bluffs crisscrossed by a network of flagstone bridges, stairs and arches, courts for children, for dogs, for big guys, hundreds of bulbs, roses, flowering shrubs, large well tended lawns, an esplanade by the river. Gracie Mansion, the mayor's house abuts its northern end.

The next morning I call the agent to confirm our 2 o'clock appointment, leaving my name and number on his machine. Twice. He never calls back.

I get a call and apology the following day from the agent who's hurt his knee.

Hmm! "You better be limping when I see you."

We make an appointment for the next morning to view the place, and he is limping. *Yes,* I decide when I approach him, *good energy. This man will find me an apartment.*

The studio turns out to be lovely, but so small my furniture won't all fit in it. So small, I feel trapped, choked. The circuitous stairs leading up to it increase my claustrophobia.

"Let me show you a better apartment," he says.

We get to another building, a walk-up. Traipsing through a narrow carpeted hall with doors on each side, I decide, without seeing the apartment -- *This is not for me.*

"I want the studio." I tell him.

The rest of the day is spent meeting with the owner of the realty company who will close the deal; he checks my credit with one of the bureaus, makes a copy of my driver's license, asks me to bring him two certified checks, one for his fee, and one including the deposit and first month's rent for the landlord. He wants part of his fee in cash, $500; he wants a copy of my certificate of deposit; he wants copies of recent statements from my personal checking account, my business account and two canceled rent checks of my present apartment. It takes me most of the day riding trains and buses, with a pastrami sandwich and a coffee on the run, to get all this done, the papers are signed and I now have an apartment on the Upper East Side.

Let's see, what is it I had asked for? My list of requirements were, 1), a respectable looking building with attractive entry, stairs and landings on, 2) a residential street and 3), sans spray painted decor. Oh, and I forgot 4), nothing above 14th Street. Three out of four ain't bad. Instead of the funk downtown, I get to have a front room for my clients, and my own private entrance in a building that is essentially mine most of the time. In Manhattan!

Trust the Spirit, it works every time.

THE STAR

-XVII-

Breasts, thighs, a small protruding belly, the naked woman kneels one leg to the land while her other foot is planted in the stream before her. She pours water into the brook from a blue pitcher she holds in one hand, while also nourishing the earth with water that she pours from a red pitcher. There is a large golden star, directly above, shining down on her. Its cool white light seeps into the earth and into the woman's belly, inseminating both.

From the back of her head emerges, like a set of antlers, a chevron of smaller stars reminding one of the mysterious horned figure in the cave at Lascaux. Deep underground, beyond the eye of careless onlookers, dressed in hooves and tail, the shaman performs his ritual, seeking the good hunt, plentiful bison for the long winter.

Star Woman is unguarded. Her horns are nature's own heavenly bodies. She too seeks to uncover the mysteries of nature, calling forth the spirits of fertility and congress, melding one element with another. This ritual of ablution and fertility occurs in the dark, in the cool night air where a red bird perched in a nearby tree is witness to the marriage of opposites. Such a blissfully peaceful face, one wants to make love to her perfect body, to fuse one's essence with the night, the earth and the waters.

Upright: Fertility, mystery, completion; finding inner light.

Reversed: Working against one's best interests.

Moving is an interesting process. You become almost feral as you devote yourself daily to packing. At night, I canvass the neighborhood for boxes. Lots of boxes in Chinatown, I look for big ones to pack the electronic equipment. My colleagues on these jaunts are people who collect bottles from trash, those who pick the spotted fruit vendors throw out; we are roamers of the night rummaging through life's detritus. Home being taken apart every day till all there is left is a bunch of boxes in a gutted flat. My emotional commitment, which was not strong at first, increases the closer I come to my goal. It takes a week to get everything ready, working till midnight with last minute things to pack. The moving crew arrives the next morning at 7:30; I have slept 3 hours.

And then comes the horror of the move itself. No doubt, stuff gets damaged. Once everything is in the studio, the boxes are lined up like skyscrapers on the floor and furniture. I'm able to find a wee spot to open up the love seat and crash. It is evening when I awake to what looks like a storage room.

Gotta get some air!

I make my way through the maze of boxes and out the street door that I close, but presumably don't lock. A one-way street, apartment buildings, a presbytery, a Catholic Church plus school to my left, and trees, trees, trees, up and down the street.

It's going to take me at least 6 months to get the apartment in order. Major shelf building chores ahead of me!

A cool night, not a soul on the street, *Hello neighbors, my name is Lorraine. I've come with an open heart, ready to offer my talents, to be of service to our community.*

I will start unpacking the toiletries, a pot to boil water for tea immediately . . .

Oh god, I have locked myself out!

After much hand wringing and babbling I connect with the Yemeni guy at the corner convenient store who loans me his ladder. It doesn't quite reach the balcony, and grasping courage by the handrail, I haul myself up to it, throw one leg over its side and I'm up!

I bring the ladder back to Yasir, rambling on about my adventure, hands still shaking from the experience as I pace back and forth; he is taking this in somewhat amazed and offers me a Dove ice cream bar as reward for my act of courage. I have made my first friend.

Since I do not believe in the possibility of accidents, I have to ask myself, *What is the meaning of locking myself out of my apartment? Is it a warning?*

The next morning, I clear a work area, set up my desks, my filing cabinet and the electronic media of computer, printer, modem, credit card authorization machine, my phones, and I'm back in business. Later, I take my bruised and battered body to my hair stylist for some much needed pampering. Afterward, I have lunch at Dan Maxwell's steak house in my new neighborhood, mussels cooked in a white wine bouillon and then a steak with red wine. An ecumenical meal, as they say "surf & turf," the mussels velvety and sensuous like a woman's vulva, the steak, bloody, red, from a bull. Good food, reasonably priced and the wait staff, friendly and helpful.

On my second day in my new surroundings I head straight for the park. I'm in culture shock and

I am happy to be here. Later, I become fearful in bed at night.

Someone could break in and I'd never see him till he was half way up the winding stairs; since there is only one exit I would be trapped, my only escape through a window to the balcony, and a bone smashing jump to the concrete pavement below.

Mostly I attribute this fear to my claustrophobia in the small studio. I have, since moving to New York, had a number of nightmares where I am overwhelmed, trapped, suffocating, trampled. There's a presence in the apartment, things fall for no logical reason, or they disappear. One day, coming back from market, I enter the building, place my key in the studio lock -- *it won't open.* Feels as if someone on the other side is messing with the lock. I try it again and get it unlocked on the second attempt, but someone on the other side is pushing against the door, then a release and I hear footsteps running up the stairs.

I get the door open and enter -- *A psychic force inhabits my apartment.* I take these events, the locked doors, the missing or damaged objects as omens. I entered the city under similar circumstances. There again, entry was denied. In both cases, I am challenged, as if the Spirit, knowing of the adventure ahead, wants to point it out to me. I'm forced into an emotional response that weds me to the situation like a lover to her paramour.

Yes, I rise to the challenge, and will do what needs to be done to claim this city, this apartment.

In my current metamorphosis from downtown girl to East Side seeress, I check out the neighborhood. When I signed the lease for my new apartment I asked my broker, who also lives nearby if he knew of a place where I could go for a celebratory drink. Cronies, where at a later date the then married Mayor Giuliani and his secret lover Judi are exposed by the press having a romantic little dinner, is his suggestion. I sit next to an older, florid, somewhat flamboyant, couple at the bar. They are entertaining a younger man with stories about horses, adventures and near disasters they've encountered on their journey through life. To my right a sophisticated fortyish twosome are eating oysters and whispering conspiratorially. I like to believe it's about their love for each other.

Taking in the scene, sipping on my red wine, the barman, a young, good-looking guy, brings me the tabloid paper someone left behind. I nod in appreciation, but I don't read it. The waiters are hanging out by the kitchen door at a quiet moment before the evening customers have them hopping. Cronies is a big restaurant. The decor is traditional New York, mahogany wood behind the bar, etched glass, white linen on the tables, huge bouquets of flowers -- muted. I order some munchies. Good food but lacks imagination. The owner is not interested in flash. Making a steady income from the neighbors seems a more important goal.

At the end of my first week, after I've chased all over creation to accomplish my errands, and a full half hour before my laundry has been promised to be ready for me, I come across Fionna's, an Irish bar around the corner from my apartment. I've seen their board on the sidewalk advertising "soccer nights." Jocks, I thought, people who watch games on TV and get rowdy. They have opened the front, which is all doors, and one can see the complete rectangle of restaurant and bar, a small place, polished, with good ambiance. I enter, take a seat at the bar and am served by an older gentleman, yes, gentleman, white hair, good build, friendly, gallant. Mom, Dad, and their little girl come in and join us. Everybody makes a fuss over the girl, which they all seem to know. Some man sits next to the opened doors with the Wall Street Journal splayed out in front of him, but he's not looking at it. Rather, he is smoking a big cigar and holding forth to his neighbors, right and left.

The smell of that cigar wafting in my direction brings with it vivid memories of my father at his club probably smoking that very brand and drinking Seagram's on the rocks, a social animal in his realm. Someone from the kitchen brings baskets of freshly made potato chips and places them before us. Finding the right bar, where the company is interesting and one can be at ease is a blessing. My father would have been right at home at Fionna's.

I can't believe my luck; I have the luxury, in New York City, of having my own front door, of being a recognized neighbor, somewhat like a property owner.

I've given some thought to the people who will come seeking counsel, and the kind of energy I want to create in the apartment. If driving across America is a rite of passage, arriving in Mexico was transcendence for me, as I discovered that my assumptions about life were just an ignorant arrogance born of a narrow worldview. Here were a people who did not share my assumptions, a sensuous folk whose artwork, on the sides of buildings, in the park, the highway, surrounded them.

I met Miguelangel in Vera Cruz. We had a drink and after a bit of conversation, I realized that with culture shock I was wide open to the world, and spoke more freely because of it. We spent several days Mexico City before I left the country, those last hours, talking, talking. It was as if, knowing I would never see him again, I wanted to share every bit of knowledge I had about the world that could be of help to him in his life, and he did similarly. I left Mexico with the thought that meeting someone like Miguel back home was akin to winning the tri-state power-ball lottery.

Mexico has come to represent true conversation, an open mind and heart for me. My

House of Spirits shall be decorated in Mexican shades of burnt orange, deep yellow, and ochre, the colors of the earth.

I get my first telephone bill and discover there are 5 long distance calls attributed to me amounting to $210.

"That's not possible," I say, "I don't know a single person in Des Moines. I'm not paying for the calls."

After deciding against paying it, I spend long hours pushing buttons on the phone, forced to endure inane music, or speak to people working at jobs they despise, who more often than not do not follow through on their word and months go by in which I donate a great deal more than the $210 of my precious time getting the matter straightened out.

How to live in the modern world for anyone of intelligence and sensitivity takes a certain amount of stamina and willfulness. Think of the Luddites in the eighteenth century smashing machinery they believed were turning us all into miserable automatons tied to mechanistic monsters, or more recently the unabomber sending his deadly packages to prominent technological researchers and professors. He saw technology as reducing the human race to passive bovine creatures grazing in the fields. And he was especially worried about cloning and other human manipulations.

It is much worse than they imagined. What is really killing us is not technology but technique, the means and ways developed wherein we interact with technology and acquire services. Example: The police have guns. There is a technique for the operation of these guns. Amadou Diallo, an innocent young African immigrant in New York, gets shot 41 times in the lobby of his apartment building. At the trial a professor, expert in police procedures, avows that the officers applied the correct technique taught to them at the police academy. They behaved appropriately under the circumstances.

I could in a huff, leave the company, but that is only the workings of pride. They all employ the same techniques and I could possibly jump from the frying pan into the fire. All the loopholes have been plugged. The method by which services or products are delivered is what's killing us. What with computers, faxes, the Internet, we will surely be buried by technique. How many times do you face some officious bureaucrat, or civil servant who tells you about something you have to perform or acquire which on the face of it is utterly nonsensical, and when you point out the ludicrousness of their demand, they simply reiterate: *That's the rules; I don't make them.*

One has no choice but to go through the charade feeling powerless and humiliated. How often can one go through such experiences without losing some fundamental integrity? Technique is not answerable to individual scenarios. We are eating cardboard tomatoes because a technique has been found wherein red tomatoes can be presented to the supermarket in the dead of winter.

There comes a time, for whatever reason one chooses, that a line is drawn in the sand.

I have invested too much of myself, or my money to retreat. I stand my ground. I will not pay the 210 dollars!

Having done so, I am now on the outside looking in, in the dark. There is no technique to assist me. I am dismissed as a crank, or worse, unbalanced, a troublemaker.

Get with the program!

But I don't. I enter the realm of magic. Magic is also a technique wherein I play by different rules. I become super vigilant, like an animal in the forest. I hear every noise, perceive all unusual movement; I understand that the world speaks to me in ways I hardly pay attention to when I am grazing contentedly in the fields. I am most alive at such times, living in the present. The cold wind bites at my cheeks, I look directly into people's eyes. They see the hunter in me and pay homage. I am the wolf.

THE MOON

-XVIII-

A large low moon the color of fresh cream, thick and silky, straddles the countryside's horizon. On either side of it, like gate-keeping sentinels, stand massive stone towers. The invitation to enter a dream unfolds like the footpath bisecting the two fortresses. At the beginning of the lane a purple crayfish, claws distended, reaches up out of its pond. The buttery planet seems so close to earth, one could almost walk up the winding foot path and reach out to grab it like the crayfish is attempting to do, leaning to it, surrendering to that force.

Part way along the path, a dog bays at the moon. Its cousin, the wolf, on the other side, howls with abandon. Like some prehistoric crayfish, the dreamer envisions a world turned inside out. In it, the dog's allegiance and the wolf's voracious appetite carry equal baffling weight.

Lunatics, those moon struck individuals, are afloat in this realm of symbols. Every action, every word is freighted with arcane significance. Having traveled beyond the towers, the somnambulist delves deeper and deeper into the mystery till a loosening occurs, a derangement.

Upright: Approaching the dark night, the incomprehensible.

Reversed: Clarity after a period of confusion.

I have received a contract from an agent asking to represent me. He loves 53's story and thinks there's a movie in it. This is my first business dealing with an agent, an older man, sweet, courtly.

When I read the contract and realize that I am entrusting my beloved property to another human being for the expanse of two years, it gives me pause. I, who have faced the world and taken care of myself for lo these many years, am taken aback. I put the contract aside for a bit to consider this matter.

As I sit contemplating a two-year commitment, from the window I see the Catholic Church's doors debouch and out pours a bridal party. Since this is New York, most of the women are dressed in black, long gowns, very chic, the men in tuxedos. The bride (she's in white) and groom stand on the church steps surrounded by their guests. Having crossed the divide into commitment, there's a stillness about them holding hands amidst the hoopla. They smile for the camera, and soon they are shuffled off to a cream colored limousine.

My agent has included a note along with the contract. He will need three more copies of the manuscript. He also has a bunch of questions about my professional versus given name. He requests appropriate title pages that favor his agency, and he wants to know if I'm at work on another novel. Ambitious man. The first thing to be done is to respond to his note. Once that's completed, I walk over to Barnes & Nobles to research the appropriate form of the title page once one is represented by an agency. I'm doing these things on an "as if" basis. As if I have accepted him, *but I really want to sleep on this.*

Back home at 6 pm, I start printing the scripts he requested. Printing 3 novel manuscripts each containing 13 chapters is a big job that takes me till 1:30 in the morning to complete. Halfway through the evening I realize there's no waiting till morning, I've already decided what my answer is, or I wouldn't be going through all this work. I sign the contract, include my note and seal it in an envelope with a love stamp on it.

Malcolm Gladwell wrote an interesting article in the New Yorker about failure. In it he posits two descriptions of failure, choking and panic. Learning skills generally occurs on two levels, explicit and implicit. For example, one learns to write a check by following the example provided by the bank or the company where the checks were bought. Carefully, one indicates the date, the amount in numbers and in script, being mindful to draw a line after the script so no one can change the amount, signing it, including a notation as to the purpose of the check. In a few months, this process is hardly thought of as one goes about one's business. Whereas, one explicitly sets out to learn how to write checks, implicit learning takes over after one has accomplished the task a number of times. It becomes second nature.

Choking in the phenomena of failure occurs because implicit learning fails to kick in. Say you're taking a test about material you know inside out. The test is important and a prerequisite to advancement in your career. You sit at your desk and look over the exam papers; the questions are about material you know well, but you cannot for the life of you formulate answers, your mind working like a washing machine set on the spin cycle. You simply keep looking at the paper in front of you . . choked. Under less pressured circumstances implicit learning would kick in and the test would be easily completed.

Failure attributed to panic is the opposite of choking. Whereas, in the former situation one's mind spins with a million inappropriate thoughts, there is a perceptual narrowing in panic. Only one thought dominates, one solution, excluding other more viable options. A musician friend provided me with his example. He had an audition with a prestigious symphony. Preparing for his audition, he focused solely on his ability to carry it off with calm and grace. He was so anxious that his fear would overwhelm him that he did not give enough attention to his music.

"The only thing I could think of throughout the audition was that I should look at ease. Over and over again, the thought reverberated through my head."

I am a choker. In moments of stress I freeze, cannot remember the most basic facts of my existence, the name of the president, what I had for breakfast, my street address. Many years ago in college when I entered therapy, I had a dream that assesses this choking phenomenon:

> I, along with a group of women, am standing at the foot of a spiral staircase looking up. We are dressed in formal gowns awaiting the men coming down the stairs. And when they do, we all pair off and enter the dining room. Four of us sit at my table; I am wearing a smart neckerchief (my choker) that I remove and proceed to ingest. Then I get up and walk out to the lobby where nuns are running a concession stand that sell lemons.

Bitter fruit indeed, what the dream conveys, not too subtly, is that I've been indoctrinated to believe whatever nourishment and rewards I am to receive in life will come down through figures of authority. I've been taught to obey. And my attempt at rebellion even furthers my submission by incorporating it in me (eating the choker.) Outside of this world of obedience, the nuns point out is bitterness and negation.

Fear of rejection chokes me up every time.

My Upper East Side apartment has placed me in a situation to cure that fear. I am developing serious enemies. The tailor below me attempts to place a sign advertising the replacement of watch batteries, attaching it to my balcony and blocking my view of First Ave. When I call the landlord to put a stop to it, he tells me to resolve it myself. I make a lot of noise overwhelming the tailor and his sign maker. They are nasty with me, but I hold my ground and the sign is removed.

Thus begins a never-ending battle. The man sees himself as the building's primary tenant because most renters, apparently, do not stay long in my apartment. (Does he drive them away?) He works 7 days a week from 8 in the morning till 9 at night, 365 days a year; Christmas, Thanksgiving, New Year, nothing stops him. Not that he works during this time, mostly he hangs in front of his shop gossiping with passersby.

A petty man who delights in causing trouble, he sets about to make my situation untenable, I find feces smeared at my entrance, or rotting food. He dumps water in the business card holder I've installed next to my door. There are mouse droppings and a nest in it one morning. Friends and clients receive glowering stares at my door, and he regales the neighborhood with stories about what a bad person I am. If I try to talk to him about our situation, he will stop passersby to inveigle them in our discussion. Obsessed, he's constantly on the lookout for my every movement, who I talk to, my deliveries.

And then there's the Pigeon Lady.

I go out to speak to her about the fleas I'm getting inside my apartment from her feeding the pigeons across the street.

"Who cares!" she says.

I contact four, five agencies to put an end to her feedings, to no avail. So I figure I'm on my own with the problem. The next time I see her out spreading her seeds I go out with a broom and dustpan.

All hell breaks loose.

She grabs hold of my broom and will not let go. This tug of war goes on for over a half hour, grabbing hold of my dustpan, overturning the city trashcans where I have deposited her bird feed. A crowd gathers on each side of the street. At some point, a man comes over to send her away and he bangs on the broom to make her let go. She throws herself on the ground and tries to blame him for it. Most of the people in the neighborhood do not want her feeding birds. It is dangerous, filthy, and attracts rodents.

Thankfully, someone finally calls the police. I feel like I'm in the middle of an Italian opera. When they arrive, I don't have to say a word in my defense, neighborhood women from the crowd explain the situation for me.

"Let go of the broom," the officers tell her.

"Who do you think you are?" she says.

One of the officers gets right up to her face and screams, "LET GO OF THE BROOM!"

She drops it real quick, and I proceed with my clean-up job, so upset, my body is shaking. I can hear her screaming in the background.

"I have the mayor's permission for what I'm doing. Furthermore, the sanitation department has given me their blessing."

The police have had dealings with this woman before and they don't buy any of her stories.

"Don't come back here," they tell her. "You want to feed the birds? Go to the park."

I hang around the corner till she leaves fearing she will find out where I live. I'm freezing in my sleeveless shirt and leggings so decide to walk around the block figuring she'll be gone by the time I come back. She's not. Spotting the business card holder outside my door, she takes one and the calls start coming in. Thankfully, I am able to screen them with caller ID. The following morning, I march down to the police station to file a complaint against her, and I also ask about getting a protection order. That might keep her out of the neighborhood. I can't get a protection order until I am assigned a case number. A detective will call me. I get the case number and head downtown to Criminal Court to get my protection order. No dice, she will have to be arrested in order for me to get that order.

Meanwhile the Pigeon Lady calls me several times a day and has gone back to feeding the birds across the street. She walks by my apartment, a bevy of birds hovering above her head. *The queen and her retinue!* I go back out once to sweep up the seeds after she leaves, but then don't go back the next day, figuring it's in the hands of the police, no sense taunting her. When I don't hear from the detectives in a couple of days, I call and am told the case is closed. They shuffle me over to the Community Affairs man.

"Oh yeah! She's the woman with the birds flying above her head following her down the street," he says when I tell him my story. "She used to be on 61st Street till they got rid of her."

"How?"

He doesn't know.

Back to square one. It means sweeping the seeds up after her. She doesn't show up all week. I figure she doesn't know what I'm up to and is probably playing it safe. Meanwhile the bird population, which figures in the hundreds, diminishes a bit. I'd say a good third of them have gone elsewhere looking for food. When she comes back on Saturday morning, I pick up my broom, bucket and dustpan, and when I think she is gone, head out to clean up. But she is not gone. My heart is going boom, boom, boom, in anticipation of a fight that I decide I cannot avoid. What she's doing is dangerous to my health and I have no choice but to act. What's more, I've had a Bear dream about it.

Its message? The Bear stands at the very spot where the pigeon lady feeds her entourage, *You have to fight for yourself* it lets me know.

The last thing I want to do is have scenes on the sidewalk with a nutty old lady, but there seems to be no choice in the matter. Since the Bear is connected to my writing, somehow the pigeon situation has something to do with it. Am I willing to make a fool of myself for what I deem important? I guess so.

She places the seeds between parked cars in three different locations making it harder for me to sweep them up. It also allows the birds some feeding time as I scurry from one pile to the other. But she does not say a word and does not try to interfere or stop me. She has deposited over 20 pounds of birdseed. The price one pays for ego is no bargain.

A woman stops to talk to me as I do my work, "Why are you taking food away from the birds? God put them here," she says.

"Yes, but God didn't put all these seeds here for them. He made them forage for their nourishment," I explain about the fleas, the diseases, encephalitis, histoplasmosis, etc. She continues assailing me.

"Alright," I say, "here's what I'll do once I finish picking up this bird seed. I'll bring it over in front of the building where you live."

Naw, she doesn't want that. I haul the bucket to my hallway wondering what I will do with all this seed. In my mail packet is a letter from Community Board 8 informing me that they sent an investigator from the sanitation department to check the scene where she feeds the birds. And they report that no pigeons were seen in that area. I look at the date of the investigation: the day of our big fight when hundreds of birds were waiting to be fed, hanging in apartment window sills, in trees, on the traffic light pole extending onto 1st Ave. like vultures, waiting, waiting.

I meet her on the street one day. I can tell she's not happy to see me as she pretends I'm not there by looking down and fumbling with her bags, her birdseed holding bags. It's been relatively quiet for a month now and the pigeon population has diminished considerably. I was hoping I had finally gotten rid of her, but seeing me on the street is too much of an affront; I am the person who has made her back down, give up her feeding spot on the corner. She comes by the next morning and dumps her seeds and bread cubes around the tree facing my entryway.

So it's back out there with the bucket and the push broom to pick up her mess. And she of course does her thing, while I sweep away the seeds and bread, screaming profanities. For some reason, probably my red hair, she thinks I'm Irish.

"Get out of the country -- We don't want your kind here, you Irish lesbian, you AIDS infected whore. Go back where you belong. I hope you die."

It goes on and on; she, like the tailor, inveigles passersby including them in her scenario. I never talk to her, never say a word, just go on with my job. She eventually gives it up and does not return, probably because of the expense and the empty gesture.

When the tailor sees the Pigeon Lady isn't coming back he starts feeding the birds, bringing back the fleas. I give him a warning, but he doesn't stop. After one of his feedings, I get some sunflower seeds from Gristede that pigeons are crazy for and dump them in the stairway leading down to his shop; hundreds of birds gather. That brings an end to his bird feeding forays, but it doesn't stop him. He then places a big sign on the side of my door. Its positioning makes it look like I'm the one offering to repair watches by replacing their batteries. It's the same sign he tried to attach to my balcony. I stop by his shop and ask him to remove it.

"Fuck you!" he says.

I repeat my request several times, same response.

"Either you take it out, or I will!"

Out comes the screwdriver and I'm ready for action. Finally, after going back and forth, and in which he becomes physically threatening to me, he gives up and removes the sign letting me know that he will do harm to my property while I'm sleeping.

I resolve the situation by calling the Department of Buildings and reporting his illegal signs. Having all the signs removed, the lawyer, the fines, the permits, cost him a small fortune getting the matter straightened out. And that marks the end of his encroaching signs. But his dirty tricks do not stop.

I have won my battle and can afford to ignore his petty behavior. After a while when he sees I will not react, he, like the pigeon lady stops the trouble, undoubtedly moving on to other victims.

The Sun

XIX

A young blond couple stands below a huge orange ball of sun. The pair looks directly into each other's eyes exchanging arcane knowledge. Their yellow hair and blue eyes, their slightly amber skin identifies them as Children of the Golden Garden.

Framing their quotidian pleasures, are large cheerful sunflowers. They entwine themselves round, and face the young lovers rather than the sun. It's a phenomenon similar to cats who, knowing their great beauty, choose only the most auspicious surroundings to repose in. Elegance must have its counterpart. One yearns for the proper setting. All beings are naked, exposed to the caressing yellow globe. In the background a high stone fence provides boundary, a magic circle wherein beauty abides.

The young people have never left this enchanted realm; don't have an appetite for cruelty. It's the story of Adam and Eve without the apple, a road to excess deflected. The sultry orb is so large, so close to earth resting just above the stone wall that all of life within flourishes in its embrace. Acceding to its brilliance, young love unfolds like a blossom, fragrant, delicate.

Upright; Happiness, fulfillment, loving relationships.

Reversed: Disconnected, illness, fear of intimacy.

I got off the plane at 10:30 this morning having been in the air for 7 hours after a sleepless night.

Diagnosis: Agitated Jet Lag.

What was most delightful about my trip to Paris was finding that I am able to converse at length in French and be understood. It had been a long time.

I was the distant cousin coming to check on the old country and the family, for the French truly are my family. I manage to control an urge to kneel on the tarmac and kiss the ground when I get off the plane. These are my people, and we connect from the start. What impresses me most in my exchanges with those I meet are their impeccable manners, and when we connect, their joie de vivre.

I go through a range of emotions during my stay. Some mornings, I wake up horribly depressed and then move out of it by lunchtime to a spirit of adventure. The French world I grew up in is forever lost. Grandmère, les oncles, les tantes, les amis et copains, les voisins who all spoke French were replaced by English speaking offspring, myself included, who either disdained their family's culture or folklorized it, making a fetish of its food, customs and language.

A week goes by like the blink of an eye. By the time I start knowing my way around I am packing to leave. I'm a zombie the first couple of days and I sleep for 16 hours to catch up with what I lost in the sky.

Being a zombie is a good thing at first because, in order to get into the country's particular rhythm, which is not like ours, I need to slow down and pay attention. In such a state on my first day, I stop at a corner cafe near my hotel and sit at one of the outdoor tables. By American standards, the service is slow. I am so exhausted, that I'm glad for the time to sit back and look at the neighborhood, its people, their style, and listen to my neighbors at adjoining tables. The food is so much better after I've had this time to calm down. What's more, I can come and sit outdoors for hours with an iced tea. I have to ask for l'addition, or they would never bring it. *Rude.*

What I find to be a very good meal on the go is a salad and a glass of wine at an outdoor café. The French make great salads with all manner of ingredients, textures, colors and the perfect, subtle sauce. One day on my way to Notre Dame I stop at a café by the Seine, very close to the island where the church stands, and have some lunch. A middle-aged big-bellied, over-coifed, couple takes a table nearby. *Americans.* He orders a hot dog and fries and she asks for a slice of pizza.

Their drink? Coca Cola! His hot dog comes and it's about a foot long, made with crusty bread and has melted cheese covering the dog. *Looks delicious.* He gives it his best shot and asks for mustard, and ketchup for the fries. How is he going to put mustard on a dog covered in melted cheese? He chooses, after some fumbling, to eat the dog without most of its crusty bread and cheese. And off they go very quickly, sorely disappointed in French food.

My task one evening is to become acquainted with Paris' Metro system, the underground trains. Its map looks like Medusa's hairdo with routes that zigzag throughout the city. I buy a bunch of tickets;

push one into the slot and it comes back up before I get past it to the gate.

"What's wrong with my ticket?" I ask.

Nothing. The machine does not eat the canceled ticket, that's my responsibility. I would imagine a pile of these now voided tickets on the ground underfoot, but not a one.

I choose the bar at Hotel Lutetia, in the 5th arrondissement, on the other side of the Seine as my destination. It will require a change of train midway. Probably read about its jazz bar in Pariscope, a "what's happening in Paris" weekly. La belle Deneuve is reputed to drop in at the bar.

Tackling the Metro on my return, I make the wrong connections and have to double back (train lines are identified by the name of their last stop which I hadn't a clue about) but from that evening on, I have no problems with the Metro.

On my last night, I go to Le Meurice located in the Hotel Meurice for dinner. The dining room is a replica of the Chambre de Paix in Versailles where many international peace agreements were sealed. I marvel at the professional staff's great knowledge about the preparation of food, and the quality and choice of appropriate wines. First serving is an offering from the chef, an unexpected treat, bread pudding that is chewy and crisp at the top with a meat sauce baked in. A perfect match for my glass of white wine which the sommelier suggests after we talk a bit about what I like.

My chief waiter and I get along famously. He speaks English quite well, but understands that I prefer French and though it takes us a bit longer to communicate as he explains, at my request, how each dish is prepared, it's more fun. With such a feast, I can't possibly eat everything, but rather I want to be able to sample as much as possible.

I sit all evening being served dish after dish of the most exquisitely prepared food, potato crusted salmon, caviar (a first) served with a pale green mousse that has a taste of earth, shrimp in a buttery sharp sauce, lamb with roasted vegetables and wild mushroom, a dessert soufflé, then a mousse served in a sea shell shaped ramekin made of sliver-thin chocolate.

Seeing the staff at their work is like watching a piece of art being composed. It isn't just about food; it's the total enjoyment of the experience. The sommelier is there to advise, but his assistant is the presenter and server. I notice that she pours herself the first ounce when she uncorks a bottle at table. I assume to make sure the wine has not gone off. She must have a good buzz by the end of evening

I top off my queen's repast with café crème that I have learned to enjoy the last few days.

Coming in to Grand Central after my experience with Paris' great architecture, its art, I'm surrounded by buildings the French call "grate-ciel" whose literal translation is sky-scratchers, I perform the act which never ceases to delight me; a hand in the air summons my yellow taxi and as the driver loads my luggage in the trunk another cabbie pulls up trying to hustle my fare -- *Yes, I'm back in town!* New York is a truly beautiful city, its style grand, yet understated and elegant. It is like no other city in the world. I left Paris early this morning in a cab driven by a woman and am picked up at Grand Central by another woman cabbie. Good omen.

Bijou called.

He left his number should I want to see him. I do call him several weeks later and we meet at Eli's for brunch. We are served coffee that turns green when I pour cream in it. The waiter forgets to bring my cabernet, and Bijou has brought his own walnuts in a zip lock bag to sprinkle over his pancakes.

The noise level is such that it makes conversation a task. I do still love him and agree to other meetings. No expectations, I'm just happy to be with him. Our new intimacy has the effect of making him impotent; he pumps and pumps, but he can't ejaculate. We meet on a few more occasions, hurtful times with angry, blaming words, yet our desire for each other is still strong. At our last good-bye, he French kisses me, bodies entwined, in the hallway before he walks out the door.

The only love wisdom I possess is that it comes into one's life at a time when it's least expected, from a source one would never anticipate, and seems predestined. In that person is a piece of the great mystery of life and you don't want to lose it. You are connected in some way that you can't explain. Losing this intimacy leaves you with a wound. Some heal fast and move on, not me.

Love and money, the way one deals with either is a true reflection of how one relates. The interactions of giving and taking, and those of giver and taker never change. It is the role one has either chosen or been consigned to play. Balance is not easy to maintain, one overeats, over drugs, over sexes, over dominates, gives it all away. If one's balanced financial account is a state of grace, a loving relationship is also a state of grace. One has taken the time to take care, to be responsible.

To hold back is to entrust the relationship to a netherland of petty power plays and eventual bitter estrangement, but not maintaining a certain distance, a sense of privacy, is to consign it to doom out of sheer overexposure and boredom. Bijou and I obviously fall in the former category.

Since we've split up I have lost interest. Every date I go on becomes the one and only time I care to see my escort. So I give it up.

I place my faith in money to tell me if I am on the right path, if I am being of assistance, if I am learning and growing. I find that when I am not focused, money dwindles, as it has during this last unhappy time with Bijou. I don't think of money as a place one arrives at, but as the fuel that energizes one's journey and this is also true of relationship. Up till now, I haven't had a great need for relationship or money. I'd like to have more, but as long as there is bread on the table, a little music, a bottle of wine and some good books, I'm happy.

But that, as always, is subject to change.

JUDGMENT

XX

At close of day on the lake, a few flickers of red on the deepening yellow water; the sky a flat amber to orange, as dusk approaches. A lone coffin floats by carrying a man, woman and child, dead, living dead, their bodies blue. The coffin glides on water so calm one could walk on it. Save for the lapping of water against the open casket and the creaking of wood, hardly a sound is heard from this still life. Cobalt spectral forces are all that remain of the substance that was once flesh.

The family stands in its wooden box. Father holds a trumpet aloft, in the center of which, wedged firmly in the circular tubing of the instrument, is a red Maltese cross, an ancient symbol of redemption and glory. The horn and cloud, from which it appears, spew out tongues of fire.

Mother stands before her man arms crossed in front of her bosom, hair billowing in the wind. If father looks concerned and she appears doubtful, the child's face beams with joy. *Hallelujah!* the outstretched arms and youthful body seem to proclaim. Like small flickers of fire the wide-open fingers are greedy to consume this new beginning, put it in its mouth, rub its face in it. *Hallelujah! Sound the brass trumpet redemption is at hand.*

Upright: Redemption, emancipation, transcendence.

Reversed: Fear of death, the unknown, isolation.

New York -- the city of no foreplay.
anon.

A friend brings me ground leaves from a psychedelic plant to smoke. Although curious, I've never tried hallucinogens, was leery since my desire to explore other states of reality is so strong. I was afraid I might not want to come back from such a "trip."

The product is salvia divinorum, a mild hallucinogen whose effects persist but a half hour. Last time I checked it was still a legal substance, easily acquired over the Internet.

I smoke once with my friend and then another time by myself, afraid I will run out of my apartment and be lost in the world. My first symptoms are distortion of depth perception and an inability to get my bearings; I give it up and stretch out on the sofa.

I can deal with this. It's not altogether unpleasant seeing the world from this new perspective, where I'm not sure if I've gotten bigger or my surroundings got smaller; I can almost reach over and touch the opposite wall.

Shortly, I have a strong impression that my self-importance, considering my humble station, is monumental.

A little more ominous is the realization that there is "nothing out there." Out of my window, civilization, society, the world of men and women is a mirage that I project on the world. "I" am alone creating it all.

I feed the birds from a wicker basket on my balcony. They visit among the marigolds, and begonias the color of milk to which has been added a single drop of raspberry juice, a couple of geraniums, one a pink and the other a very sharp red, its blossoms appear like a wound in the body of the world. Little birds. At midsummer, a pair of elegant and courtly mourning doves come to visit. Most birds leave the feeder if I move about near the windows, not these doves. They are curious and watch my every move. It appears they are mates, (I checked them out in "Birds of North America") the female smaller and less decorated than her partner. Late afternoon, when I am writing is their time to visit. I lean in to hear them sing their mournful song, but they do not sing, or if they do, it is drowned by the traffic on First Avenue as workers are heading home at that time of day.

Are they an omen of death? These two lovebirds don't just eat and run, they hang around, they preen, perform their ritual dance, check out the neighborhood, all the while taking note of my habits. They give me such pleasure how could they carry bad omen. I don't know why they've chosen to visit me -- I'm sure I'll find out at some point.

For several weeks I have had free floating anxiety, nothing in my life upsetting me, and then Tuesday, the 11th. I generally wake up slowly, write my dream before getting out of bed and read the cards. Not this time, I immediately get up and do something I consider akin to receiving electroshock therapy; I turn on the radio. The announcer explains that an airplane has crashed in one of the twin towers of the World Trade Center. Then a second one. And then the Pentagon! I run to the window.

We're the greatest power on earth; what country could possibly attack us?

I sit most of the day listening to my radio trying to understand what is happening. We are told all air traffic has been halted in the country, yet there are still planes roaring above, military jet fighters, nevertheless, still frightening. I get on the Internet hoping to find more information. There's an email from Meredith in Brooklyn, a former Farm colonist and Kate's current right hand woman. We communicate back and forth throughout the day describing the happenings in our respective neighborhoods. Her view is of a bedraggled pilgrimage of workers crossing the Brooklyn Bridge. The street is crowded in my region with people carrying briefcases, obviously coming from the financial district.

No trains! I don't know how they made it home; did they walk all the way up here?

Mayor Giuliani, a true hero throughout this ordeal commends the people of New York for behaving purposefully and maintaining composure when getting out of the line of fire. He reassures us that everything is being done to insure our safety. I leave my computer on all day to keep open a line of communication. One-eight-hundred telephone numbers are not working, and I continually lose my Internet connection. A number of radio and TV stations have been knocked off the air.

News throughout the day gets worse and worse; people have been seen jumping off the towers driven off by the intense heat. Police and fire workers who go to rescue others in the tower are killed when the building collapses on them. And the horror stories, Mayor Giuliani loses an officer he had thrown a party for at Gracie Mansion the week before; a man in the tower knowing he's going to die momentarily calls his wife to tell her he loves her and the children, his last thoughts being of them. All day, I sit and listen to these sad stories, numb. By evening, I, a vegetarian, decide to go and get myself a steak at the market. I feel a need for extra protein. It's rush hour, but there are no cars in the street, and the few people are silent and dazed. Cadets from the police academy are directing whatever traffic there is. Inside the supermarket, silence, no Muzak today for a line of grim people standing with their purchases, waiting to be served.

This is what it's like for citizens experiencing war within their borders.

The following morning, I go out to get the NY Times and the Daily News.

I'm going to sit, have my coffee, and read the papers, then start my day slowly.

"No papers till later," says Yasir, "*The trucks can't get through to deliver them.*"

I turn on my computer and find that my hard drive has finally given up the fight.

Throughout the crisis yesterday, the man who spends every morning watching me from the stoop across the street was at his post looking up at me. Today when I see him take his seat, I grab my camera, walk across the street and just as I'm about to snap his picture, he puts his hands to his face. I walk right up to him, furious, and kick him in the shins, all the while screaming to a man who is deaf/mute -- YOU'RE NOT GOING TO TERRORIZE ME, YOU SON OF A BITCH! I get a really good shot of him, a stunned look on his face.

Jeez.

The computer news is grim. I travel the trains to get down to the shop; not many on board . . . a certain fragility in people, still very quiet. Everyone eyes me carefully as I enter the car, and I do likewise to others.

Who's the killer, the bomber among us?

No one is above suspicion, not even a 102-pound woman in a dress and high heel shoes. The routes are a mess, no trains travel below 14th Street. I have to make several changes to get to my destination. I was exhausted when I got up this morning, exhausted all day, big headache, feeling vulnerable and sad. And still, stories of horror and dying continue. The old monitor stands mute on my desk along with the exterior modem.

A whole week without my computer!

Traffic entering Manhattan has been severely curtailed and by Thursday, markets are starting to run out of food. Most of the milk is gone except for the gallon jugs of whole milk; meat supplies are dwindling. I am still on a high protein diet. The wind has changed direction and I breathe and smell the horrible stench of pulverized bodies, smoke and burned rubble. I now shut my radio off and put on music, Telemann, Vivaldi, and even French songs of my childhood, Edith Piaf, Jacques Brel. Around 6 in the evening, I go out and pass St. Joseph Catholic Church with its open doors and people streaming in. I pause for a moment, but continue on to my church, the park. Although part of it is cordoned off around Gracie Mansion, and there are some police, the rest of it is open. Mothers with children have come out, people are walking their dogs and young men shoot baskets. People look directly at one, not common in NYC, but we are coming back to life. Back home, the tears come at last.

Trains are packed on the way down to the computer shop, jam-packed. Posted at bus stops and train stations are computer printed pictures of men mostly, young twenties and early thirties, with their names, the clothes they were wearing, identifying material they were carrying and a message from the wife, sweetheart, or parent asking for any information. Another sign tells of the 6 firefighters in my district that have been killed, and then the police officers. People stop and look, there is nothing we can do but look into these innocent faces and know the suffering their families are undergoing. These signs are grim, but important. Real people have died, not just numbers. At the Union Square Station, a picture of a truly beautiful woman, open, radiant, a lawyer who worked in the WTC. Her lover seeks information. It breaks my heart.

Coming back on the #6, packed in like sardines, I stand in a circle of people grasping a pole, a woman across from me unfurls her NY Times in all our faces. I tap the newspaper and say, "Get real, lady."

She responds by remarking, "I guess this disaster has had no effect on you!"

How dare she! I want to kill her, blow her dirty mouth out with a shotgun.

Anger is kicking in, yet I can't help but have concern for this anger and flag waving that we are experiencing. I cannot vent my anger at the violation we have suffered on a self-involved matron who hasn't a clue in life. The same applies on a larger level, we need to find the people who are responsible for the terrorist attacks against us and bring them to justice, behaving in accordance with our own, and also international laws in pursuing justice.

I'm feeling better a month after the attack, but there are times . . . I spent all of Saturday in the apartment working on one thing, then another. At nine in the evening I decide to get out for a walk. I encounter a truck with an officer in it at the park, blocking one of the lanes leading to Gracie Mansion. We are alone in the dark night. Normally, I would pass him with a slightly uncomfortable feeling. Not this time, I call out, "Good evening, Officer," as he watches me approach.

"How you doing?" he responds.

"You have a good night, " I say.

He's going to spend most of this Saturday night sitting alone in the truck. Walking by the East River, I feel vulnerable and teary again after I thought I was moving beyond this.

Spiro Agnew was Richard Nixon's vice president from 1969 to 1973. He never finished his term because he got caught with his hand in the cookie jar, something most present politicians do with impunity. Yet there was something about Ol'

Spiro. The press took a liking to him for his outrageous and even delightful sound bytes. He's the man who popularized the phrase, "Nattering Nabobs of Negativity" when speaking about Vietnam War critics.

He once participated in a debate on TV, a famous show with a big name moderator. His opponent was a war protester. It was like seating Jerry Falwell next to Hugh Hefner at the dinner table, their viewpoints and philosophies could not have been further apart. Yet, we were treated to an excellent discussion, interesting and informative. Asked to explain his attitude, Mr. Agnew replied, and I'm paraphrasing, You start by respecting the other fellow if any discussion is to ensue. It doesn't mean you agree with him. You don't, that's why you're having the debate -- Out of the mouths of miscreants!

I understand that the policeman who I've often thought of in absolute terms as someone with a gun who stands above the law, he is also the person who is willing to risk his life on my behalf. This sadness, this vulnerability is the product of re-awakening feelings and sensitivity to others, and as

Spiro understood, respect, so that conversation is possible.

There are positive things to be gained from this horrible event. And this is what I take from the disaster. I will keep the vulnerable heart. People in and out of government are behaving and speaking outrageously during these dark, scary times. We are in a period I would label, The Reading of The Will: after the death of a family member when everybody's greed and hidden agendas are brought to light, and profit is to be made from this loss. I am diametrically opposed to everything the Bush administration believes, proposes or initiates.

The following week-end, after I've wrapped up work for the week, lovely short-sleeved, sunny day, I take a long leisurely shower then choose a dress and heels to wear, make myself up, jewelry, earrings, perfume, and I'm off. My plan for this weekend is to go check out the Signac paintings at the Met on Saturday and brunch with my group of women on Sunday.

I head first to the library where I pick up a biography of Crazy Horse, then over to the bank to make my deposit. Afterward, I stroll over to Eli's for a baguette and that's when I see it: on the cover of the Daily News, FBI WARNS OF EMINENT ATTACK, and on the Post, RED ALERT with a big bull's-eye. Instantly, my mood crashes.

What the hell is this? Why are they telling me this? If it's known that an attack is about to happen, how is it supposed to occur? Are we going to be bombed? Biological attack? What am I supposed to do about this warning, go home, tape the windows and doors to keep out the poisonous fumes and hide under the bed?

I choose a couple of art books at Barnes & Nobles and head for the café. A woman sits at a table, working on her computer her feet up on another chair.

What is this? Not enough chairs for people to sit in and this bitch has to use one as a footstool?

I walk up to her and point, "The chair."

She removes her feet wordlessly. I drag the chair to another table where a man sits by himself.

"This your stuff?" I motion to the books and magazines sprawled on the table. He nods and picks everything up and deposits it on the floor.

What am I doing, snapping at people and creating bad energy?

An uncomfortable minute and then, "Thank you."

He nods.

After he's gone, I notice that he's left his newspaper behind. It's the RED ALERT bull's-eye Post. I bring it over to the trashcan.

At the Met the following day, looking at Signac's pointillist paintings, I think that we are up close to all the little dots of our present situation. We haven't stepped back far enough to make out what the picture is about. Signac started his career as an impressionist until he met Seurat and then his style gradually evolved. His first paintings pulse with emotional coloring in comparison to the progressively formal pointillist works whose characters and scenes lose their substantiality and become symbolic objects poised on a piece of canvass. A lot of my stories start with a kernel of an actual event, a real person, but as the story unfolds I've traveled so far from the initial facts that it becomes like a Signac pointillist painting. The initial event, whether it is the WTC attack, or the kernel of a story is not the half of it.

One has to look at the whole picture and the whole picture is too complex to be rendered by what actually happened. Later the dots will coalesce and a formal abstract picture will emerge capturing the essence of 9/11.

My women friends and I have long, soulful conversations at brunch that range all over the "facts" of the World Trade Center attack and have no clear purpose or direction other than to vent, to try and understand, to finally see the truth of the situation. Stepping back and letting the soul do its work of processing recent events is about all that can be done at this time. It's not always easy.

Afraid Osama's got a Bomb pointed at NYC;
afraid hawks will nuke the Middleast.
Afraid you can't be intimate;
afraid you lack boundaries.
Afraid of the P. O. & anthrax;
afraid of opening letters.
Afraid to go to sleep at night;
afraid of sleep medication.
Afraid the world is going crazy;
afraid you'll die of boredom.

Afraid you're getting fat;
afraid of sweets and marbled meat.
Afraid of airplanes in the sky;
afraid of subways underground.
Afraid of being late;
afraid of getting there too early.
Afraid you'll run out of money;
afraid you're too extravagant.
Afraid of getting old;
afraid you're a perennial Peter Pan.
Afraid of fundamentalist fanatics;
afraid no one gives a shit.
Afraid you'll be a failure;
afraid of success.
Afraid you've lost your cool;
afraid you've become shallow.
Afraid you're out of style;
afraid you lack distinction.
Afraid of global warming;
afraid of cancerous growth.
Afraid of the sun's rays;
afraid of the moon's power.
Afraid no one will love you;
afraid they may, then what'll you do?
Afraid of being exposed;

afraid of being unnoticed.
Afraid to be alone;
afraid of unsuitable companions.
Afraid the costume's too revealing;
afraid you look frumpy,
Afraid you've lost your talent;
afraid you never had it.
Afraid what they say is true;
afraid you'll prove them right.
Afraid you're going to die
afraid you missed the best of it.

THE WORLD

XXI

Encircling the naked woman, in the vast emptiness of the cosmos, a million stars twinkle. She hangs suspended in the void performing her Dance of Life. Twirling and twirling, a wand in each hand, she conjures the awful magic of the universe with her presentation. There are no stumbles, no faux pas. With the grace of an accomplished ballerina she lifts the green gauze of illusion to expose a firmament with no beginning and no end.

Her cosmos is flanked in the four directions by the beasts of the Apocalypse. An eagle sets the course, soaring at rise of light. In its train are the poems, the stories, the soul that creates. While at full sun, a mighty lion roams the veld, the fire of its passion coursing through its body, impelling it to devour and to feast. When light plunges deep into the great waters, it unleashes emotions that, like the bull, are powerful, intemperate.

Man, the fourth beast of the Apocalypse, represents earth, matter, that which brings forth life, decays and reforms itself. It is the home of dreams and darkness, the mystery that confounds us. These four powers: the unknowable, the ability to create, a keen appetite and an implacable heart are the gifts of life, the wonders that impel the naked woman to perform her ballet.

Upright: Success in all spheres, fulfillment, happiness, well-being.

Reversed: Superficial view of situation, wrong expectations.

The present in New York is so
powerful that the past is lost.
John Jay Chapman

Is making money your goal in life?

The thought *w*akes me up in the middle of the night. *Oh god, I'm going to start losing money!* The dream is an omen of change. Something's missing.

True to form, a crisis presents itself and challenges me to make a commitment. It hits me on the head, literally. The roof comes crashing down into my studio. I love how the Spirit adds a metaphorical touch to its disasters. Ceiling too low, a need to expand? - - Roof collapse and the sky is limitless.

A week later I hit the rental powerball lottery and find a dream apartment. To acquire such a home is a mark of distinction among New Yorkers. This is not about money, style, or status. It's about the deal, and luck, which is judged as real indicators of a person's potential. Again, I'm making this move on a wing and a prayer. I will have to find a way to afford it.

It's a real apartment with a front parlor that has an elegant brown and black marble fireplace, French doors, a bedroom, a work area, a dining room, an eat-in kitchen with a dishwasher, a frost-free refrigerator, and . . . a backyard! All this in a lovely pre-war building with a gargoyle above its front entrance, I'm only one block from the old studio, but a world away in a tonier neighborhood of elegant brownstones, manicured properties and streets, half a block from the park. After I've secured my old studio, locked it up with the last of my keys inside, and my belongings are deposited in my new home, I pay off the movers, close the door and head straight for the backyard.

At last!

On my block are young families, upper middle class, genteel, loving of their children, respectful. Well-being emanates. There is that moment when your children are young and you are involved in their care that you are most at peace with yourself and with life. Later it will turn out that you don't like your wife or your husband anymore.

I can't live with you. I'm leaving.

When I left my husband, I assumed that since I could not love him, it probably wouldn't work with anyone else. I saw my choices as, life with Roger, or life alone. The light went on in my head one day and I found myself a virtual slave to the institution of marriage, and by extension, to him. It had been going on for years. I, who had never uttered a peep throughout our long and difficult marriage, exploded in the parking lot of the supermarket.

"You lying, son of a bitch!"

He smashed the windshield of the car. I was angry and remained so for two years, after which I became depressed, then I divorced him.

Getting out of marriage is an interesting phenomenon. Aside from the broken heart and volatile emotions, one returns to the age at which one married, as if single and married are two spheres that develop independently of each other. I became a 17-year-old girl and a single person. My goal was to make a happier, more natural life for myself. I wanted to do something interesting, meet good people. And I did achieve my goals, but basically, I'm alone.

This isn't the plan. I'm supposed to go back into marriage . . .

But I don't go back. I fall in love, madly, desperately; life is finally delivering the happy times, the tender moments, the music. We even consider moving in together. The relationship deconstructs after two years, and I am broken-hearted.

I will never have another relationship like that because I loved him so.

Then later someone shows up when I'm feeling pretty good and BAM! I'm in it again. There are no road maps, no permanent safe harbors. At a gathering of old friends with married folks and their concerns, I decide I no longer belong to this world, I have nothing in common with the women or men, furthermore, my life's more interesting than theirs. I take my new life to heart.

I*t's what I wanted all along.*

There is a time of harvest and a time to nurture seedlings. Nurture, being the time I give to myself, to replenish, to assimilate experiences, to shed old skin, old attitudes and ways of being. The harvests are the good times that do come, over and over. It's like breathing, inhale, exhale, a life of relationship, a life alone, coils of the same helix, with their particular gifts and pleasure. I have no interest in pursuing romance, and have been without a lover since Bijou left a few years ago.

I never saw him again. But one night last year, he called while I was writing and I answered the phone, my thoughts still on the story I was working on. A man's voice at the other end said, "Hello."

"Who is this? What do you want?"

"Is that you, Lorraine?"

Then his fax machine kicked in and we were cut off.

My work evolves in ways I would not have anticipated. I am the subject of a documentary film "In The Cards" about my work and my life. The director, Pedro Suaraz, his sound technician, Maggie, a camera woman and a lighting technician come to my studio to film it. The script entails my giving someone a reading after which I am to be interviewed.

I have some questions about which person this might be, and the authenticity of their desire to consult a seeress. In order for a reading to work, the person has to have a question, a reason to consult me. I suggest Pedro might do it himself. In the end Maggie volunteers.

"Have her give me a call."

Maggie is indeed interested in getting a reading. Her questions focus on her career as a sound technician in films. At the start of my weekend, Maggie's reading descends on me like a spider engulfing me in its web. She's all I can think of. What kind of visualization would be appropriate for Maggie, and all of us, as psychic energy has drawn us together? It comes to me on Saturday morning, minutes before the crew arrives.

I have her sit in the love seat, eyes closed, and have her perform a breathing exercise. Thus begins the process of her detachment from the everyday world. I then have her visualize herself in another realm.

An adaptation of a Zhuzhanna Budapest visualization is what I use for Maggie:

> There is in all of us an Ancient One who knows everything, and sees everything.
> But she is quite primitive, below brain level, at the hypothalamus. She knows nothing of the modern world of money, careers, machinery, etc.
> What pleases her is drama and ritual; she likes dance, costumes, passion.
> You must feed and nurture her in your everyday life.
> On this journey, you are going to meet her. She has something to show you . . .
> You may also have questions.

I tell the crew that there's a purpose behind the four of us coming to meet, and because of it the reading will speak to us all. Maggie freezes at the beginning and gives only yes or no answers. The visualization has taken her to her grandmother's image, but she will not say more than that.

Once we move to the sofa and I give her a reading, she opens up, and the reading goes well. It speaks to us about craft, about dedication, the insecurities and heartbreaks that hold us back.

The camera peruses my books, my kitchen, my altar, the clippings and pictures on the corkboard above my desk. Talking about myself, my philosophy, my work is similar to writing a book. The written page never approximates more than a third of the wisdom, poetry and beauty I know in my heart.

On first watching "In the Cards," my reaction is one of shock seeing myself so exposed and vulnerable. I've acted in another independent film last year, but I was playing a role in that one. It was no great stretch as I played the part of a psychic, but it was a role, not me up there on the screen.

I immediately watch the documentary again, so clear and so obvious has my path been all along. Finding, or accepting, who one truly is, is no minor task. Had I ever in my wildest imagination perceived myself in New York City serving people as seeress? Watching the film, seeing myself expound on my knowledge and beliefs, I'm reminded of the work and study I've dedicated myself to all these years. It has not been a fluke. I was preparing, but I didn't know I was preparing.

At a large witches' conference, I once had a vision that I would indeed be helping people spiritually. Whenever I get such messages, my reaction is ambivalent, but then I continue to follow through on its objectives. Perhaps because the prediction is so accurate, one has no objection and it is accepted as fact on a subliminal level.

That's interesting, I thought at the time. *It might happen; it might not.* I could not have borne the responsibility for bringing it about.

My ambition was to be a writer. At some point these two goals meshed. And now it's a layered casserole with ingredients blending and melding; what I talk to seekers about, what I write about becomes the message that I learn from, as does the seeker, and hopefully the writing reflects it.

I am so out of the loop, and have been for years now, that it has made me a little peculiar, but that's OK. I am an innocent in that I have not been shaped by the rules, mores, and etiquette that society imposes. And then I am truly right, and correct in my beliefs (which takes people aback) regardless of the particular knowledge or received truths facing me. It doesn't matter that others don't agree, because I have no choice but to respect my knowledge and convictions.

After the film viewing, I wake up the next morning and the person I take to the coffee shop is a seeress working on the Upper East Side of Manhattan New York.

It starts with a call from a young man named Giuseppe, a representative of Metro Pictures Gallery downtown. He's looking for a psychic to work with the artist Gianni Motti.

"Sounds interesting."

I meet with a group consisting of Gianni, his interpreter Giuseppe, and Ivo the camera man, for my interview.

Gianni Motti sits on a sofa across from me and there is a table between us. "I am a bit hard of hearing," I say. "Could you come and sit by my side?"

True, my hearing is off, yet I know that my invitation, which he accepts, binds him to me. Sitting on the sofa next to me, I discover that he speaks fluent French and we are able to communicate.

"No," Gianni tells Giuseppe, "I don't need to see other psychics. I have a good feeling about Lorraine."

He wants to contact John Lennon, who at one time, said he would come back and make an appearance after death. Gianni is going to film the event that will play in the next room via a continuous loop. These rooms will be dark, accenting the energy of the séance.

A chauffeured car waits the next day to take us to the Dakota where John Lennon was killed so as to pick up any energy remaining in the area. Then we cross over to the park's Strawberry Fields with its memorial plaque honoring the musician. Our crew has been augmented to include a photographer. Many pictures are taken of me at both venues, eyes closed to conjure John's spirit. Standing by the plaque in Central Park posing for Ivo filming the event, the photographer snapping away and Gianni in his black clothes, wild silver hair styled in a disheveled afro, directing the action with Giuseppe at his side translating. The crowd standing nearby furiously snap pictures of me, assuming I am a star, or a celebrity.

When Giuseppe first called, I thought it would be a simple matter of giving a reading, but that no longer seems appropriate. What I end up doing is creating a ritual, casting a circle with candles in the four directions, calling in the allies, raising a cone of power, and channeling. It lasts about 40 minutes. I already knew John Lennon was in a bad way. Dying in a violent, unexpected manner with many issues unresolved traps the spirit somehow. The ritual upsets me. My body shakes and I sob when it's over. It is much as I expected; in my journey, the scenes I view seeking John's spirit are dark and foreboding, yet there is still creative energy there with many bright colors and configurations.

Gianni wants to contact Lennon because of the man's honesty as an artist; John wasn't in it for money, or glory. It was his ability to speak from the heart that captivates Gianni.

The gallery director takes us to dinner in Chelsea afterward. Still not down from my ritual, I sit for the first fifteen minutes speechless, listening to people talk and feeling quite outside the situation. Gianni surreptitiously looks at me with concern. I have steak and a hot fudge sundae and the world returns.

For the shows' opening, I put on my little black dress, strappy high heel shoes and head down to the opening party at the gallery . . .

My god! I don't know what I expected, but I am the whole show! Gianni's sole presentation is the loop of my performance in one room and the room itself where the event occurred.

I'm the star!

The experience has a strong effect on me and I realize a need to make changes in my work. The "spirit" behind questions asked of me is what interests me most and I must explore it. I have been wandering through the safe, predictable life lately. Making money as a goal, as the dream chided me, indicates that I've become complacent, focusing on my work as business, rather than the creative/spiritual endeavor that it needs to be.

I came to New York a penniless grad student with thoughts of a career in writing, and possibly teaching to allow me a writing life. What I found caught me off guard, a part-time job as a psychic counselor for a company advertising on late night television. I saw it primarily as a way to make money, but my attitude changed as I started getting my own clients. I became a "seeress," one who "sees," with a business card and a web site. Where this would lead, fame or ignominy, was questionable, but there was no turning from it.

I imagined that people in the city were more sophisticated, and I would be free to express myself more fully. By sophisticated I don't mean, rich, jaded, above the din of everyday life. I mean sophisticated as in experienced, knowing, able to hold a multiplicity of opposing ideas. It comes from the word sophist, an expert, a wise person. That is not to say that everyone in New York is wiser than those from other areas, but I doubt that you would find in most small towns in America, people riding public transportation reading books of philosophy, literature, art, criticism; yet this is so common in the subways of NYC as to be ubiquitous. There are just too many of us from various backgrounds with different ideas not to question established beliefs. We are forced to be democratic, in the true sense of the word, in order to get along.

I looked for a haven in New York, a place where I could exhibit my talents, and hopefully find acceptance for views difficult to accept in the rest of the country, where being different is seen as a sign of creativity, intelligence, gumption, and even profundity, and I found it.

The first indication I had that there was more to life than what I was taught, or what we call reality, occurred when I was 5 years old. My stepmother, and her sister familiarly known to us as l'As de Pique, the Ace of Spades, were dressing me. I sat at the table singing the song, "Take me out to the ball game," as stepmother slipped the dress over my head, "Take me out with the crowd . . .

"You'd like that," said l'As de Pique. "You'd like to get away from us, wouldn't you?"

Through the dress concealing my head and face, which offered me some protection, past my little singsong, into my brain, the Ace of Spades had read my thoughts.

It was an "aha" moment where the idea of reading someone's mind was born in me. The world held unfathomable secrets that I had yet to uncover. Since I despised both stepmother and her sister, it was no great leap for her to conclude I wanted to get away from them. Yet I understood that I had just made an important discovery: It was possible to tap into secret things about others, and the world.

Fin

Made in United States
North Haven, CT
27 January 2023

31704806R00252